PRAISE FOR *SOLVED!*

'In a time of chaos, there are answers all around us if we take the time to look. Which is exactly what Wear does in this invaluable book.' —**Annabel Crabb**

'A terrific idea, brilliantly executed … Deserves to spark a national conversation.' —**George Megalogenis**

'A welcome dose of optimism that we can create change. Buy it if you are over gloom and doom and ready for action!' —**Rebecca Huntley**

'Wear offers something valuable and rarely present in such a practical book about politics: determined optimism, and real hope.' —**Van Badham**

'In a world of endless outrage, armchair critics and keyboard warriors, *Solved!* is that rarest of things: a book that actually offers solutions to the planet's problems instead of just listing them.' — **Joe Hildebrand**

'Fascinating … it's a good book to read if you're stuck at home and the world seems a bit bleak because it shows how human ingenuity, evidence-based policy and cooperation can help us to get ahead and do a much better job.' —**Peter Mares**

'Optimistic, clear, compelling and realistic ... An uplifting and timely guide that show how policy – and citizens – can tackle even the largest challenges.' —**Glyn Davis, distinguished professor, Crawford School of Public Policy, ANU**

'Wear shows why in pessimistic times there are reasons to feel optimistic about our capacity to solve the big problems the world is facing.' —**Robyn Scott, co-founder and CEO of Apolitical**

'A refreshing, cup-half-full approach to inspire each and all of us we MUST and CAN do the work "to make the world a better place".' —**Dana H. Born, Harvard Kennedy School of Government**

'Evidence-based and immensely readable ... Anyone inter-ested in designing and implementing public policy that works should read this book.' —**Professor Helen Sullivan, director, Crawford School of Public Policy, ANU**

'Wear has much to say not just to policymakers, but to business and other travelers to countries he profiles. Insightful.' —***Kirkus***

'An important book which puts forward realistic and achievable solutions to humanity's ills.' —***New Internationalist UK***

'A valuable book on practical possibilities for a better world ... Wear passionately believes in what he is telling us, regarding it as an optimistic engagement with humanity.' —***The Canberra Times***

RECOVERY

ANDREW WEAR

ALSO BY ANDREW WEAR

Solved!: How Other Countries Have Cracked the World's Biggest Problems and We Can Too (2020)

RECOVERY

How we can create a better, brighter future after a crisis

ANDREW WEAR

Published by Hero,
an imprint of Legend Times Group
51 Gower Street
London WC1E 6HJ
hero@hero-press.com
www.hero-press.com

First published in in Australia by Black Inc., an imprint of Schwartz Books, in 2021

9781800313408 (paperback)
9781800313415 (ebook)

Cover design by Ditte Løkkegaard
Text design and typesetting by Typography Studio
Illustrations by Alan Laver
Author photograph by Paul Hermes

Printing managed by Jellyfish Solutions Ltd.

For Claire

CONTENTS

PREFACE

I n late February 2020, I received a phone call from the chief executive at the City of Melbourne. He was offering me a job, leading the organisation's economic development branch. But there was a note of concern in his voice. The World Health Organization had recently declared a 'public health emergency of international concern'.[1] The world had been watching with horror as a novel coronavirus killed thousands of people in Wuhan, China, and now it had begun to spread. The first COVID-19 cases had been confirmed in Australia in the last days of January. A sense of anxious anticipation hung over the metropolis.

'This is going to hit the city hard,' he said. Already, with the borders closed to China, two of our biggest industries – international education and tourism – had ground to a halt. That alone would be enough to seriously disrupt our economy, but he warned that there was worse to come. 'This is like nothing we've experienced before,' he said. 'We'll have to look back in history, to wars and natural disasters, to get a sense of how we need to respond.'

A few weeks earlier, when I had interviewed for the role on a baking hot day, there was no sense of what was to come. The questions I had been peppered with were filled with optimism.

How could the city best manage the pressures of population growth? What should we do to shape development in new city precincts? How could we support growth in emerging sectors such as advanced manufacturing and biotechnology?

By the time I started my new role, office workers had abandoned the city for dining-room tables and hastily assembled home offices. Shortly after, Australian borders shut completely to non-residents, and lockdown restrictions were progressively enacted by the state government. The central business district emptied out, leaving a disconcerting vacuum. 'The city feels strange and unfamiliar,' Melbourne's lord mayor, Sally Capp, said. 'The city hasn't been this empty for this long in living memory.'[2]

In the months that followed, I worked from the granny flat in my backyard, with a team that I had never met in person, using Zoom to support the councillors who were leading the city's recovery. While my children grappled with remote learning, the team and I worked urgently, rolling out whatever support we could for desperate small business owners who had seen their customers disappear or had been forced to shut their doors. If they could survive through lockdown, their employees might just keep their jobs and the city might rebound once we eventually reached the other side of this thing.

Melbourne has been largely successful in containing the virus. While many places around the world have experienced the deaths of tens – or hundreds – of thousands of people, we have been fortunate to avoid this trauma.[3] Yet, confined to our houses for 112 straight days and allowed a daily maximum of one hour outside for exercise, within a 5-kilometre radius, before the 8.00 p.m. curfew, much of 2020 was an intense, anxious time. Central Melbourne's economy was hit hard, with output declining by

53 per cent during 2020.[4] Consumed with the present, I gave little further thought to any parallels the COVID-19 pandemic might have had with past crises.

Yet it soon became clear that we could not spend all our energy responding to immediate challenges. The pandemic would end at some point and the city would have a long recovery ahead of it. We would need to plan to ensure activity in Melbourne was able to recover and to grow in the years ahead. What does it take to bounce back from a global pandemic? How might we even begin to think about this task? Our city had never experienced anything like this before. The challenge my boss set many months before began to gnaw at me – the past seemed an obvious place to look for insights relevant to the coming recovery.

Throughout history, cities and nations have emerged from devastation to prosper and thrive. Whether pandemic, war, natural disaster or recession, the examples are plentiful. The United States recovered from the Spanish flu to enter the boom years of the Roaring Twenties. After being hit by the Great Depression at the end of the decade, it eventually managed to recover from that too, building a prosperity that was to last decades. Germany and South Korea both expanded their economies in the decades following war. Aceh, Indonesia, and Christchurch, New Zealand, suffered terrible natural disasters and managed to build back better than before. What are the lessons from these recoveries that we might draw on?

Almost six months into the pandemic, the need for this book became overwhelming. And while it was a crazy time for me to write a book, it was also a project imbued with a driving purpose.

Whereas the pandemic has been a dark and overwhelming experience, this book has a bright sense of optimism running through it. That's because in each of the recoveries I investigated, cities and nations have been able to rebound strongly. Recovery was not always easy, of course. But looking at the outcomes with the benefit of hindsight gives me confidence that – if we make the right choices now – we too can recover from this historic moment of crisis and build a better, brighter future. So join me to find out how.

INTRODUCTION
A BRIGHT DAWN

I n the pre-dawn light, a magnificent bird builds its nest. The size of an eagle, with brilliant red and gold feathers, it is roughly one thousand years old. Carefully assembling a bed from cinnamon, sage and myrrh, it pauses to sing a haunting melody. Just as the sun rises, a spark falls from the sky, igniting a fire that destroys both bird and nest, leaving only a pile of ashes. Yet after three days, a new phoenix emerges gloriously from the residue, ready to restart the cycle.

The phoenix was said to live in Paradise, the perfect world beyond the sun, and would enter our world only to be reborn. Mostly associated with Greek mythology, the story of the phoenix is also present in some form in Egyptian, Russian, Indian, Native American and Jewish mythology. The story symbolises renewal, rebirth and hope – the idea that a difficult period is followed by better times.

The desire to believe that disaster contains within it a seed of possibility is a reflection of human optimism. Throughout history, the world has periodically experienced times of intense difficulty. Large-scale natural disasters, such as earthquakes, floods or bushfires, that devastate communities. Economic recessions or depressions that disrupt whole economies. Wars that cause mass devastation. Pandemics that lead to death and severe disruption. But our literature is filled with aphorisms expressing hope for the period that follows our lowest ebb. English theologian Thomas Fuller was the first to record the phrase 'the darkest hour is just before the dawn'. In one of my favourite quotes, American author Hal Borland writes that 'no winter lasts forever; no spring skips its turn'.[1]

The COVID-19 pandemic is a crisis of enormous scale: a health emergency that has killed millions of people and an economic calamity resulting in the deepest recession since World War II. In many parts of the world, it has also been accompanied by a crisis of democracy, with governments letting people down badly. In the midst of such bleakness, this book is a reassurance that after this intense period of turmoil, we can recover. It explores how we can rebuild physically, economically and psychologically from what seem like serious setbacks. By learning the lessons of other recoveries, we can shape the path ahead. With the right choices, a bright dawn beckons.

From crisis to recovery

The word 'crisis' does not only mean unmitigated disaster. It contains the idea of facing a crossroads. Depending on which dictionary you consult, a crisis is 'a turning point for better or worse', 'a decisive moment' or 'an unstable or crucial time in which a decisive change is impending'.[2] This is a moment of truth for us. We will be different after this pandemic. It is up to us to determine if things will be better or worse.

'Recovery' is another interesting term. My favourite dictionary, the Cambridge, defines recovery as 'the process of becoming successful or normal again after problems; a process in which a

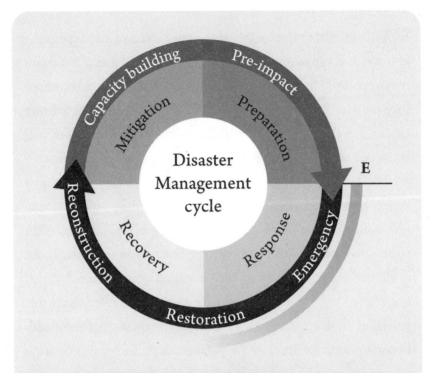

Figure 1. The disaster management cycle involves four key stages: response, recovery, mitigation and preparation. It is a useful tool for thinking about the effects of a crisis and what comes next.

situation improves after a difficult period'.[3] Recovery is one of four stages in the disaster management cycle used by agencies all around the world.

During or immediately after a crisis, the response phase is about saving lives and minimising the immediate impacts. In a natural disaster, this might involve the provision of medical assistance, drinking water or shelter. In the context of COVID-19, it involves widespread testing, contact tracing, social distancing requirements and treatment of those who contract the virus.

After response comes recovery, which is about resuming normal operations. But anticipation of future crises is important too. Two stages in the disaster management cycle involve getting ready for calamities that may befall us in times to come. 'Mitigation' is about reducing the impacts or risks of future disasters. This might mean ensuring houses are built to withstand storms or bushfires, for example. 'Preparation' is about being ready to manage a future crisis, for example by ensuring that emergency services are well trained. Each phase in the cycle is of equal importance.

While it's tempting to think of the word 'recovery' as meaning simply getting back to normal, that understanding isn't quite correct. After an enormously stressful event, we will be changed. That applies to communities and nations, but also to individuals. As resilience expert Dr Michael Ungar writes, 'We are transformed, hopefully for the better, by our experience. We re-evaluate our priorities ... Recovery usually means a new regime that eventually becomes our new normal.' Or as German philosopher Friedrich Nietzsche wrote in 1888, 'What does not kill me makes me stronger.'[4] So in this book, let's think of recovery not as a return to the past but as a move to the future.

It's possible to draw parallels between personal and national crises. In his book *Upheaval*, geographer Jared Diamond builds an elaborate framework that does just this. 'Individuals in crisis often receive help from friends, just as nations in crisis may recruit help from allied nations,' Diamond writes. 'Individuals in crisis may model their solutions on ways in which they see other individuals addressing similar crises; nations in crisis may borrow and adapt solutions already devised by other nations facing similar problems. Individuals in crisis may derive self-confidence from having survived previous crises; so do nations.'[5]

Yet I'm sceptical about relying too heavily on the psychology of individual crises. Cities and nations are not individuals; they need to grapple with different questions. For example, what are the implications for political and economic institutions? What role should our leaders play? How do we make collective decisions? Should change be implemented incrementally or as part of a radical overhaul? How can we achieve reconciliation between parties in conflict?[6] These questions are not analogous to those faced by individuals. They require a different frame of reference.

By exploring past recoveries, I hope to generate insights into the crisis we're in and how we might approach our coming recovery. Germany today is a manufacturing powerhouse with the world's largest trade surplus, and South Korea is on its way to having the longest life expectancy in the world. New York City is the finance and media capital of the world, and Taiwan has handled COVID-19 better than almost anywhere else in the world. All of these places were devastated by crises in the relatively recent past, and all have recovered strongly to become better than before. Crisis has not stopped them growing to become quite amazing places.

The circumstances of each of these recoveries, and the others described in this book, are very different from those facing us today. The past is not an instruction manual for the future, but the lessons of history offer us something of value nonetheless. 'History doesn't repeat itself,' Mark Twain is reputed to have said, 'but it often rhymes.'

History has been influential in informing our response to the pandemic. From quarantine to lockdowns to masks, many of the policy decisions responding to the virus have been informed by lessons from previous pandemics, including the Spanish flu of 1918–19 and SARS (severe acute respiratory syndrome) in 2003.[7] Historical consequences also remind us of the risks of easing restrictions too early – in the next chapter, for example, we'll explore the horrific results in Philadelphia when its mayor decided to proceed with a large parade during the Spanish flu. Similarly, times past can help inform our coming recovery. Countries that have successfully recovered from crisis have much to teach us.

My starting point in writing this book was to identify cities, regions and countries that had recovered from a major crisis within the last century to become even better than they were before. Each chapter focuses on a different type of crisis – pandemic, recession, natural disaster and war – and includes at least two examples of successful recoveries. I sketch the background and history to each place that I investigate, and the interventions that led to the successful recovery. Most importantly, I draw out the potential implications for our recovery. What can we learn that we might be able to apply?

Of course, crises aren't always followed by successful recoveries – improvement is not inevitable. Throughout the book I briefly touch on some less successful recovery attempts, including the decade of stagnation in the United Kingdom following World War I and the Spanish flu, and stalled reconstruction efforts following civil wars in sub-Saharan Africa, to examine what we can learn. However, my focus is on the positive case studies, which act both to inform and to inspire.

While public policy is what I do for a living, I am not a historian and am far from an authority on most of the countries covered in this book. So, in addition to drawing extensively on studies and reports, I sought out a range of experts from around the world to hear their perspectives on my chosen case studies. Some, like Australian immunologist Professor Peter Doherty or German historian Professor Ulrich Herbert, are renowned academics. Others, like Christchurch mayor Lianne Dalziel or former Indonesian public servant Dr Kuntoro Mangkusubroto, played key leadership roles in their city's or nation's recovery. Learning from such an experienced and knowledgeable group of people was one major reward of this project. The insights they generously shared were fascinating and at times surprising.

As I immersed myself in interviews and data, I wondered if it was possible to determine the common elements of a successful recovery. Is a top-down, government-led approach most effective? Or is it better to support communities to establish their own recovery efforts? How and where should financial support be directed for best results? In my home of Australia, many argue that business and other tax cuts are the best approach to get things moving. Others suggest that addressing inequality by supporting the most disadvantaged in society is a better strategy. Proponents of each position present their opinions fervently, but often with slim data. I was keen to understand what the evidence says about the most effective approach.

As we commence our recovery, we won't only be dealing with COVID-19. The end of the pandemic will coincide with a host of other serious challenges. While many of these have plagued nations or the world for years, the virus has shone a light on or even exacerbated them. This makes the task of recovery more complex, requiring us to consider a great many factors – from deep structural inequality to geopolitical tensions to long-term economic stagnation. Yet while the task is large, there is also a once-in-a-lifetime opportunity here. The accelerating decarbonisation of the economy, for example, may provide the perfect catalyst to stimulate post-COVID economic development. Overlaying the lessons of past recoveries onto the current context, the final chapter provides some practical things we can do to set ourselves up for a strong recovery, at the local, national and global levels.

This book is not intended as an academic exercise. I have imbued it with a determined focus on action. The central question driving the text is simple: what do we need to do?

Prosperity is not inevitable. It's not a given that the phoenix will rise. Still, there is a lot to be optimistic about. The stories in this book demonstrate that over the longer term, the nature of a crisis is less relevant than the steps cities and nations take to address its impacts. The places described in this book have rebuilt to be wealthier, more productive and more resilient. They now know peace when before they were at war; they are healthy when once they were sick. If those who came before us could leverage their misfortune to create a better future, we can too.

If we make the right choices, a bright dawn will follow the darkness. The lessons of past recoveries show us the way.

1

PANDEMIC

In September 1918, American doctor Victor Vaughan was surveying the scene at Camp Devens, some 50 kilometres northwest of Boston. The hastily constructed camp was home to soldiers preparing to fight in the Great War. Just a couple of months earlier, engineers had built some 1400 buildings, including an 800-bed hospital. The camp was capable of housing 30,000 men, but as tens of thousands of soldiers arrived from across the country, the rough wooden barracks were quickly filled, forcing the erection of tents for the overflow.

Vaughan was grappling with the fact that the camp had suddenly, explosively, been overtaken by influenza. By 10 September, more than 500 men had been admitted to the hospital. Within four days, that number had tripled. On 15 September, a further 705 were admitted, and on 16 September beds had to be found for 1189 more. Another 2200 presented the day after, meaning that more than 6000 servicemen were crammed into the 800-bed facility.[1] The body count was rising quickly.

'I see hundreds of young, stalwart men in the uniform of their country coming into the wards of the hospital in groups of ten or more,' Vaughan wrote. 'They are placed on the cots until every bed is full and yet others crowd in. The faces soon wear a bluish cast; a distressing cough brings up the bloodstained sputum. In the morning the dead bodies are stacked about the morgue like cord wood … such are the grewsome [sic] pictures exhibited by the revolving memory cylinders in the brain of an old epidemiologist.'[2]

By the end of October, one third of the camp's population – some 15,000 men – had contracted influenza, and 787 had died.[3]

The United States was in the midst of the second – and most devastating – wave of the Spanish flu, the deadliest pandemic in modern history. In the United States alone, the virus killed some 675,000 people; in France, possibly up to 400,000; and in Britain, 228,000. Globally, the death toll from the influenza pandemic was somewhere between 50 and 100 million – about 2.5 to 5 per cent of the world's population, and at least five times as many as died in the fighting in the war.[4]

The pandemic had been enabled by the mobilisation of troops for war. As Mark Honigsbaum writes in *The Pandemic Century*, 'by bringing together men from so many different immunological backgrounds and forcing them to live at close quarters for weeks on end, the mobilisation greatly increased the risk of communicable diseases being spread from one to another'.[5]

The world's first case of the Spanish flu – so named because Spain was one of the first countries to publicly report cases of the disease – was at a military base in Kansas in March 1918.[6] American servicemen brought this comparatively mild first wave to Europe when they were deployed. But 'Northern France was a vast biological experiment – a place where large masses of men from two continents converged and mingled freely with men from a host of other nations', Honigsbaum notes, and it seems likely that the brutal second wave was introduced to the United States by troops returning from Europe.[7]

The second wave hit violently, with nearly 200,000 Americans dying from the flu in October 1918 alone. Cremation was an uncommon practice, and the sheer number of bodies overwhelmed undertakers, casket makers and grave diggers.

The mayor of Philadelphia made a serious error when he decided to proceed with the Liberty Loans Parade on 28 September 1918. More than 200,000 people jammed the streets, cheering wildly as marching bands, boy scouts and uniformed troops marched to promote the sale of 'liberty loans' – government bonds issued to pay for the war.[8] Sadly, Philadelphia recorded more than 2600 flu deaths within two weeks of the event, and by the third week of October, deaths had climbed to more than 4500. At the peak, flu deaths in Philadelphia approached 1000 per day, and 'bodies piled up in morgues for lack of undertakers, the stench became overpowering and the city resorted to digging mass graves'.[9] Corpses draped in sackcloths and blood-stained sheets were left on porches and footpaths. Bodies collected by police and priests were piled atop each other on horse-drawn wagons, limbs often protruding from the sheets.[10]

Yet as quickly as the pandemic arrived, it ended. By November 1918 and the armistice signalling the end of the war, it 'was already once more on its way to becoming a familiar seasonal ailment'.[11] A milder, third wave of the pandemic hit during the northern winter and spring of 1919. By the summer of 1919, it had mostly fizzled out, a sufficient proportion of the population having developed immunity.

The world moved on. While in many countries the pandemic was accompanied by a recession, in the United States and some major European nations it was followed by the Roaring Twenties.

The flu was effectively the preamble to a decade of radical change. The place of women in society shifted in many countries as they were granted the right to vote and sought professional employment in roles such as nursing, some having gained experience in World War I or the American Revolutionary War. The introduction of the assembly line turned the United States into a manufacturing powerhouse, making cars affordable to the masses. The US economy grew by 42 per cent during the 1920s, while unemployment rarely rose above 4 per cent.[12] Due to the widespread adoption of electricity during the period, new technology such as radio and film became widespread. Jazz music and the rejection of stuffy pre-war attitudes might have originated in the United States, but they soon swept through Europe too.

The US experience shows that it's possible to recover quickly after a devastating pandemic. With the right policy settings, the years following a pandemic can even be a period of flourishing. The United States was probably the source of the Spanish flu, some 28 per cent of Americans were infected by it and the disease killed nearly 0.8 per cent of the country's population.[13] Yet in the decade that followed, Americans became healthier than they had ever been, and life expectancy increased – males born in the 1920s could expect to live some six years longer than those born in 1914.[14] This was a period of enormous economic prosperity and carefree living for many.

Similarly, in this chapter we'll see that Taiwan's experience of the 2003 SARS epidemic informed the policy responses that have equipped it to respond impressively to COVID-19. Taiwan demonstrates that a pandemic can in fact leave a nation's health system better placed to face the next crisis, making us more resilient to future health and economic shocks.

But this brighter tomorrow is not guaranteed. As the world mobilises to defeat COVID-19, we need to make the right policy choices as we recover from the health and economic impacts. We need to respond to the profound social changes that have been brought about, and make the most of the opportunity to learn from this experience in order to prepare for future pandemics.

In the next chapter, we'll look at the decisions we need to make to ensure we recover quickly from economic recession. This chapter draws on the experience of past pandemics to explore the decisions we need to make as we recover from the health and social impacts of COVID-19.

Learning from the past

In a normal flu season, infants and the elderly are those most likely to die, as they have the weakest immune systems. The graph looks like a U, with mortality highest on the left side (infants) and on the far right (the elderly).

The Spanish flu was different. As shown in Figure 2, its mortality curve was shaped more like a W, as otherwise healthy adults aged twenty to forty died in large numbers. Adults in this age bracket accounted for half of all deaths from Spanish flu. The reasons for this are unknown, but some researchers speculate that those over forty had developed immunity through previous exposure to a similar virus.[15]

The death rate among men was much higher than for women, meaning it was often the family's primary breadwinner who succumbed. This placed enormous pressure on the rest of the household. Many survivors faced the complete destruction of their family unit, and millions of children were orphaned.[16] This was at a time when the United States had little formal social welfare and no

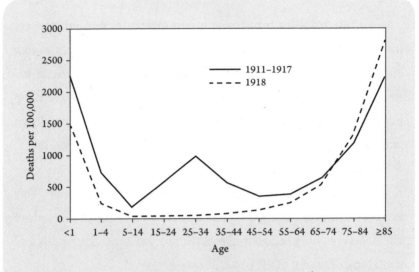

Figure 2. During the 1918 Spanish influenza, the combined influenza and pneumonia mortality among those aged twenty to forty was particularly high.

organised system of adoption. Similarly, in the absence of support from their adult children, many of the elderly and infirm were left destitute and went in their thousands into poorhouses.[17] These were shelters designed to care for the poor, though they were often degrading to residents, routinely grouping people into 'deserving' and 'undeserving' poor and imposing strict discipline.[18]

The flu killed at different rates in different settings. In New Zealand, the Maori population died at seven times the rate of British settlers. Across large parts of the Pacific, similar discrepancies between indigenous populations and those of European descent were evident. In Guam, the flu killed 5 per cent of the local population, but only one sailor at the US naval base. In South Africa, the virus killed 2.6 per cent of infected white South Africans. For the black population, the rate was nearly 6 per cent.[19]

The country most impacted by Spanish flu was India, where 17 to 18 million people died – about 6 per cent of its population.

This is a phenomenal number – at that time equivalent to losing the combined populations of New Zealand, Denmark, Norway, Greece, Switzerland and Australia. Women – who were more likely to be undernourished and cooped up indoors caring for the ill – died at a greater rate than men.[20] The mortality rate in India was truly terrifying. Among Indian troops, for every hundred that caught influenza, twenty-one died. One hospital in Delhi treated 13,190 influenza patients, with 7044 of those succumbing to the illness.[21] Normally, corpses in India are cremated on riverbanks, with the ashes given to the river. A lack of firewood made this impossible and the rivers became clogged with bodies.[22]

Victor Vaughan, the American doctor we heard from at the start of this chapter, watched the virus move rapidly across the earth and feared for humanity's future. 'If the epidemic continues its mathematical rate of acceleration,' he wrote, 'civilisation could easily disappear … from the face of the earth within a matter of a few more weeks.'[23]

In India, it quickly became clear that the British rulers were incapable of handling a crisis like this, with the country's health-care infrastructure in shambles. So local organisations mobilised to assist, raising funds, removing corpses, organising cremations and running relief centres to distribute medicines, blankets and other supplies.[24] While local caste-based and community organisations had existed across India for some time, the flu united them in common cause. 'Once the pandemic passed, emotion against the British was even higher than it had been before,' Laura Spinney argues in her book *Pale Rider*. 'Those people were far more united than they had been. And now they came together behind Gandhi. He found that suddenly, he had the grassroots support that he had been lacking.'[25] And so, the flu became a catalyst for

India's independence movement, which culminated with the end of British rule nearly two decades later.

As devastating as it was, the flu didn't cause widespread panic in the United States and in most parts of Europe. Concern in early 1918, during the first wave, was muted. 'Compared to typhus, a deadly blood-borne disease spread by lice that lived in soldiers' clothing, or the septicaemia that bred in gunshot and shrapnel wounds,' Honigsbaum writes, 'influenza was a trifling infection from the point of view of army medical officers.'[26] In the United States, Spanish flu was thought of as an exotic disease, largely impacting on those elsewhere. This view was reinforced by public health officials, who were keen to downplay the toll on American servicemen and talk up the impact it had on German troops. It was only during the most significant wave of deaths, in October 1918, when hospitals were 'flooded with pneumonia cases' and the dead 'had become impossible to ignore', that Americans recognised it as 'some kind of plague'.[27]

This is perhaps because most ordinary Americans were unaffected by the pandemic. While the Spanish flu was twenty-five times deadlier than a normal flu, the population had recent memory of outbreaks of diseases such as cholera and pneumonic plague, which had a much higher mortality rate. At least two-thirds of the population escaped infection altogether, and of those who caught the disease, just over 2 per cent died. Come 1920, the flu faded from the public consciousness.

Another reason for the lack of panic may be the limited perspective on the death toll that was available at the time. There were only a few places in the world that aimed to keep accurate statistics, and even they were quickly overwhelmed. Many people died without ever having sought medical aid. Outside of the developed world, good records were more or less non-existent. The first attempt to collate a global death toll didn't come until 1927, when an American study estimated that 21 million people had died. Every revision of the death toll since then has been upwards.[28]

The Spanish flu had a significant impact on economies worldwide. As we've seen with COVID-19, many cities imposed health measures that closed shops and restaurants. They also banned public gatherings, restricted transport and staggered business hours.[29] Researchers at Harvard concluded that the flu led to worldwide declines in gross domestic product of between 6 and 8 per cent.[30] Following the pandemic, the globe went into a severe economic recession in 1920 and 1921, accompanied by deflation and large drops in productivity. This economic crisis was so significant that English economist T.E. Gregory described the world in 1921 as 'nearer to collapse than it has been at any time since the downfall of the Roman Empire.'[31]

People living through this era endured an enormous amount. First, a four-year global war, killing some 15 to 22 million combatants and civilians. Then, a pandemic, killing 50 to 100 million people. And to top it off, a major recession, leading to huge falls in output and rises in unemployment.

At the end of it all, it's no surprise that people cut loose a little. While many had retreated into isolation during the waves of sickness, the 1920s saw a manic flight into sociability, characterised by parties and concerts. The flu had not reduced humanity's determination to socialise. Given the level of collective trauma, you'd hardly blame them for being a little nihilistic. If you might die in a war or get wiped out in a pandemic, why not get drunk and dance the night away?

America's economy boomed during the 1920s, with national wealth more than doubling, propelling many Americans to hitherto unknown levels of affluence. Recovery was enabled by a surge of investment in technology. In the United States, mass electrification rolled out across the country. With this came household appliances, such as washing machines, refrigerators and radios. Mass production made cars more affordable and accessible. Electricity and the automobile both had their beginnings before the war, but the recovery facilitated a rapid uptake. By the end of the decade, there was one car on the road for every five Americans, giving more young people the freedom to go where they wanted and access to 'bedrooms on wheels'.

The long-term pattern of increased life expectancy resumed after the pandemic. The war and the flu had significantly impacted average life expectancy at birth, which dropped 11.8 years in the United States between 1917 and 1918. But the rebound was quick, and life expectancy at birth was higher in 1919 than in 1917. Male life expectancy at birth, down to below forty in 1918, was approaching sixty by the early 1920s.[32]

Another trend that continued apace, seemingly unaffected by the pandemic, was urbanisation. There was no sign that people carried any lingering anxiety about living in densely populated cities. In the United States, the share of the population living in urban areas rose from 51 per cent in 1920 to 56 per cent in 1930.[33] The Roaring Twenties was a decidedly urban phenomenon.

In 1920, American women were granted the right to vote. With more than a quarter of employed women working in office jobs,[34] many – particularly those in urban areas – could afford to participate in the burgeoning consumer culture. Birth control became respectable and more readily available, meaning women (at least those of a certain economic status) could choose to have fewer children.[35] One of the defining images of the era is the flapper – a sexually liberated woman who smoked in public and danced the new dances in jazz clubs.

The fervour of the Roaring Twenties was experienced across America and much of continental Europe. While Italy saw Benito Mussolini, the leader of the Fascist party who established a one-party police state, and the Russian Empire transformed into a communist state, the Weimar Republic of Germany developed a cabaret culture and became a centre of artistic innovation, creativity and experimentation. The United Kingdom as a whole endured stagnation and recession, but in London and Paris, the Bright Young Things – bohemian aristocrats and socialites – threw decadent costume parties, engaged in pranks, consumed alcohol to excess and had drug-fuelled orgies.[36] All of this was catalysed, at least to some extent, by the terrible experience of the Spanish flu. While writing this book, more than one friend has enquired hopefully as to whether that's the type of behaviour we can anticipate after this pandemic is over.

Some eighty-four years after the end of the Spanish flu, another pandemic was spreading rapidly around the world. Severe acute respiratory syndrome, SARS, was a coronavirus from an unknown animal species – perhaps bats – that first infected humans in the Guangdong province of southern China in 2002.[37] By April the following year, the World Health Organization was reporting some 4000 cases worldwide, with 229 deaths. At that time, Taiwan, a highly developed East Asian economy with a sophisticated public health system, had just 29 probable cases and no deaths. Most cases were among those who had arrived from mainland China or Hong Kong, and the growth rate seemed relatively low. The virus looked to be manageable. Yet by May 2003, cases had grown exponentially – to 683 – and there had been 181 deaths.[38] Most cases had come from mass infections at hospitals.[39] With the disease killing more than one in every four who caught it, Taiwan experienced the highest SARS fatality rate in the world.

Once the crisis in Taiwan was over, there was much soul-searching, with attempts to understand how the virus was able to spread so rapidly. Inexperience in containing outbreaks was thought largely to blame, along with inadequacies in the health system, hospital mismanagement and some degree of human care-lessness.[40]

When the world confronted the next major coronavirus, Taiwan was ready. On 31 December 2019, staff at the Taiwan Centers for Disease Control (CDC) were monitoring social media posts about a pneumonia of unknown origin in Wuhan, China. Close ties between many in Taiwan and mainland China provided Taiwan with excellent early intelligence. The CDC quickly fired off an email to the World Health Organization seeking additional information. On the same day, Taiwan started instituting health screenings for all passengers arriving from Wuhan, with foreign minister Joseph Wu telling *Time* that 'we were not able to get satis-factory answers from either the WHO or from the Chinese CDC, and we got nervous and we started doing our preparation.'[41]

In early January 2020, well before it was confirmed that the virus could pass between humans, Taiwan classified the new strain of flu as a statutory infectious disease and implemented manda-tory health checks on passengers from China. It quickly integrated its national health insurance database with the immigration and customs database, which provided doctors with real-time alerts. If someone who had recently returned from China presented with flu-like symptoms, they could be identified quickly. Strict travel advisories and entry protocols were introduced, tiered by the risk level of the country in question.[42] Patients with severe respiratory symptoms who had tested negative for flu were sought out through the national health insurance database and re-tested for COVID-19.

The story of Taiwan's successful response to COVID-19 begins with Taiwan's recovery from SARS, when it learnt the lessons of that experience and put in place the changes that would ensure it was prepared for the next pandemic.

Tsung-Mei Cheng grew up in Taiwan, where she studied law before moving to the United States for graduate study. An expert on health policy and economics now based at Princeton University, she was previously a member of Taiwan's Science and Technology Advisory Group, which informed the Taiwanese premier on policies relating to the development of science and technology, including healthcare. Over a scratchy phone connection, she tells me that the impact of SARS 'spooked' the Taiwanese government. As a result, 'the government made legal and institutional changes in anticipation of future emerging infectious disease'.

After SARS, Taiwan sent the health minister, together with the head of the Taiwan CDC, to the United States Centers for Disease Control and Prevention to seek advice. 'After they came back, they established a super war room against infectious diseases,' Cheng says. 'And so they have a nerve centre to respond to any pandemic in future.' This body, called the National Health Command Center, is described by the government as 'an operational command point for direct communications among the central, regional and local authorities' aimed at addressing public health emergencies. It brings together multiple command centres, including the Central Epidemic Command Center, the Biological Pathogen Disaster Command Center, the Counter-Bioterrorism Command Center and the Central Medical Emergency Operations Center.[43] It accommodates 100 people, a situation room and a coordination centre, supported by cutting-edge technology and advanced communications.

In January 2020, when the first COVID-19 cases were reported from China, Taiwan quickly established the Central Epidemic Command Center to oversee and implement the national plan – 'headed by the health minister himself, with CDC heads', Cheng tells me. This body was able to coordinate efforts across the ministries of Transport, Labour, Education and Economics, as well as cabinet-level executive agencies such as the Environment Protection Authority, to ensure there was a comprehensive government response.[44]

In the wake of SARS, Taiwan had introduced a raft of legal measures to enable management of future pandemics. These included provisions for compulsory physical examinations, short-term detention or quarantine. In 2011, the constitutional court reviewed these provisions and found them valid.[45] So, when COVID-19 hit, a robust and agreed legal framework was in place, meaning that 'everything that the government has needed to do since has been in accordance with both the law and the constitution', according to Cheng. 'It's been very helpful.'

One of the most important factors underpinning Taiwan's pandemic preparedness is its healthcare system, which on some measures is ranked the best in the world.[46] After SARS, the Taiwanese government invested hundreds of millions of dollars in the healthcare system to increase preparedness for the next pandemic, including the construction of hospital isolation wards equipped for patients with new infectious diseases.[47] Because it is a government-run system with universal coverage, 'there are no financial barriers preventing access to needed care', Cheng says. This makes a big difference in a pandemic. 'In Taiwan, the minute you have symptoms, you go to a doctor or a hospital. If you land in Taipei and you have fever, cough, et cetera, you are checked right there and then. If tests come back positive, you're taken to the hospital right away.'

Taiwan's success in containing COVID-19 was further enhanced by the extensive adoption of face masks. As in many East Asian countries, it was common for people in Taiwan to wear masks long before COVID-19. The experience of SARS had led the Taiwanese to see that wearing face masks was an easy and practical way to protect themselves in the case of a pandemic. Consequently, once COVID-19 arrived, masking up was second nature. From very early on in the pandemic, the government recommended that healthy people wear masks in crowded spaces. An enormous national stockpile of masks, and the capacity to scale up production, meant that Taiwan was able to export millions of masks to other countries.[48]

Taiwan has experienced relatively few deaths from COVID-19. While most of the world suffered through hundreds of millions of cases, Taiwan went 250 days without a single case.[49] This is made all the more remarkable by the fact that Taiwan is located just 160 kilometres from mainland China, where the disease originated. Given the extensive travel between Taiwan and mainland China, many expected Taiwan to be severely impacted. But, with a population of some 24 million, it has a death rate of just thirty-two per million people. By comparison, at the time of writing, the

United Kingdom had a death rate of 1885 per million, the United States had a rate of 1876, and Peru had experienced 5828 deaths per million.[50]

This success is not just about lives saved and trauma reduced. It has meant that life in Taiwan was mostly able to continue without significant disruption. Unlike many other countries around the world, throughout 2020 Taiwan was able to avoid having to go into lockdown.

Taiwan's experience of the pandemic has not been without challenges. It has suffered from a severe shortage of vaccine doses – in part due to geopolitical tensions with China – and its vaccine rollout was particularly slow to get going. In mid-2021, underestimating the virulent new strains of the virus, Taiwan experienced its first significant COVID-19 outbreak. While nowhere near the magnitude experienced elsewhere around the world, it led to hundreds of deaths and blemished its previously near-perfect record of COVID-19 control.[51] Still, Taiwan's success in controlling the virus at a time when it was running rampant throughout much of the world has been impressive. It is a clear demonstration that lessons learnt from a past crisis can better equip us to respond to the next one.

Preparing for the future

Pandemics are not a recent phenomenon. Since pretty much the beginning of recorded history, humans have been writing about being struck down by infectious diseases. In the Old Testament, the prophet Jeremiah describes how 'death has come up into our windows; it has entered our palaces, cutting off the children from the streets and the young men from the squares'.[52] The Antonine Plague afflicted the Roman Empire in 165–180 AD, killing an

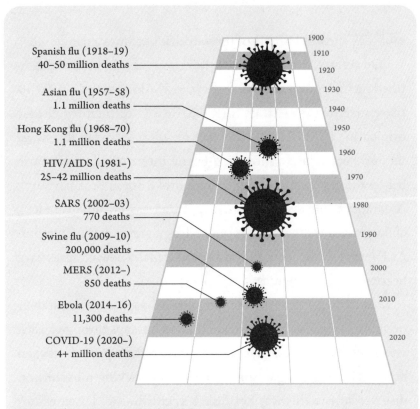

Figure 3. Deadliest pandemics of the past 100 years

estimated five million people. From 541 to 549, the Plague of Justinian devastated Europe, the Mediterranean Basin and the Near East, dispatching some 50 million people. Plague felled some 200 million in Eurasia and North Africa between 1347 and 1351. In 1520, the Spanish brought smallpox to North America (yes, a plague they did actually have responsibility for spreading), killing millions of Native Americans. And bubonic plague struck again in 1855, killing 12 million, including ten million in India alone.[53]

Emerging infectious diseases are those that have recently appeared within a population or whose incidence or geographic range is rapidly increasing. An outbreak occurs when the number of cases exceeds what would normally be expected. When an outbreak spreads to most of the world, it becomes a pandemic.[54]

On average, a significant new infectious disease has been identified each year over the past forty years.[55] Along with COVID-19,
these include HIV/AIDS, SARS, MERS (a respiratory disease
originating in the Middle East in 2012), Ebola, avian flu, swine
flu and zika virus (a mosquito-borne infection that can harm
babies during pregnancy, which first broke out in Brazil in 2015).
A number of old diseases have reappeared too, including cholera,
chikungunya, yellow fever, plague, dengue fever and meningitis.
As Figure 3 shows, over the past century many new diseases have
become large pandemics.

About 75 per cent of emerging infectious diseases have their
origins in animals and are transmitted to humans through a variety of infection routes.[56] Diseases can also be transmitted between
humans by living organisms such as bloodsucking mosquitoes;
diseases spread this way are called 'vector-borne'. Diseases can
also be spread through indirect contact, such as through chicken
coops or soil, consumption of contaminated animal products
or drinking water contaminated with the faeces of an infected
animal.[57]

Sometimes, in a phenomenon called 'zoonotic spillover',
viruses mutate to allow transmission from an animal to a human.
Usually, a virus starts in a primary host species, say a bat. When
another animal species comes into contact with the bat, it may
contract the virus. If the virus can overcome the immune response
of the new species, transmission occurs. It can now spread from
one species to another, including humans, and in the right circumstances it may lead to sustained human-to-human transmission.
Coronaviruses – which SARS, MERS and COVID-19 all are – are
known to cause regular spillover events.[58]

To learn more about zoonotic diseases, I sought out Laureate Professor Peter Doherty, an Australian immunologist. He won the 1996 Nobel Prize in Physiology or Medicine for his discovery of 'killer T-cells', which the body produces to destroy infected cells so that viruses cannot reproduce. In his eighties, and with a medical research institute named after him (The Peter Doherty Institute for Infection and Immunity), he's showing no signs of slowing down. Speaking with me on Skype from his home in Melbourne – he resides just a few suburbs away from me, but I can't visit as the city is in lockdown – he says, 'I'm not going to sit around and do nothing. I don't think that's the way to survive.' He spends his time writing, working a day a week at the University of Melbourne and explaining the science of COVID-19 to the public. A frank and somewhat uncensored science communicator, he speaks to the media regularly and has an active social media presence.

Doherty tells me that zoonotic diseases are increasing in frequency because people travel more often and over greater distances than in the past and live together in densely packed cities. Destruction of habitat also means people are coming into contact with wild animals more often. 'It's not going to be a one-in-100-year pandemic,' Doherty says of COVID-19. 'It's going to be a pandemic every ten or twenty years, if we keep down the road we've been going – with this massive global population, deforestation and people moving more and more into wildlife areas – and if the Asian societies continue with live animal and live bird markets, which are really dangerous.'

Air travel is also a key risk that needs to be managed. 'Real viruses don't move themselves,' Doherty writes on his blog. 'They don't blow across the oceans like dust plumes from the Saharan Air Layer and they are not, like computer "viruses" and conspiracy theories, disseminated via 5G networks. SARS-CoV-2, the virus that causes the disease COVID-19, flew around the world in people travelling in Boeings and Airbuses.'[59] As a result, Doherty argues that 'the very first thing we need is a global agreement that any country that detects what looks to be a new pathogen spreading rapidly immediately notifies the World Health Organisation and shuts down air travel'.

While new diseases present an enormous threat to humanity, other infectious diseases – many of which are curable or preventable – continue to kill millions of people around the world. Tuberculosis killed 1.5 million people in 2018. Measles killed 140,000 people, mostly in low-income countries, despite a safe and effective vaccine being widely available. In 2018, there were more than 228 million cases of malaria, mostly in Africa, leading to 405,000 deaths. Seasonal flu kills up to 600,000 people globally each year, and diarrheal diseases kill around 525,000 children each year.[60] Annual deaths from many of these causes are reducing, but there are some big risks.

'With climate change, you're looking at diseases that are insect-borne moving further away from the Equator or further up into cooler mountain regions,' Doherty says. For example, in Kenya malaria moved 'from Mombasa to Nairobi'. While malaria is the most obvious example, this concern relates to any insect-borne disease. 'A whole lot of insect-borne diseases that were confined essentially to Africa or Southeast Asia – dengue, chikungunya, zika – basically moved across the planet in the mosquito belt. And so those diseases that were confined to the Western Indo-Pacific are now in the Caribbean and up into the United States and down into South America.' His concern is backed up by the Intergovernmental Panel on Climate Change, which argues that 'risks from vector-borne diseases are projected to generally increase with warming, due to the extension of the infection area and season.[61]

Epidemics 'underline the key role played by environmental, social, and cultural factors in changing patterns of disease prevalence and emergence', Mark Honigsbaum writes. 'Most cases of disease emergence can be traced to the disturbance of ecological equilibriums or alterations to the environments in which pathogens habitually reside.'[62]

With future pandemics almost certain, it's essential that we prepare for the next one.

The Spanish flu gave rise to a greater focus on epidemiology, the branch of medical science that studies the distribution and determinants of diseases, and to a host of measures that paved the way for preparedness.

One lesson that health authorities took away from the 1918 catastrophe was that it was no longer reasonable to blame individuals for an infectious disease or to treat them in isolation. Pandemics are a social problem. The 1920s saw many governments embrace the concept of socialised medicine – healthcare for all, free at the point of delivery. Soviet Russia was the first to put in place centralised public healthcare in the early 1920s, with the government providing state-funded healthcare to all citizens. Germany, France and the United Kingdom eventually followed with their own socialised healthcare systems.[63] The United States took a different approach, preferring employer-based healthcare insurance schemes, which saw employers paying for their employees' health insurance as part of a benefits package.[64]

Globally, there was more interest in tracking the progress of disease, too. Without an early warning system, the United States was caught unawares by the flu in 1918, so a national morbidity scheme was introduced across the country. By 1925, all states were reporting on the prevalence of infectious diseases in the community.[65] A number of other countries followed.

The world had learnt that viruses don't respect borders. After a series of meetings and conferences, the Health Committee of the League of Nations was established in 1920 to advise and facilitate international cooperation on health matters. This – along with the Paris-based International Office of Public Hygiene – was the forerunner of today's World Health Organization.

But the influence of pandemics on medicine hasn't all been positive. I spoke with a historian of twentieth-century medicine and technology, Dr Caitjan Gainty. A Chicago native, Gainty is now based at King's College London. From her home office, she tells me on a video chat, 'It's amazing how quickly medicine moved on from Spanish flu.'

Gainty says that medicine, rather than retaining a focus on public health, became obsessed with science – with 'finding a cure' and 'individualised care that is focused on acute illness rather than preventative care focused on chronic illness'. The medical fraternity, caught up in the Roaring Twenties exuberance, concentrated on 'marketing medicine in terms that they thought would sell at this moment of massive consumption. Medicine does a great job of promoting itself as something that people want to buy, as the thing that cures what ails you.'

That focus dogged medicine throughout the twentieth century. 'We committed to a particular direction in healthcare right around this period,' Gainty says. Doctors and medical scientists 'turned towards looking at things through the microscope' and focused on finding 'something that makes those diseases disappear'. As a result, they neglected 'the notion that we need to think about, for example, the kind of social determinants of health – poverty, housing, nutrition'.

Gainty is far from exuberant about the legacy the Spanish flu had on healthcare. 'The kinds of things that we attended to after the Spanish flu were really not the kinds of things that would help us long-term in terms of health and wellness,' she says. 'They are things that were industrially focused. They are about offering consumers a very particular product that they could then use to cure themselves.'

In thinking about the response to infectious diseases, there is a tension between two different – but complementary – approaches.

On the one hand there's the scientific approach, with its focus on the development of vaccines, treatments and cures. Medical researchers and the biotech industry are absorbed with the quest to understand the virus and to develop a technology that can control the pathogen. This is the world of laboratories with high levels of biosecurity, high-tech equipment and highly trained scientists.

Yet COVID-19 reminds us that no matter how brilliant the technology or the scientists behind it, there are inherent limitations with the scientific approach. Before we roll out new vaccines or treatments to millions of people, testing needs to ensure they are both safe and effective. This process typically takes years, even if expedited. 'No matter how clever we are with the technology, basically we've still got to go out and test it in people,' Peter Doherty says. 'If you were just going to bang it straight into people you could have had a vaccine almost straight away, but you've got this totally unavoidable testing in the way.'

On the other hand there's the non-pharmaceutical approach. While the scientists are developing vaccines and therapies, those focused on public health are more likely to use bureaucratic tools to understand and manage the disease. These tools include restrictions on travel, quarantines and lockdowns. The countries that have been most successful in containing the spread of COVID-19 have typically relied on non-pharmaceutical approaches to do so. Earlier in this chapter, we explored Taiwan's early success in containing the disease through travel advisories, innovative use of data, robust public healthcare systems and effective governance.

The two approaches work best in tandem. In many countries, the public health response has been enabled by widespread testing, made possible by the rapid development of technology by scientists and industry. And while an effective public health response is absolutely essential to bring a pandemic under control, it is probably not sufficient to end it. It seems that only pharmaceutical responses will be able to permanently neutralise the threat of COVID-19. As we recover from this pandemic, it will be important that we remember the value of both approaches.

We see the tension between these two approaches most clearly when it comes to the role of experts. In places such as Taiwan, Australia and New Zealand, governments have been prepared to take specialists' advice. In many, the declaration of a formal state of emergency has provided chief health officers with extensive powers to enforce public health orders, without the normal processes of parliamentary scrutiny.[66]

Experts are fallible. They don't know everything. Throughout the course of COVID-19, experts have changed their minds – and their advice – numerous times. For example, early in the pandemic the wearing of face masks was often actively discouraged – due to concerns about the shortages of masks available for health workers, yes, but also to concerns that the potential risks (such as self-contamination resulting from touching a contaminated mask) could outweigh the potential benefits to the user.[67] Yet when new evidence that widespread mask wearing could slow the spread of the virus came to light, the World Health Organization updated its advice to 'encourage the general public to wear masks' in areas where there is community transmission. Mask-wearing was even made compulsory in many countries.[68]

Scientific understanding matures with time. Initially it was believed that COVID-19 was transmitted through droplets – large mucus or saliva particles heavier than air. This informed guidelines about the need for 1.5-metre separation, as droplet transmission occurs most readily at these short distances. However, if it was the case that COVID-19 could only be spread by droplets, why did more than 700 passengers on the *Diamond Princess* cruise ship in Yokohama, Japan, contract COVID-19 when isolating in their cabins? Why were mysterious outbreaks emerging where, for instance, fifty-two members of a choir in Skagit Valley, Washington, were infected by one super-spreader?[69] By July 2020, the World Health Organization had updated advice to acknowledge that COVID-19 could be spread through the air, causing an increased risk of transmission in indoor spaces, particularly those with poor ventilation.[70]

Confronted with the fallibility of expert advice, how much should we rely on it? As Caitjan Gainty says, 'We shouldn't say, "Okay, so science knows and gives the right answer all the time." We should instead say, "Okay, so this is a process by which we are drawing conclusions about something that we had no prior experience with."' In responding to a pandemic, expert advice is the best hope we have. But we need to cut experts some slack – they are drawing on their knowledge and experience to respond to a pathogen the world hasn't seen before. Every new insight builds

on what came before, meaning it takes time for an expert understanding to mature.

In *The Pandemic Century*, Mark Honigsbaum argues that every
outbreak over the past century 'undermine[d] confidence in the
dominant medical and scientific paradigm'. In almost every case,
'what was "known" before the emergence event ... was shown to
be false'.[71] Medical researchers assumed that the Spanish flu was
transmitted by bacteria and that they would be able to develop a
vaccine. As Honigsbaum describes it, the flu was initially dismissed
a nuisance – but history shows us it was far more than that.[72]

It's also worth remembering that a diverse range of experts are
offering advice on different aspects of a pandemic. The immunologist in the lab, the epidemiologist exploring disease transmission
and the science communicator all contribute a unique perspective. As these expert views collide, there are judgement calls
and decisions that need to be made. Different factors need to be
weighed up. It's important that appropriate mechanisms are in
place to ensure that a diversity of expert voices can work together
to lead the pandemic response. Taiwan's Central Epidemic Command Centre is one such mechanism that enables this.

Other types of expert advice are valuable too, not just that of
scientists. This is especially the case when shaping the broader
public health response. Even in my country, Australia, where the
pandemic response has been mostly impressive, governments
have had to learn to draw on the advice of a broader range of
experts. Scientific voices led the public health response, but as
the pandemic progressed, it became clear that governments had
not been engaging with multicultural organisations or ethnic
associations in a coordinated way, meaning their expertise was
underutilised. As a result, many communities found it difficult

to access up-to-date public health information in a timely manner or an appropriate form.[73] It is important to consider the full breadth of the knowledge that we may need to draw on.

Given the enormous upheaval that pandemics generate, the world is inevitably different afterwards, with changes that are often indirect and unexpected. We can expect transformations of our economy, politics, cities and gender relations. Even Peter Doherty, author of a book called *Pandemics*, has been surprised by the impacts of COVID-19 so far. 'I vastly underestimated the human factor,' he writes. 'Though I was aware of economic projections that a global influenza pandemic could cost trillions of dollars, I hadn't translated that to job losses, personal isolation, effects on social and psychological wellbeing, broader health consequences and so forth.'[74]

Some of these changes may end up being positive. The Spanish flu, for instance, enabled women to play a new and valuable role in the workforce. The disproportionate share of men killed by the Spanish flu, together with the deaths of World War I, led to a shortage of labour in many developed countries, enabling women to move into jobs typically occupied exclusively by men, such as manufacturing. And with more economic power, women agitated for political rights as well.

By 1918, women in New Zealand, Australia and Finland had been able to vote for more than a decade. Yet in the United States, despite a long campaign, the women's suffrage movement had not yet succeeded. The flu helped elevate women socially and financially, giving them a greater voice in political affairs. The Nineteenth Amendment was ratified in 1920, finally granting American women the right to vote.[75] COVID-19 may yet bring an opportunity for new groups to move into parts of the workforce or society previously denied to them.

Another area in which pandemics have a profound impact is urban form. Cities are the epicentre of pandemics. The sites of major ports and airports, they are the virus gateways. Urban areas provide more opportunity for viral transmission, with greater contact between larger numbers of people. Pandemics have decimated cities in the past – from the plague in Europe in the Middle Ages to the Spanish flu in Philadelphia in the twentieth century. During the Spanish flu, city residents experienced empty downtowns, wore face masks and went through quarantines and lockdowns – just like we are during COVID-19. Some people fled cities for the countryside.

The perversity of this is that while viruses hit cities hard, urban residents actually tend to fare better than those in suburban or rural areas. In urban communities, less than one in 100 inhabitants died of Spanish flu, whereas in isolated communities, nine in 100 died. The mortality rate from Spanish flu was higher in Alaska than anywhere else in the United States. These outcomes might be because people living in cities have a higher degree of pre-existing immunity from past infections.[76] Rural areas also tend to be home to older, more vulnerable populations and have fewer, smaller and lesser-equipped hospitals. If you fall sick, you will have a better chance of survival in a city. While the analysis is ongoing, it may be that rural areas were disproportionately impacted by COVID-19, just as they were by the Spanish flu. For example, a detailed study of the American state of South Carolina found that while the majority of cases and deaths were in cities (not surprising, as that's where most people live), after adjusting for population, the case and mortality rate was much higher in rural areas.[77]

Cities change in all sorts of profound ways as a result of a major health crisis. In 1793, a yellow fever outbreak in Philadelphia killed 5000 people and led to the establishment of a municipal rubbish collection service and the introduction of laneways to facilitate ease of that collection.[78] The cholera epidemic of the mid-nineteenth century led to the development of London's modern sewer system, meaning the Thames River was no longer an open sewer. Tuberculosis contributed to modernist architecture, with its emphasis on hygiene, fresh air and sunlight.[79] These are all things that would probably have happened anyway. But a crisis accelerated and magnified their arrival.

Pandemics always lead to predictions of the demise of cities, but great cities will survive. They always do. The urban centres of Paris, London and New York boomed in the years after the Spanish flu, and the relentless global growth of cities continued with barely a pause. As urbanist Richard Florida writes, 'urbanization has always been a greater force than infectious disease'.[80]

Similarly, but less optimistically, the legacy of a pandemic lingers long after the final wave has passed. If we are to recover quickly from the COVID-19 pandemic and enter a period of newfound flourishing, we will need to ensure we respond appropriately to the virus's after-effects.

In many cases, viral infection is followed by long-term illness. These illnesses can be devastating. Of those admitted to hospital with bird flu in China in 2013, more than half still had long-term lung damage two years after they were discharged. Similarly, of the previously healthy patients admitted to intensive care suffering swine flu in Europe in 2009, more than 50 per cent had lung incapacities a year later. More than half also had symptoms of anxiety, and a quarter had depression.[81]

In the decade following the Spanish flu, the American Medical Association reviewed hundreds of research reports from around the world and concluded that there was 'general agreement that influenza may act on the brain'. 'From the delirium accompanying many acute attacks to the psychoses that develop as "post-influenzal" manifestations, there is no doubt that the neuropsychiatric effects of influenza are profound and varied,' the report said.[82] The impact of viruses on the brain has been subject to further research in recent decades, and it is now well established that many viruses – including herpes, polio, influenza and coronaviruses – are capable of invading nerve cells. This can manifest in ways ranging from delirium or abnormal behaviour through to 'seizures and coma.'[83]

The impact of viruses on the brain may also lead to an increased risk of disorders such as Parkinson's disease. Individuals who were born or were young at the time of the Spanish flu 'had a two- to three-fold higher risk of developing Parkinson's disease than those born outside of that range'. Researchers at Melbourne's Florey Institute of Neuroscience have proposed long-term screening of people recovering from COVID-19 for any signs of degeneration of the central nervous system, including Parkinson's disease.[84]

While the evidence is still accumulating, it's possible that COVID-19 will leave behind a wave of post-viral illness. 'What's worrying me about the virus at the moment is I'm realising more and more there's going to be a lot of long-term consequences to this infection in people,' says Peter Doherty, 'especially those who are hospitalized and then don't go on to a fatal outcome. A lot of those people are going on to all sorts of chronic disease problems.'

Tens of thousands of 'long-haulers' – those suffering lingering illnesses after COVID-19 – have set up their own support groups. Some research is underway, but more is needed. Many sufferers report symptoms similar to chronic fatigue syndrome, while others have lung damage and breathing problems.[85] It will be critically important that longitudinal studies on survivors are undertaken, and that if evidence of significant chronic illnesses as a result of COVID-19 comes to light, health-system planning takes the long-term implications of this into account.

Similarly, there are good reasons to expect that the pandemic will be followed by a tail of mental-health challenges. Drawing on data from Norway, researcher Dr Svenn-Erik Mamelund found that in the six years following the Spanish flu, 'the number of first-time hospitalized patients with mental diseases caused by influenza, compared to normal situations, increased by … an average annual factor of 7.2'. A similar but smaller effect was documented during the Russian influenza of 1890–94. While it's not possible to determine what caused the increase in hospitalisations – we don't know whether it was related to post-viral illness, social isolation, individual pain and depression, fear and discomfort, or perhaps the interactions of these factors – the trend is clear.[86]

The pandemic has caused isolation, disruption of routines and a mass psychology of fear. A global review of academic studies conducted by Iranian researchers concluded that the COVID-19 pandemic has contributed significantly to psychological disorders in the general population. About 30 per cent of people experienced stress; 32 per cent, anxiety; 34 per cent, depression. The incidence of mental-health concerns was significantly higher among those aged twenty-one to forty – a group particularly concerned with the economic consequences of the pandemic.[87]

During the acute phase of the COVID-19 pandemic, many governments increased funding for mental-health support. For example, the Australian government funded ten additional psychological therapy sessions for those in areas impacted by lockdowns.[88] It seems likely that increased funding for mental health will need to be sustained over the longer-term. The World Health Organization argues that countries should allocate resources to mental health 'as an integral component of their response and recovery plans'.[89]

The psychological stress and social isolation associated with lockdowns has also led to an increase in family violence. While lockdowns sometimes reduce the number of reports, due to women and children being confined in close quarters with their abusers, anecdotal reports from China, the United States, Europe, Australia and Brazil indicate that family violence increased by up to 30 per cent.[90] Governments will need to ensure that adequate funding for the services and institutions that protect women and children from family violence is built into their recovery efforts. While lockdowns have ended for most, severe financial stress and unemployment is likely to cause heightened levels of anxiety throughout the recovery period, intensifying the danger.

While some countries have been successful in containing or controlling the virus, they have been unable to return to life as normal. Their international borders have remained closed, their supply chains continue to be disrupted and their economies are in disarray. 'We cannot rebuild health systems, economic systems, educational systems, and food systems – to say nothing of making them better than they were,' the Gates Foundation writes, 'until the virus that is tearing them all down is under control.'[91]

There is a critical need for international action to control the virus, helping those countries without the resources to adequately tackle it. Diagnostic tests, treatments and vaccines need to be developed and manufactured at enormous scale, and then distributed equitably, to those who need them the most, no matter where they live and regardless of their capacity to pay. The pandemic is a global problem, and until it is controlled globally, no country will be able to recover completely.

How to recover well from a pandemic

Like Taiwan following its experience with SARS, we can use the experience of the COVID-19 pandemic to ensure we are better prepared for the next. With the right insights and a determination to act, we will be able to face the future confidently, knowing we are equipped to respond to whatever novel pathogen emerges.

The World Health Organization says a key goal of the post-pandemic period is 'to address the long-term health and social impact of the pandemic'. Its Pandemic Influenza Preparedness and Response guidelines suggest that as part of this phase, countries should evaluate the effectiveness of responses, review the lessons learnt and revise their pandemic preparedness and response plans.[92] According to Peter Doherty, it's important that this process draws on the perspectives of experts from multiple disciplines, including 'economists, sociologists, epidemiology people, infectious disease people'. As Taiwan shows, if we can do this well, we will be in a much better position for the next pandemic.

Each country will reach different conclusions about what worked and what didn't in their pandemic response. Some may need to improve governance, while others may need to invest in healthcare, or hospital isolation wards. Improving supplies of medical products and personal protective equipment (PPE) may be a priority, but so may be updating legislation to better support the type of decision-making required during a pandemic.

Developing countries may not have the capacity to work through this process on their own. They will need technical support, capability building and transfer of technology from more developed countries.

We will also need to move quickly to ensure that public health capacity is retained into the future. Vast amounts of resources have been invested in preparedness and boosting infection control capacity, and it's important that this is not lost. For example, staff have been trained in the relatively intricate processes of donning and doffing PPE. As healthcare workers treat fewer and fewer cases of COVID-19, the challenge will be to maintain that level of preparedness. 'It is enormously important to maintain strong public health systems,' Doherty writes. 'In general, the pandemic has been less catastrophic in countries that did that, providing the politicians were prepared to listen to, and act on, informed advice.'[93]

As another way of improving preparedness, Doherty suggests we should consider making antiviral drugs – that is, drugs that can be taken after a positive diagnosis to reduce the severity of the illness – ahead of time. While vaccines tend to be specific to particular viruses, antiviral treatments often work against multiple variants of a virus. 'It's a matter of stopping people getting sick and dying, that's what they do,' Doherty says. He suggests that we could make antiviral drugs against all the potential threat viruses we know of. 'It would be comparatively low-cost. And we could test them in our current situation against those families of viruses and have drugs ready to go. But it takes time to do.'

It also relies on well-funded, high-quality laboratories and medical research institutes. Thanks to existing scientific capability, Doherty says, when it came to COVID-19, 'we had a specific diagnostic test within days'. The obvious lesson here is that we are protected by having institutions 'that can rapidly build capacity in the face of any pandemic threat'.[94]

As pandemics are global, building preparedness will involve improving the capacity of the global health community. Through a coordinated international effort, countries around the world will need support in vaccination, disease surveillance and improving public health networks.[95] A report from the independent think tank Commission on a Global Health Risk Framework for the Future concluded that nations commit only a 'fraction of the resources' to preparing for, preventing or responding to infectious disease crises that they devote to strengthening national security or avoiding financial crises. We can see the flaw in this approach, especially when the economic costs of a pandemic are enormous, along with the health consequences. The commission recommended a global investment of some US$4.5 billion per year, to enhance prevention, detection and preparedness. This would equate to just 65 cents per person per year.[96]

To ensure we are really prepared for the next pandemic, we'll also need to address the social determinants of health – what the World Health Organization describes as the 'conditions in which people are born, grow, live, work and age'.[97] Globally, COVID-19 has disproportionately impacted people from disadvantaged and marginalised communities, including black, Asian and minority ethnic groups, older people and those with pre-existing health conditions. These populations already experience a disproportionate burden of disease, with greater exposure to risk factors such as tobacco smoke, air pollution, obesity and dangerous jobs. As a result, they have a higher prevalence of lung cancer, asthma and chronic obstructive pulmonary disease – a progressive illness that makes it hard to breathe. More likely to be living in over-crowded housing, these groups were disproportionately impacted by lockdown.[98]

Through the COVID-19 pandemic, we've learnt that 'the poor and inadequately housed are the most at risk', Doherty writes. 'And, as people who work at bottom-level jobs in, for example, aged-care facilities, the security industry, restaurant kitchens, food processing and supply and so forth, are generally poorly paid, their vulnerability can potentially extend to all of us.'[99]

Understanding and responding to the factors that contribute to these inequities will need to be part of our efforts to prepare for the next pandemic. Strategies to reduce poverty, improve educational attainment and lessen inequality will be essential. Progressive taxation and redistribution through the welfare system is the most obvious way to do this, along with a strengthening of universal service provision, including in areas such as childcare and aged care. Improved access to affordable housing, and public health interventions such as smoking cessation programs and reduced air pollution, will also be important.

Caitjan Gainty tells me that the United Kingdom grappled with this challenge in the decades after the Spanish flu: 'One of the things that you see they understand by this point is that the social determinants of health are really problematic – that these are some of the deep reasons why we have poor health outcomes.' The solution put in place was universal access to healthcare, with the birth of the National Health Service in 1948. This was a crucial step forward. However, 'every time there's an epidemic ... the co-morbidities are always revealed,' Gainty says, 'and increasing access to care did not improve the social determinants of health. So, it did not improve health in general.'

Tackling the social determinants of health means reducing inequality. In general, people from poorer social or economic circumstances are at greater risk of ill health, have higher rates of disability and death, and live shorter lives than those who are more advantaged.[100] COVID-19 has spread fastest and furthest in countries with the greatest levels of inequality: the United States, Brazil, Mexico and Peru collectively account for 39 per cent of the world's deaths from COVID-19, despite being home to less than 9 per cent of the world's population.[101]

By taking the time to reflect upon the experience of COVID-19, we can put in place the conditions that will mean we are better prepared for the next pandemic.

After SARS, Taiwan undertook the work of analysis, policy implementation and reflection, and it reaped the benefits when it faced COVID-19. By July 2020 – when the United States was experiencing 70,000 new COVID-19 cases every day – on the streets of Taipei, there were few visible signs the world was in the midst of a pandemic. Diners were packed into restaurants, large groups were exercising together, bikes filled the pathways.

While much of the world was experiencing a deep recession during 2020, Taiwan's economy grew by 3 per cent.[102] Taiwan led the world in its initial response to COVID-19. As a result, it was also able to lead the world in opening back up.

FIVE STEPS FORWARD

1. **Conduct a post-pandemic review.** A thorough evaluation of all
    public health interventions is needed to determine how well the
    health system coped with the COVID-19 pandemic and where
    improvements can be made. Initiating a royal commission or
    commission of inquiry is one way to do this. It will be important
    for countries to share their lessons internationally, including
    with the World Health Organization and via international
    conferences and staff exchanges, so all nations can benefit
    from the insights gained.

2. **Develop an alert system coupled with the ability to rapidly
    shut down air travel.** Viruses are spread internationally by
    movement of people, particularly through air travel. As a global
    community, we need to be ready to shut down all flights
    from places that identify new, rapidly spreading pathogens.
    International agreements will need to be negotiated,
    committing countries to quick notification of new diseases on
    the understanding that this may lead to the suspension of air
    travel. Countries can also put in place protocols that enable
    them to unilaterally suspend arrivals and departures.

3. **Ensure we're ready for next time.** We need to improve our preparedness and response plans. Countries could establish a multi-agency pandemic preparedness committee that meets regularly. Legislation could be enacted to support proposed interventions; national infectious diseases surveillance systems could be improved; and further investments in the health system (for example, additional isolation wards) made to ensure it is ready to quickly scale up.

4. **Address the lingering health effects of COVID-19.** Millions may have long-term physical or mental-health effects due to COVID-19. We must monitor COVID-19 survivors and ensure health services are ready to manage their needs over the long term. Investment in mental-health services will be needed. Increased funding for organisations that offer practical and emotional support for women and children in family violence situations should be a key national priority too. Furthermore, with COVID-19 likely to remain with us, we'll have to learn to co-exist with the virus. While it's not yet clear what this will involve, as a minimum it seems we will need regular vaccination booster shots, as with the seasonal flu.

5. **Address the social determinants of health.** Poverty, housing and nutrition play an important role in determining health outcomes. At-risk groups in our community are more likely to die from infectious diseases. Reducing inequality – for example by redistributing tax revenue through targeted welfare payments or by investing in social housing – needs to be at the heart of our planning for the next pandemic.

2

RECESSION

Outside the back door of a Chicago restaurant, some fifty desperate men fought over a barrel of garbage, clawing 'for scraps of food like animals'. In Stockton, California, others scoured the rubbish dump for half-rotten vegetables, while coal miners in Kentucky resorted to eating plants from the roadside – 'violet tops, wild onions, forget-me-not wild lettuce and such weeds as cows eat'. In the coal fields of West Virginia, families shivered in tents in winter, with children going barefoot.[1]

The years of 1932 and 1933 were incredibly hard in the United States. At the height of the Great Depression, families whose electricity and gas had been disconnected were forced to cook over wood fires in back lots, some even without candles. In New York City, a couple moved into a cave in Central Park and stayed there for a year; the people of Cameroon, West Africa, raised $3.77 and sent it to New York as relief for the starving. Thousands of European migrants boarded ships to head back to Europe, where they believed there were better prospects.[2] Millions wandered the country in a fruitless search for work, while thousands lived in villages made of cardboard or scrap metal on vacant blocks or on the outskirts of cities. Regardless of where they were, these shanty towns were known as 'Hooverville', after Herbert Hoover, the president widely blamed for the Depression.[3]

The capitalist system did not appear to be functioning. People wore threadbare clothes, yet farmers couldn't sell their cotton. Millions of people were starving, but crops were left rotting in the fields. In response to low prices, farmers desperately produced more in an attempt to raise total income, which had the effect of driving prices still further down. However, the excess production made it harder to find buyers. Thousands of farmers who were unable to pay mortgages or taxes lost their land. On a single day in April 1932, a quarter of the entire land area in Mississippi went under the auctioneer's hammer.[4] The country was beset by farm strikes, miners' strikes and communist-led demonstrations by the unemployed. Some speculated whether revolution might be imminent. 'In the eyes of the people there is the failure,' novelist John Steinbeck wrote, 'and in the eyes of the hungry there is a growing wrath.'[5]

Yet while anger was evident, the predominant sentiment was despair. Society seemed to be disintegrating. Barely anyone had confidence in the ability of President Hoover's administration to improve things, but there was 'less an active demand for change than a disillusionment with parliamentary politics'.[6]

Industrial production had been cut in half and steel plants were operating at just 12 per cent of capacity, with the number of full-time steelworkers down from 225,000 to zero. Almost no construction was taking place in the industrial sector.[7] The bottom had fallen out of the stock exchange and five thousand banks had crashed, wiping out nine million savings accounts. By the end of Hoover's presidency in 1933, more than fifteen million Americans had lost their jobs. Unemployment rose from 2.9 per cent in

1929 to 22.9 per cent in 1932. Between the pre-Depression peak of August 1929 and March 1933, national output fell by 52 per cent.[8]

Yet only a few years later, growth in gross domestic product was the fastest ever experienced outside of wartime, increasing by an average of 8 per cent per year between 1933 and 1937, even after adjusting for inflation.[9] By 1936, output was back to where it had been in 1929 and unemployment was down to 10 per cent. By 1941, the economy was almost back to its long-run trend. Policies put in place by Franklin D. Roosevelt, successor to Hoover, had set the country up for success. Roosevelt's New Deal programs have their legacy, even today, in America's social security system and various labour protections. This chapter investigates the US experience during the Great Depression, the longest, deepest and most widespread depression of the twentieth century. It shows that with the right policy response, an economy can come roaring back to life.

In more recent memory, the Great Recession of 2007–09 reinforced this lesson. Two places on opposite sides of the world responded adeptly to the crisis. Australia, with rapid and decisive policy action, was able to avoid a national recession. New York City, the global epicentre of the financial sector, was deeply impacted by the recession, but used the experience to reform the city's economy, ensuring it would be more resilient to future shocks. These stories show that the policy initiatives put in place in response to economic crises can lay the foundation for long-term prosperity.

From depression to development

By mid-1929, in what would subsequently be seen as the tail-end of the Roaring Twenties boom, the share market was subject to wild speculation. A reckless sense of overconfidence led people to buy stocks with easy credit. Yet production had begun to decline, unemployment was rising and many stocks were priced well in excess of their real value. In September, prices on the New York Stock Exchange began to fall, accelerating on 18 October, triggering panic. The following week, the market lost 11 per cent of its value at the opening bell, in an event that became known as Black Thursday.

A moderate rally followed as institutional investors attempted to stabilise the market by buying up big blocks of shares. However, the market soon went into freefall: with Black Monday, followed by Black Tuesday, the market lost 23 per cent of its value in just two days. Billions of dollars were lost, wiping out thousands of traders, many of whom had borrowed heavily to buy shares. Newspapers reported terrible suicides by those who had lost everything. John Schwitzgebel, an insurance salesman, shot himself twice in the chest after the words, 'Tell the boys I can't pay them what I owe them.' Down to his last four cents, Wellington Lytle left a suicide note in his hotel room: 'My body should go to science, my soul to [Secretary of Treasury] Andrew W. Mellon and sympathy to my creditors.'[10]

The market continued to slide, and by July 1932 it had lost 89 per cent of its value. It took until 1954 for the share market to recover to the highs of twenty-five years earlier.[11]

The share-market crash triggered profound psychological shock and a loss of confidence among both consumers and businesses. This uncertainty about the future led to declines in consumer spending and business investment.[12] Big drops in industrial output resulted, along with job losses and declining prices, further amplifying the downturn. A series of banking crises exacerbated the situation, with customers withdrawing their deposits as they feared for the solvency of their banks. These runs on the banks further weakened the financial system, and by 1933 one in five American banks had failed.

At the time of the Depression, the world's economies were based on the gold standard – currencies were backed by gold. For every dollar, pound or yen in circulation, there was an equivalent amount of gold stored in a bank vault. This linked the world's economies intimately and meant that the crisis in the United States spread quickly to other countries. Americans were buying far fewer goods and American exports had become extremely cheap due to declining prices. As other countries bought US exports, their gold flowed into America, depleting their own supplies. Foreign central banks attempted to arrest this trend by raising interest rates. This had the effect of reducing output and increasing unemployment in those countries. Around the world, gross domestic product contracted by some 15 per cent between 1929 and 1932 (by contrast, the World Bank estimates the global economy contracted by 4.3 per cent in 2020).[13] Ultimately, the Depression was almost as long and severe in Europe as in the United States. However, in places such as Latin America it was far milder.[14]

In Europe, the Depression was accompanied by the spread of totalitarianism. Financial insecurity created political instability and a vulnerable populace. This enabled the Nazi Party in Germany to build a nationalistic fervour that brought disaffected masses together across the lower and upper classes, to seize power and to commence the process of building a fascist empire. Similarly, Asia in the 1930s saw the rise and brutal effects of Japanese imperialism. So while Americans were preoccupied with their domestic hardships, European and Asian countries were facing quite different challenges.

Through the early years of the Great Depression, President Hoover sought to avoid direct federal intervention, believing that supporting business was the best way to strengthen the economy. He was also resistant to assisting the unemployed through welfare payments, believing it would permanently weaken the country. He came to be widely perceived as cold, incompetent and out-of-touch, and his opponents accused him of being indifferent to the suffering of millions.[15]

At the election in 1932, Hoover's opponent, Franklin D. Roosevelt, swept to victory with 57 per cent of the popular vote, carrying all but six states. Earlier, as part of his speech accepting the Democratic Party nomination, Roosevelt had pledged himself to a 'New Deal for the American people'.[16]

After declaring at his inauguration in March 1933 that 'the only thing we have to fear ... is fear itself', Roosevelt responded to a series of rolling bank closures by shutting down the entire banking system. He used this time to rapidly create a deposit insurance scheme, which was in place when the banks reopened a week later. Roosevelt commenced a series of regular 'fireside chats' on radio, during which he communicated with Americans about the actions being taken and plans for the next steps.

Much of the New Deal was legislated within Roosevelt's first 100 days. It focused on alleviating the suffering of the country's unemployed. Hundreds of millions of dollars were provided for short-term aid in the form of soup kitchens and blankets. Temporary jobs were created with new construction projects and youth were set to work in the national forests through the Civilian Conservation Corp. Cash subsidies were given to farmers and farm production quotas were introduced in an attempt to raise prices. Industrial codes governing trade practices, wages, hours, child labour and collective bargaining were established. The administration commenced major infrastructure projects too, including the Tennessee Valley project, a series of dams and hydroelectric generators across seven states to control floods, generate electricity and improve navigation.[17]

In 1935, when the recovery was gathering momentum, Roosevelt initiated a second stage of the New Deal. Legislation enshrined the rights of private-sector employees to organise into unions, engage in collective bargaining and take collective industrial action: to strike. Maximum working hours (forty-four hours per week) and minimum wages were set and child labour was prohibited.[18] The *Social Security Act* established a permanent system of retirement pensions, unemployment benefits and welfare provisions for widows and people with a disability. At Roosevelt's insistence, these were funded from payroll taxes rather than general revenue: 'We put those payroll contributions there so as to give the contributors a legal, moral, and political right to collect their pensions and unemployment benefit,' he said. 'With those taxes in there, no damn politician can ever scrap my social security program.'[19] The Works Progress Administration, a government agency founded in May 1935, employed millions of jobseekers to carry out large public works. Prominent projects included the Lincoln Tunnel and LaGuardia Airport in New York City and the San Francisco–Oakland Bay Bridge.[20]

There was never a master plan for the New Deal. Instead, it adopted an incremental and experimental approach. Roosevelt listened to a wide variety of voices to inform the administration's actions, including experts, union leaders and everyday Americans. In the year before his election, he had assembled an informal group of academics to advise him – *The New York Times* dubbed it a 'brains trust'. This group consisted of law professors and an economics professor, as well as a broader group of 'associate members' who were academics, lawyers and business executives. Never paid for their efforts, this brains trust interviewed experts and hammered out campaign speeches, and later legislation.[21]

The New Deal represented a bold break with the past, but given the enormous hit to the economy, its stimulatory effect was relatively small. Despite the spending, the budget deficit only increased marginally – and this was largely due to a tax rise that had been implemented at the end of the Hoover era. Both sides of politics were broadly committed to balanced budgets. Nevertheless, the New Deal was central to the recovery, as it provided a massive boost to confidence. The election of Roosevelt and New Deal policies created the expectation of higher incomes and higher inflation, which in turn stimulated demand and investment. Economist Gauti Eggertsson calculates that the changing expectations flowing from the election of Franklin D. Roosevelt accounted for three quarters of the recovery in output between 1933 and 1937.[22] Roosevelt's political skills perhaps contributed as much to recovery as his economic policies.

Ever since the end of the Depression, there has been debate among economists about why it was so long and so severe. They point to a few things. First, the collapse or near collapse of financial institutions led to panic and undermined investor confidence. Second, government's failure to borrow and spend large sums to stimulate consumption and investment meant economic activity remained subdued. Third, constrained by its commitment to the gold standard, the Federal Reserve choked the economy by restricting the supply of money. Given the extreme uncertainty, people were driven to hoard funds, limiting the amount of currency in circulation, but the gold standard meant the Federal Reserve couldn't create more money unless it had the gold to back it (which it didn't). Finally, falling prices and deflation increased the real value of people's debts, which in turn increased the effective cost of borrowing. Although interest rates were low, deflation meant the effective rate of interest was much higher, making investment less likely.

The big intervention that kicked off the recovery was the abandonment of the gold standard – the value of currency was delinked from gold. Around the world, there was a remarkable correlation between the timing of recovery and abandonment of the gold standard.[23] The change allowed countries to expand their money supplies without worrying about gold, and more money circulating meant greater stimulation of the economy.

Shortly after assuming office, Roosevelt began to urge Congress to abandon the gold standard, arguing that 'the free circulation of gold coins is unnecessary, leads to hoarding, and tends to a possible weakening of national financial structures in times of emergency'. This was a controversial suggestion, with critics labelling the proposed reforms 'immoral'. Some claimed it would lead to a speculative boom bigger than in the 1920s and cause another disastrous recession.[24] Yet he also received backing from some heavy hitters, including banker J.P. Morgan. 'It seems to me clear that the way out of the depression is to combat and overcome the deflationary forces,' Morgan argued. 'Therefore, I regard the action now taken as being the best possible course under existing circumstances.'[25]

Roosevelt suspended gold exports, prohibited banks from paying out gold coins or bullion except under government-issued licence and required people and corporations to deposit any gold they had or face fines or imprisonment. Through legislation in

1933, the president gained the power to reduce the gold content of the dollar by as much as 50 per cent, and to back the dollar with silver rather than gold. The value of the dollar consequently plunged against gold-backed European currencies and created expectations of inflation, thereby spurring recovery.[26]

World War II played only a limited role in stimulating the US economy. The country had largely recovered before spending on the war ramped up. But with unemployment still hovering at around 10 per cent, preparations for the war did help with the return to full employment.

Although the American economy grew remarkably quickly between 1933 and 1937, by 1937 there were just as many people employed as there had been in 1929. As the size of the workforce had increased substantially in those years, unemployment remained high. After another short recession in 1937 (triggered by a premature withdrawal of economic support), growth continued.[27] Between 1938 and 1941, annual growth in real gross domestic product was over 10 per cent. Yet unemployment remained stubbornly high, and business investment didn't really recover either. It wasn't until the boom caused by the onset of war that the poverty rate dropped to below 30 per cent.[28] The experience of the Depression had involved significant trauma, leaving scars that endured for many years.

The New Deal left a legacy that is still felt today. It reconfigured the role of government in the United States, creating the expectation that the old or the infirm should be able to receive federal income support or medical care. Prior to the New Deal, that financial responsibility fell directly to their children, if they had any. The New Deal also inspired President Lyndon Johnson's Great Society of the 1960s – a program aimed at eliminating poverty and racial injustice. A number of social welfare measures in the United

States today trace their origins to the New Deal, including old-age pensions, unemployment insurance, subsidised public housing, farm subsidies, support for the disabled and support for students from disadvantaged families. Other protections that Americans take for granted are also products of the New Deal, including bans on child labour, maximum working hours and minimum wages.

New Deal initiatives set the United States up for growth and prosperity through the second half of the twentieth century. As economics professor David Weiman puts it, 'new roads and electrical power networks paved the way for post-World War Two economic expansion built around the automobile and the suburban home. Astonishing 21st-century innovations such as next-day FedEx deliveries and Wi-Fi still rely on these aging investments.'[29]

One of the most profound legacies of the New Deal was the economic development of America's South. Through roads, hospitals, schools and rural electricity, the New Deal modernised the Southern states, allowing living standards to catch up with the rest of the country. According to economic historian Gavin Wright, these advances 'had immediate benefits, but perhaps more importantly, they set the stage for rapid economic growth during and after World War II'.[30] The New Deal funded a massive upgrade of Atlanta's sewerage system, for example. The rapid growth of America's sunbelt owes much to New Deal investment.

Stanford University professor David Kennedy argues that by enabling sustained economic growth and spreading the benefits of prosperity widely throughout the country, 'it helped set the stage for the civil rights movement that brought at least a measure of long-delayed social justice for African-Americans'. Ultimately, the New Deal 'revitalized American life in the second half of the twentieth century'.[31]

One of the outcomes of the Great Depression was the development of macroeconomic policies designed to prevent or moderate recessions. John Maynard Keynes is a name you've probably heard of. With only eight weeks of formal undergraduate study in economics, Keynes went on to become one of the most significant economists of the twentieth century. His ideas remain highly influential with central banks and governments today.

Keynes' central insight was that once an economic downturn starts, the fear and gloom that sets in among consumers and investors becomes self-fulfilling, engendering a full-scale depression, leading to prolonged periods of high unemployment. In his *General Theory of Employment, Interest and Money*, he argued that government spending, tax cuts and interest rate cuts could be used to counteract economic downturns. At times when private sector spending is in retreat, government interventions are important to stimulate demand. When people and companies are subject to lower taxes or lower interest rates, they have more money in their pocket and so are likely to spend more. Similarly, when government spending increases – through transfers to citizens or directly – there is more money circulating through the economy, increasing confidence and breaking the cycle of economic despondency. During recessions, governments should ideally run a budget deficit, spending far more than they raise in taxes.

Governments are in the strongest position to provide such support when they have a good medium-term policy framework. Keynes was adamant that government budgets should remain balanced over the medium term. This means that governments should ideally run budget surpluses during prosperous times, so that there is sufficient scope to run large deficits during downturns.

This use of government budget spending to influence the economy is known as fiscal policy.

The other intervention Keynes advocated was monetary policy – the expansion or contraction of the money supply, influencing interest rates. When interest rates are lower, individuals and firms are more likely to borrow money to invest because borrowing costs them less. However, as interest rates approach zero – as they are currently in many countries – there is less scope to use them to stimulate investment, as it's not really possible to have interest rates lower than zero per cent. In this circumstance, governments need to rely on other measures – usually fiscal policy.

Keynes studied classics and mathematics at the University of Cambridge. He loved Cambridge life and famously only went into economics because he was offered a lectureship and a chance to get back to Cambridge. He was bisexual but he was (happily) married to a Russian ballerina. He was a pioneer of women's rights, particularly over their own body.[32] But his enduring legacy is the notion that governments can and should act to prevent recessions. Recent government action around the world during recessions is due directly to Keynes and the lessons from the Great Depression.[33]

Looking back to see forward

Almost eighty years after the Great Depression, the world was once again plunged into economic and financial turmoil. The Great Recession of 2007–09 was a global economic downturn that devastated financial markets, along with real estate and banking industries. The crisis caused millions of people to default on their mortgages, and led to lost jobs, savings and homes. It was experienced most severely in the United States – where it originated – and in Western Europe and South America.

The recession was caused by vulnerabilities in the financial system and was triggered by the bursting of the housing bubble in the United States. A complex web of financial securities was backed by 'subprime' mortgages (risky loans issued to borrowers with low credit ratings), and when large numbers of people defaulted on their repayments, these securities dramatically declined in value. This, in turn, led to the collapse or bailout of banks. In 2008, the investment banking giant Bear Stearns collapsed, and a few months later Lehman Brothers did too, creating the largest bankruptcy in US history. This led to major panic among bankers, and many large and well-established commercial banks across the United States and Europe suffered huge losses or even bankruptcy. With banks unable to lend and people focused on paying down debt rather than spending, the globe fell into a deep recession. Governments around the world responded with enormous fiscal and monetary stimulus measures, designed to rouse national economies and reduce financial risk.

The United States experienced a decline of 4.3 per cent of gross domestic product, and would not return to pre-recession levels of output until late in 2011. The number of people with jobs fell by 8.6 million, with the unemployment rate peaking at 10 per cent. The Baltic states of Lithuania, Estonia and Latvia suffered declines in gross domestic product of between 11.9 and 21 per cent. In 2009, Russia's economy contracted by 7.9 per cent. Years later, many countries were still struggling to recover, with the unemployment rate in Spain and Greece at 26 and 27 per cent respectively.[34] 'The 2009 episode was the most severe of the four global recessions of the past half century and the only one during which world output contracted outright,' Ayhan Kose from the World Bank and Marco Terrones from the International Monetary Fund wrote in 2015.

It was 'truly deserving of the "Great Recession" label'.[35]

Not all countries felt the recession in the same way, though. More recently developed countries suffered less. China, India and Indonesia actually grew substantially during this period – principally because their large populations served as a source of domestic demand, making them more resilient.[36]

Australia – along with Poland, Israel and South Korea – was one of the few developed countries to avoid recession. Australia's then treasurer, Wayne Swan, spoke with me about how Australia's experience might inform our approach to the recovery ahead. Swan looks every bit the accountant, with his well-fitted suit, glasses and silver hair. Yet, as he punctuated his recollections with rather colourful language, I was forced to rapidly recalibrate my assumptions of him.

Swan recalls the moment when the implications for Australia became clear. In April 2008, he was in Washington, DC, for the annual spring meeting of the International Monetary Fund. Bear Stearns had been bailed out by the US Federal Reserve a month earlier. Lunching at the Australian embassy with a group of Wall Street investors, Swan recalls saying, 'Oh well, Bear Stearns is over now. It doesn't seem to be looking too bad. Everything's settled down.' The response from an executive at a large New York hedge fund was unsettling. 'It's not the end, it's not even the beginning of the end,' he said. 'It's just the end of the beginning.'

'From that time on, things began to deteriorate,' Swan says. 'By the end of June, we were pretty sure we were in trouble, although the world didn't know it. Things slowly started to rock in the global economy in July, August and, of course, September – when Lehman Brothers fell over and the whole world changed.'

The collapse of Lehman Brothers, a massive global financial

services firm, involved US$600 billion in assets – more than the annual GDP of Poland, Thailand or Belgium.[37] With the world economy in crisis, Australia's Reserve Bank reduced interest rates by a full percentage point to inspire investor confidence. The Australian stock exchange suffered its second biggest fall on record and there were fears that there would be queues outside banks, with people rushing to withdraw cash. The government moved quickly to guarantee all deposits held by Australian financial institutions. After an emergency cabinet meeting, Swan found himself presiding over an initial stimulus package of A$10 billion (US$7.7 billion), assembled in just a couple days. Cash payments to pensioners and families were the first order of business, drawing on advice from Treasury secretary Dr Ken Henry, who advised the government to 'go hard, go early, go households' with 'timely, targeted and temporary' stimulus measures.[38]

In February 2009, Swan announced another, more substantial package. The A$42 billion (US$32 billion) included more cash grants, A$14.7 billion (US$11.3 billion) for a massive program of school building, A$6.6 billion (US$5.1 billion) for new social and defence housing, and A$3.9 billion (US$3 billion) to insulate 2.7 million houses.[39] At its height, the stimulus measures equated to about 2 per cent of GDP.

Swan tells me the government's response was influenced by Australia's experience of recession in the early 1990s. 'They had been too slow or too late to respond,' he says. 'And the consequence of that had been a lost decade of economic growth and prolonged high unemployment. So, all of those things went through my thinking. I was absolutely determined not to be a treasurer who was going to preside over the sort of scarring that we'd seen – either after the '90s recession, or the scarring that happened in my own family, or for hundreds of thousands of people during the Great Depression.'

While the government was infusing the economy with cash through the budget, the Reserve Bank continued to provide stimulus in the form of interest rate reductions. Between September 2008 and April 2009, interest rates came down from 7 to 3 per cent.[40] Yet Swan is convinced that the spending in the budget had the greater impact. 'The main lever is fiscal policy, not monetary policy,' he says. 'It was then, and it always has been.'

The government not only responded quickly and forcefully; stimulus was sustained over a number of years. One of the largest programs involved the construction or refurbishment of school halls, classrooms and libraries across the country. New buildings, with open-plan, fluid spaces, facilitated widespread adoption of innovative teaching methods. Rather than a single teacher in a classroom, teams of teachers were able to bring students together, teaching across disciplines. In the months after the new buildings were occupied, university researchers observed groups of teachers and students in the new environments, measuring comfort and acoustics. They observed a quiet buzz of activity and a positive response from teachers. 'The students just work well in there,' one teacher observed. 'They're relaxed, they're proud of their building. The surprise is how well the students have adapted to the new environment.'[41]

Millions of homes received ceiling insulation, which sought to save 1.9 million tonnes of carbon emissions each year, equivalent to 0.4 per cent of Australia's emissions in 2007, and billions of dollars were spent on infrastructure projects, including railway lines and freeways.[42] By 2012, the stimulus still amounted to 0.6 per cent of GDP. 'We'd effectively built a bridge from both sides of the river at once,' Swan writes in his biography, *The Good Fight*. 'Infrastructure from the long-term side and payments from the short-term side – meeting up in the middle to provide a pathway forward.'[43]

Much of this spending was criticised by Swan's political opponents. They claimed the funding on school infrastructure did not deliver value for money. The home insulation program (popularly known as the 'pink batts' scheme) resulted in the deaths of four workers. After a change in government, a royal commission inquiry found there had been serious problems with the design and implementation of the program.[44] Yet Australia was lauded internationally for its response. In 2011, Swan was named Finance Minister of the year by European banking and finance magazine *Euromoney*. They admired his 'careful stewardship' and his role in making Australia 'the best-performing economy among the world's richer, developed nations'.[45]

The impact of the Australian government's policy response was profound, with the economy remaining relatively strong throughout the crisis. Growth eased off only marginally and the increase in unemployment was slight (from 4.4 per cent in 2007 to 5.6 per cent in 2009). Analysis conducted by the Australian Treasury concluded that without fiscal stimulus, growth would have been negative for three consecutive quarters.[46]

New York City was ground zero for the Great Recession. As the world's top financial centre, it experienced the collapse of a number of investment banks and insurers, such as American Investment Group and Merrill Lynch, in addition to Bear Stearns and Lehman Brothers. Consequently, the city was hit hard. Although the finance sector employed less than 10 per cent of New York City's workforce, its employees took home an average of US$280,000 a year each, so the loss of 32,000 finance jobs between 2008 and 2010 had a significant impact.[47] Unemployment rose from 4.4 per cent in February 2008 to 10.3 per cent in September 2009, with 413,000 people out of work. But the city bounced back relatively quickly and – at least until COVID-19 hit – it was booming. Between 2009 and 2017, it added 702,000 jobs – the longest and largest expansion since World War II.[48]

To understand how New York City achieved this feat, I spoke with the man who oversaw the city's economic recovery, first as president of the New York City Economic Development Corporation (NYCEDC) and then as deputy mayor in charge of economic development, when mayor Michael Bloomberg asked him to step into the role. Robert Lieber was once a Lehman Brothers executive, a Wall Street 'real estate investment banker' who, after twenty-five years, decided he was ready for a career change. The NYCEDC he went on to run is a unique non-profit. Founded in the 1990s, it is geared to promoting economic development in the city. It owns and operates an enormous amount of real estate – 66 million square feet (6.1 million square metres) across 200 city-owned properties – and uses the revenue it generates to invest in strategic development projects.[49] Although at arm's length from City Hall, its board is appointed by the mayor, borough presidents and the speaker of the council. As well as managing and developing city assets, it negotiates firm-specific tax incentives to help attract new investment, provides economic development advice to the New York City government and conducts research into economic issues facing the city.[50]

Lieber talks with me from his apartment in Manhattan, spending much of our discussion fending off overtures from his new puppy. He does not come across as a politician; rather, he is every inch the banker, his words confident yet cautious and occasionally self-deprecating. While he's enthusiastic about helping me understand New York's journey, he seems disinclined to promote himself. He volunteers that he started at the city administration without a deep understanding of what was involved, but 'thought it'd be interesting to go learn'.

'I used to stand up and give these stump speeches all the time, talking about how great the city was doing,' he says. 'Everything was going great until September 2008. And then it wasn't.'

In assessing the economic landscape during the recession, it became clear to Lieber that the city relied too heavily on the financial services sector. 'Over 50 per cent of the taxes paid came from 7 per cent of the people who live here,' he says. Consequently, in planning the city's economic recovery, Lieber's team aimed to 'diversify the city's economy, to create demand to address the excess supply that we had of real estate and no jobs'. So they began to 'look about how to grow different sectors that we thought were going to be important to the future of New York City'. They saw opportunities in bioscience, fashion, media, technology and tourism.

But before these industries could grow, the 'fundamentals' had to be in place. 'We needed to make sure that the streets were safe and people didn't feel threatened with random crime,' Lieber says. 'The biggest issue that all the big cities face today is: how do we make people feel safe to be able to come into the city and intermingle with others? When I moved to New York in the '70s, this was not a safe place for people to be able to walk the streets. There were neighbourhoods you just wouldn't go. But by the time we got to the mid-2000s, crime was way down.' In 1990, New York City was the murder capital of the United States, with 2245 homicides.

By 2005, that number was down to 539.[51] 'Providing an environment where people feel safe is critical,' he says.

To help attract 'the STEM [science, technology, engineering and math] businesses, which we really didn't have', Lieber and his team looked to the city's universities. 'We had two great universities here, Columbia and NYU,' Lieber says, but only Columbia was competitive in engineering. 'I remember we had a session where we brought together business and education leaders from around the city to understand how to make New York City more competitive. And the president of Columbia said, "The most important thing to Columbia's success as we go forward here is to make NYU more competitive."' By building the city's capacity and making the city more attractive to the research community, everyone wins. 'That insight was an eye-opener for me,' Lieber says.

The city needed a top-rated graduate school of engineering on par with Stanford University or the Massachusetts Institute of Technology if it was going to spawn technology-based startups that could go on to become major employers. That insight led Lieber and team to plan for a new engineering-based campus on city-owned land on Roosevelt Island, in the East River. Lieber's successor, shortly after Lieber stepped down as deputy mayor, announced that universities around the world were invited to submit proposals. The winning bid came from Cornell and its partner, the Technion–Israel Institute of Technology. They won US$100 million and a spot on the island.[52] 'That was one of the hallmark transactions [in] creating the demand generators for jobs,' Lieber says. Roosevelt Island would be 'a place where the super smart students, and more importantly the super smart faculty, would come to do their research, and use those as incubators for growth businesses in the New York City area'. While the campus is still establishing, startups founded on the island have already raised more than US$100 million and employ 300 people.[53]

Other priority sectors received similar attention. Fashion saw the establishment of an investment fund which made loans to small designers to help them fulfil production orders. The city partnered with a private real estate firm to develop an enormous commercial bioscience centre on land owned by the city. The Made in NY media centre was established as an 'incubator space for storytellers, creative professionals and entrepreneurs across multiple disciplines to collaborate and create new business opportunities'. Neighborhood x Neighborhood was a tourism initiative that supported businesses and encouraged visitors to venture beyond Manhattan.[54]

Have these efforts to transform New York City's economy been a success? 'I honestly don't think we're going to know for twenty years,' Lieber says. 'But having that as a centre of focus means a lot of the technology companies have now made big inroads in New York.' Google, Facebook, Microsoft and other technology businesses are 'making big concentrated efforts in New York City because they recognise that the growth of their business is going to be enhanced by having bicoastal brain centres to help support their businesses'.

One report by the New York City comptroller (the position known as an auditor-general in some countries) found that the city's economy had modestly diversified. However, the same report also found that New York's diversification had not reduced the volatility of employment or wages, because the growth has 'occurred in sectors that are not substantially less vulnerable to economic downturns than the securities sector'. As financial services jobs are extremely well paid, diversification away from the sector has reduced average wages.[55] Nevertheless, diversification had been accompanied by 'robust growth in employment', with more jobs in the city than ever before. And the change in industry composition means there is likely to be more job growth in the future – more so than if the industry mix had remained unchanged.[56]

E conomic recessions are often thought of as short-term events: a couple of quarters of declining activity; a temporary rise in unemployment. The immediate hardships caused by recessions are acute – job losses causing people to fall back on unemployment benefits, defaults on home loans, businesses going broke, high streets blemished with vacant shopfronts. But recessions leave deep scars and a long-term legacy.[57] While an economy often sees rapid growth in the aftermath of a recession, the damage that it causes can persist for decades.

Loss of income and unemployment due to a recession can reduce educational attainment. There is a growing mountain of evidence that early childhood education plays a critical role in setting up children for later life success. Yet with participation in kindergarten often driven by parent choice or funding, recessions impact the quality of education available to children. Early childhood nutrition also plays a role in shaping cognitive development, impacting educational attainment, reading comprehension and wages later in life. In the Great Recession, 21 per cent of American children experienced food insecurity.[58]

University and college graduates who enter the workforce during a recession earn less than those who graduate in more prosperous times, and this effect lasts for ten to fifteen years on average. These graduates go on to have higher death rates in mid-life, including significantly more drug overdoses and other 'deaths of despair'.[59] People who lose their job in a recession are more likely to end up unemployed over the long term. And tragically, the impacts can persist for generations. For example, analysis of Canadian data from 1978 to 1999 (back when fathers were almost always the main family breadwinner) shows that eight years after a father lost his job, the family income was 15 per cent lower than it would have been had he not lost it. Children in these families went on to earn 9 per cent less than children whose fathers did not experience unemployment.[60]

As we saw earlier when we looked at the Great Depression, recessions also mean that companies invest far less in upgrading their capacity or developing new products and technologies. Less investment today means that companies produce less in the future than they would otherwise have been able to. Lower levels of productivity ultimately lead to slower wages growth. Recessions also temporarily slow the rise of new businesses that rely on cashed-up customers and investors. Because businesses are often formed to develop, implement and market new technologies, delays mean that technology adoption is set back too.[61]

Recessions are miserable events that should be avoided at all costs. And if they can't be avoided, we need to do whatever it takes to reduce their severity and duration.

So why do some countries experience recessions while others don't? To answer this question, I spoke with Tim Hatton, professor of economics at the University of Essex. Hatton's specialities are economic history and applied economics. I had a captive audience for my words – literally. He was confined to a Sydney hotel room, undertaking fourteen days of quarantine before heading to the Australian National University in Canberra, where he is based for six months of each year.

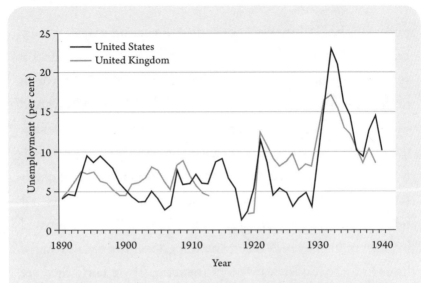

Figure 4. In the 1920s, unemployment in the United Kingdom was substantially worse than in the United States, while in the Great Depression of the 1930s, the United States suffered greater job losses than the United Kingdom.

As we saw in the last chapter, while the United States experienced an economic boom during the 1920s, the United Kingdom's economy remained depressed, with a decade of lost growth. Figure 4 shows that despite having a similar unemployment rate at the start of the decade, unemployment in the United Kingdom was much higher by the late 1920s than it was in the United States.

These divergent histories provide a fantastic basis to explore the factors that influence economic recovery. Hatton's research examines this period in detail and provides us with insight into what factors we need to consider in order to ensure the 2020s are more like the 1920s in the United States, not the United Kingdom.

One of the main ideas that I take from my discussion with Hatton is that while during the 1920s the United States was focused on progress, the United Kingdom sought to return to how things were before the war. 'The approach to the whole of economic policy was basically to say, "Look, the UK economy was very successful in the nineteenth century. Let us go back to 1913,"' Hatton says. 'In Britain, the things that were driving productivity growth in the nineteenth century were innovations like the railways and the steam engine and the gradual mechanisation of industry, urbanisation, all these sorts of things,' he says.

In this context, being the first country to industrialise didn't really help. In the 1920s, the UK economy was weak in sectors that relied on significant research and development. It was dominated by older industries such as ship building, steel and textiles. Large firms in these industries were characterised by a fairly rigid set of labour market rules – for example, certain machines and tools could only be operated by recognised craftsmen.[62] 'You get the institutions that come along with that industrialisation,' Hatton says, 'and then you find it very hard to change them after that. And these institutions become a sort of dead weight on the economy rather than something which is fostering growth.'

While the United Kingdom was grappling with its industrial legacy, the United States – unencumbered by the same sort of institutional dead weight – rapidly progressed new developments such as the internal combustion engine and electrification. Helping fuel American growth, the US Federal Reserve was priming the economy with low interest rates.

After the war, the United Kingdom was saddled with a huge amount of debt. So, despite the challenging economic circumstances the country was facing, the government ran budget surpluses, minimising its spending in an effort to pay down its debt. Like the United States, the United Kingdom operated on the gold standard and was keen to return to the pre-war rate of £1 equal to US$4.86. But to sustain this exchange rate, interest rates

needed to remain relatively high.[63] These 'very conservative policies' meant there was less money available in the economy than
there would otherwise have been.

Hatton says overly high wages were an important factor that
contributed to the prolonged period of high unemployment in
the United Kingdom. After the war, 'expectations were very high
about what wages were going to be, what prosperity was going to
be,' he says. 'Real wages ran ahead of productivity.' In the decade
to 1923, output per worker did not increase. In the United States,
by contrast, strong productivity growth saw output per worker
increase by 11 per cent over the same period.[64]

Two factors exacerbated the problem of overly high wages
in the United Kingdom – perhaps inadvertently. The first is the
amount of inflation during and after the war, when both prices
and wages more than doubled. When prices later plummeted,
wages didn't, meaning 'you had a real wage which was a little bit
too high'. The second is that around this time there was a cut in
working hours (by about 13 per cent), which was not accompanied by a cut to wages.[65] This was an effective wage increase.
While increased wages are a great thing and we all want to be
paid more, when wages went up in the context of a stagnant
economy, it meant that unemployment remained higher than it
should have.

(It should be noted that many countries currently have a different problem to the United Kingdom in the 1920s. Just as it did
in the 1920s, institutional inertia is stopping wages adjusting – but
in our case, they need to adjust up, not down. Structural challenges such as low inflation, lack of union bargaining power and
the rise of the gig economy have meant that in countries such
as the United States and Australia, wages have stagnated or even

gone backwards after adjusting for inflation. Given that consumer spending makes up half of GDP in most countries, without wages growth, economic recovery will be difficult. Consumers can't spend more unless they receive a payrise!)[66]

Recessions don't just have an economic impact; they leave a political legacy too. When people are unemployed, hungry and desperate, they sometimes turn to extreme political parties offering simple solutions to their problems.

In Europe, the country most affected by the Great Depression was Germany. After World War I, loans from American banks helped fuel German industry and enabled Germany to pay reparations. After the 1929 crash, American banks called in all their foreign loans at short notice, causing the collapse of German industry and a full-scale depression. By 1933, one in three Germans – more than six million – were unemployed and industrial production had halved. Germans began to lose faith in their democracy and turned to extreme parties on the left (communists) and the right (Nazis) for simple solutions. Whereas in 1928 the Nazis had just twelve seats in the German parliament, by July 1932 they dominated it, with 230 seats. Adolf Hitler became chancellor of Germany in January 1933, ultimately leading to World War II and the deaths of up to 85 million people, including the genocide of six million Jews in the Holocaust.[67]

Whenever depressed economic conditions are allowed to persist, there is a danger of political extremism. According to researchers at the Center for Economic Policy Research, a think tank based in Washington, DC, the danger of political extremism is greatest in 'countries with relatively recent histories of democracy, with existing right-wing extremist parties, and with electoral systems that create low hurdles to parliamentary representation of new parties'.[68]

Even in democratic countries, recession can lead to more extreme political views becoming mainstream. Wayne Swan, Australia's former treasurer, believes Donald Trump's ascension to the US presidency was a consequence of the Great Recession. 'It's pretty well documented now that the American fiscal stimulus was too small,' Swan says. 'I think that the prolonged level of high unemployment that scarred America unnecessarily for six or seven years was one of the causes of the collapse of America as a functioning democracy. It paved the way for higher inequality and the likes of Trump.' Likewise, the increased political polarisation and the rise of populist movements that followed the Great Recession gave rise to Brexit in the United Kingdom.

Professor Scott Reynolds Nelson is the author of a book on the history of American financial crises titled *A Nation of Deadbeats*. He argues that the Tea Party movement that supported Donald Trump is precisely the type of fringe group that often emerges after a major panic. Conspiracy theories flourish in the wake of crises, which can elevate extreme politicians who seek to portray their opponents as the source of economic pain. 'The fringe groups are the things to look at if we want to understand what our future will look like,' Nelson says.[69]

Swan worries about the political consequences of the COVID-19 recession. 'We don't know what the political fallout from this is,' he says. 'We didn't know what the real political fallout from the global financial crisis was until we saw Donald Trump. If this again exacerbates inequality dramatically, then we're in trouble.' In the United States, President Biden seems to share the same concerns, and in a radical departure from his predecessor, has made countering income inequality his main objective.[70]

Another fallout from the coronavirus-induced recession is likely to be a dramatic recasting of the world's economic order. While the crash was synchronised, the recovery will be dramatically different around the world. Some countries have successfully contained the virus and are opening up, while others will continue to suffer the economic consequences of isolation. Differences in the makeup of economies also influence the extent of the impact. As *The Economist* puts it: 'It is far easier to operate factories under social distancing than it is to run service-sector businesses that rely on face-to-face contact.'[71] There are large differences in the economic responses across countries too. The United States has to date provided stimulus in the form of additional spending or foregone revenue equivalent to a staggering 25 per cent of GDP, New Zealand has allocated 19 per cent and Singapore, 16 per cent. However, across the European Union fiscal stimulus packages were worth just 4 per cent of GDP, and Mexico has allocated just 1 per cent.[72]

According to forecasts by the OECD, the European and Canadian economies will still be smaller at the end of 2021 than they were in 2019. The Spanish, Italian and UK economies are unlikely to return to 2019 levels even by the end of 2022.[73] Yet Norway only experienced a minor interruption to its steady growth and will be 7 per cent bigger at the end of 2022 than it was at the start of the pandemic.[74] The Chinese economy is likely to grow by 15 per cent by the end of 2022.[75] As we saw in the last chapter, Taiwan has not seen a recession at all. The crisis looks set to dramatically reorder the global economic league ladder.

How to recover well from recession

One of the world's foremost experts on recessions is Professor Christina Romer from the University of California, Berkeley. Not only is she renowned for her research on the Great Depression, she was also chair of the Council of Economic Advisers in the Obama administration, co-authoring the administration's plans for recovery from the 2008 Great Recession. Romer argues there are three factors that account for the variation in the depth and length of recessions. The first and most obvious is 'the severity and persistence of the crisis itself: worse crises have worse aftermaths'. The second is the presence of additional shocks, such as the bursting of a housing price bubble or the collapse of the banking system. The third is the policy response: 'What policymakers do in response to a crisis has a fundamental impact on what happens to the economy in the wake of financial turmoil.'[76]

Romer's message is a hopeful one. 'There are things policymakers can do to deal with crises faster and more definitively, and to cushion other shocks and prevent such developments as a housing bubble from occurring in the first place,' she says. 'Even more obviously, the monetary and fiscal policy response to a crisis is firmly in policymakers' hands.'[77] Heading into the next recovery, there are several insights from past crises that we can use to guide us.

A key lesson that shines through from past recoveries is that size matters. As Romer puts it, 'a small fiscal expansion has only small effects'. So if it's a large effect we're after, we need a large expansion in government spending. In response to COVID-19, countries – ranging from Canada to India and South Africa – have put in place stimulus packages that are many times bigger than those deployed during the Great Recession, and the rest of the world should follow their lead.[78]

There are three broad types of spending measures governments use to stimulate economic activity.

1.   Tax cuts and other incentives provided to businesses, in the hope that it will lead them to expand operations, invest or employ more people.

2.   Tax cuts or cash payments to taxpayers or welfare recipients, in the hope that they will spend most of the money, thereby stimulating the economy.

3.   Direct spending, for example on new roads or other capital projects.

You'll recall the former Australian Treasury secretary Dr Ken Henry advocating 'timely, temporary and targeted' stimulus measures. The money needs to get out into the economy quickly – it's not much good if it's held up in planning for a year or more. Governments are also concerned with 'leakage', which occurs when not all the stimulus money ends up circulating in the economy. This can happen when people save some of their payment rather than spend it, or spend money on imports rather than local products, meaning it then effectively serves to stimulate the economy of another country.

Tax cuts or payments to individuals are a relatively quick way to get money into the economy. Wayne Swan describes 'cheques being printed' and hitting letterboxes in time for Christmas 2008.[79] However, the wealthier someone is, the more they tend to save. In March 2020, American taxpayers earning less than US$99,000 were sent cheques worth up to US$1200. One study by economists found that 27 per cent of these payments were saved, another 31 per cent was used to repay debt and just 42 per cent was spent. While it might have been a rapid policy response (and great for those who were able to pay down their mortgages!), it was an inefficient way to stimulate the economy. However, poorer people did spend most of their payments, with the bulk going on food and other essentials.[80] It makes a lot of sense to target stimulus payments to lower-income households, who are more likely to spend the money. This approach has been adopted in many countries. In Australia, for example, a 'coronavirus supplement' was temporarily added to unemployment benefits.

Because economic stimulus is a temporary measure designed to respond to economic downturn, payments should be designed as temporary also. One-off payments or fixed-term projects are ideal. In Singapore, for example, a one-off voucher program encouraged residents to holiday in their own city, supporting the tourism industry while international borders were closed. Ongoing initiatives are rarely ideal as stimulus measures as they make it more difficult to return the budget to surplus over the medium term. Permanent tax cuts for wealthy households are particularly ineffective. Not only are recipients likely to save much of the benefits, dramatically reducing any stimulus effect the tax cut might have had, but the budget is left with a reduced capacity to generate revenue once the economy recovers.

Investment in capital projects is another common form of stimulus. Because governments spend directly on these projects, leakage is minimal. However, capital projects require lots of time to plan before any construction can take place. For large projects such as freeways or railway lines, this can take years. This is obviously not ideal when the desire is to stimulate the economy in the short term. On the other hand, projects that are ready to proceed – or are accelerated for rapid delivery – are not always the most worthwhile. Wayne Swan describes the tension between 'shovel-ready' and 'shovel-worthy' projects, noting that 'shovel-worthy projects, seven times out of ten, aren't ready'.

Government investment in other labour-intensive activities may be a better option. In much of the developed world, more than two-thirds of the economy is made up of the services sector, with jobs ranging from cleaning to teaching to brain surgery. Given that service-sector interventions can be delivered with relatively little lead time, it makes sense for governments to invest here. In Australia, for example, the state of Victoria is investing A$250 million to engage 4100 tutors in schools to help students who struggled during the state's coronavirus lockdown.[81] 'There's plenty of labour-intensive areas where there's a strong community lead, and existing frameworks to train and employ people,' says Wayne Swan. 'It's not that hard.'

With interest rates at or near zero in much of the world, there's not a lot of scope to reduce them further to stimulate the economy. But Romer says a 'key lesson from the 1930s is that monetary expansion can help to heal an economy even when interest rates are near zero'.[82] She is referring to quantitative easing. This intimidating technical term can be considered the modern equivalent of printing money. Central banks use their cash reserves to buy government bonds or other financial assets, thereby increasing the amount of money in circulation. Because the central bank is increasing demand for government bonds, it leads to a decrease in interest rates for those bonds, thereby further helping to keep interest rates low.[83]

DON'T WITHDRAW STIMULUS TOO EARLY

The Great Depression shows us the risk of cutting stimulus back too soon. In 1937, the US government withdrew monetary and fiscal support, interrupting the recovery and causing another recession. 'Taking the wrong turn in 1937 effectively added two years to the Depression,' Christina Romer says.[84]

The classic case of withdrawing too early, according to Wayne Swan, is Britain. In 2010, in the immediate aftermath of the Great Recession, the UK government adopted an austerity budget, with sustained reductions in government spending and increased taxes, designed to reduce the budget deficit. Economists widely regarded these measures as 'too severe and unnecessary', contributing to the country's 'dismal' economic performance.[85] 'It condemned them to lower growth and higher levels of unemployment for a good half a dozen years,' Swan says.

With government debt mounting to uncomfortable levels, it's tempting for governments to start to reduce the stimulus and move towards budget surplus. Yet 'if there's any lesson to be learnt at all, it is to unwind the public debt very slowly, as slowly as possible,' Tim Hatton says. 'There's absolutely no reason to be really ramping down on public debt by trying to create massive budget surpluses when interest rates are basically zero.'

Modern economies are intricately linked around the globe, more so than at any time in human history. Movements of goods, knowledge, labour and capital mean that what happens in one economy shapes what happens in others. Consequently, in a global recession, economic stimulus is more effective when it is coordinated. 'The more that countries throughout the world can move toward monetary and fiscal expansion, the better off we all will be,' Romer says.[86]

During the Great Recession, the world's top economies coordinated their response through the G20, which consists of nineteen individual countries plus the European Union, collectively accounting for around 90 per cent of the world's economic output. This was a rekindling of the economic cooperation that emerged after World War II. Countries coordinated interest-rate cuts and other monetary policy measures, and nations with the capacity delivered fiscal stimulus measures amounting to 2 per cent of GDP, on advice from the International Monetary Fund (IMF). 'It was more a megaphone than it was a coordinated policy action,' Swan says. 'But the megaphone worked, because it said everyone is doing something.'

Because of the interconnected, global nature of economics and politics, there's also a good case for rich countries to support economic development in low-income countries. Strong global growth involving all countries is in everyone's interest. The IMF argues low-income countries have suffered more during the pandemic and are likely to suffer greater medium-term losses as well,[87] particularly as they have little capacity for additional spending as part of a stimulus package. Until countries such as Ethiopia, Papua New Guinea and Bangladesh are supported to beat the pandemic, with rapid vaccine distribution at affordable prices, COVID-19 will continue to plague the globe, causing restrictions and disruption. Wealthier countries will also need to ensure that low-income countries are supported with sufficient funding so that they can continue to invest in the healthcare, social services and infrastructure needed for their recovery and ongoing development. The IMF and the various development banks will play an important role in assembling the required funding, which will amount to hundreds of billions of dollars and will need to involve grants, discounted loans and debt relief.[88]

Whereas fiscal policy is about helping an economy to grow in the short term, it can't increase economic growth over the medium to long term. Long-term economic growth is determined by the 'three Ps': population, participation and productivity. The economy will grow if the population grows, if the rate of participation in the labour market increases (for example, by more women entering the workforce) or if each worker produces more output.

In the decade following the Great Recession, economic growth in many developed countries was slow. This was mainly because of the extremely slow rate of productivity growth,[89] which was caused by businesses being reluctant to invest in machinery, equipment and the latest technology; low numbers of new firms; and workers unprepared to move from low-productivity to high-productivity firms or jobs.[90] Recovery from the current recession will be intertwined with the challenge of productivity growth. While economic stimulus will support recovery over the next couple of years, economic growth in the decade following COVID-19 will be influenced mainly by productivity growth. In designing economic stimulus measures, it's important that governments keep at least one eye on the need to improve productivity. 'You should be doing structural reform at the same time as you're doing stimulus,' Swan says.

To support improved productivity, the OECD recommends stimulus interventions such as support for education and training, as well as investments in research and development, innovation and the development of new technologies.[91] This is already happening in some countries. For example, Singapore, Malaysia and Israel are providing financial support for businesses to adopt digital technologies. France's stimulus package includes billions for investments in startups, infrastructure, digital transformation and research and development.[92]

President Roosevelt led the American recovery from the Great Depression by tackling the structural challenges facing the country. His administration increased material support for the unemployed, introduced social security, supported farmers, provided temporary jobs through government-funded projects, improved labour standards and invested in major infrastructure supporting economic development. It returned confidence to the nation, breaking the cycle of despondency, causing businesses to invest and consumers to spend once again.

Ninety years later, the problems might be different, but solving structural challenges should still be the goal. The OECD recommends that governments focus on support for the vulnerable, including an increase in unemployment benefits, and workers who need to transition from one job to another. Similarly, it suggests a 'green recovery' through investments in energy efficiency, public transport or support for renewable energy.[93] Germany's stimulus package, for example, addresses climate change, innovation and digital technology, and includes investment into electric vehicle–charging infrastructure.[94]

A group of economists including Nobel Prize winner Joseph Stiglitz authored a report drawing on a survey of 231 senior economic experts from across the G20. These experts found that there are five interventions that support both long-run economic growth *and* positively address climate change: 'clean physical infrastructure, building efficiency retrofits, investment in education and training, natural capital investment, and clean R&D'. By contrast, airline bailouts, and support for large corporations and agriculture, are not likely to contribute to long-run economic growth and will have a negative impact on climate.[95]

The New Deal was as much a process as a set of policies. The Great Depression shows that recovery is a complex, uncertain, painful process, requiring the participation of many. In shaping his administration's response, Roosevelt drew on expert advisers, labour leaders, activists and ordinary Americans. There was no grand plan; recovery was not ideological but incremental and experimental, often involving failure. Many things were tried. If an initiative worked, it was kept; if it failed, it was discarded.

Roosevelt and his administration 'learned not just to lead, but to listen'.[96] By responding to Americans' needs, he earned their support. Roosevelt worked to cultivate empathy and unity: almost every New Deal program involved photography, documenting the lives of those Americans it impacted. A federal writers' program sponsored oral histories and portraits of diverse cultural communities. 'We introduced America to Americans' is how the head of the Farm Security Administration put it years later.

Today's world is different and we can't simply take New Deal programs and replicate them. But we can take inspiration from the way Roosevelt and his team went about it. As Lizbeth Cohen, professor of American Studies at Harvard University, writes: 'We can set aside ideology in favour of experimentation, fend off partisan attacks with appeals to higher principles, focus on the needs of ordinary workers, and deliberately cultivate the unity and empathy required to forge an effective coalition to do battle with the coronavirus and economic devastation.'[97]

The New Deal offered people hope in desperate times. We can learn from this as we strive to provide people with a safety net, a job to lift them out of unemployment and the confidence to build a future.

FIVE STEPS FORWARD

1. **Inspire confidence.** Consumers need to be reassured that it's okay to spend and businesses encouraged to invest. Safety – and the perception of it – will underpin economic recovery: governments will need to reassure people that the pandemic is under control and cities are safe. Governments also play an important role in reassuring people that their economic concerns are being listened to and that recovery is underway.

2. **Keep up fiscal stimulus.** Governments will need to borrow large sums of money to stimulate the economy with their spending. In the short term, that stimulus must be fast and be directed to the right targets – for example, one-off payments to low-income households. Over the medium term, stimulus should support measures that grow the economy (such as education and research and development) and address strategic priorities such as climate change – for example, by investing in electricity transmission or storage capacity. Governments should avoid winding back stimulus until economic recovery is entrenched, so as not to stifle economic growth.

3. **Allow for adjustment.** The pandemic has permanently changed our economies, and governments must adjust quickly to these new circumstances. Economic settings need to facilitate the movement of workers and capital to sectors and activities with the biggest growth potential, to allow prices to adjust and to make it easy for new businesses to establish or grow. Governments should review and adapt support measures regularly (at least every couple of months) to ensure they are not limiting growth by preventing the reallocation of resources. For example, government support for companies should be phased out over time and wage subsidies shifted from job retention to support for jobseekers.

4. **Support growth in the long run.** Successful recovery from recession means sustained economic growth over many years. While stimulus may be able to get the economy firing again, improved productivity will lead to economic growth – and raised living standards – over the next five to ten years and beyond. Measures to improve productivity, such as investment in education and skills, research and development or digital infrastructure, are crucial. Singapore has anchored its stimulus response around a massive investment in innovation to support research in biomedicine, climate change and artificial intelligence – a good example of the type of strategic response that is required.

5. **Develop a coordinated global approach.** World economies are intricately connected, and a coordinated global approach will ensure that all countries share the costs and rewards. Low-income countries need support from developed countries in both their health and economic recoveries. Rendering assistance is the right thing to do, but the global recovery also requires it. Multinational bodies such as the International Monetary Fund will play an important role in gathering the funding.

3

NATURAL DISASTER

Dr Kuntoro Mangkusubroto finally sat down, stunned by what he'd seen that day. The landscape was denuded as far as the eye could see, houses and vegetation stripped by the devastating force of the tsunami that had overwhelmed Banda Aceh two months earlier. Houses within 2 to 3 kilometres of the shoreline had been swept away or destroyed. In the coastal district of Lampuuk, the Rahmatullah Mosque was the only building that remained standing.

Some 3 kilometres inland, close to the centre of the city, a 2600-tonne ship called the *Apung 1* rested eerily. Not too far away a 25-metre fishing vessel remained perched atop two houses. In the heart of the city, the tsunami had reached the second floor; debris now piled up along the streets and in ground-floor shop-fronts.[1]

Mangkusubroto felt paralysed by the overwhelming scale of the devastation. How do you respond to something like this? Where do you start? One of the nation's leading public servants, at fifty-eight he had had a long and distinguished career that had involved dealing with many challenges. But now he felt out of his depth.

With the city devastated, survivors were living in tents. Thousands of children had lost parents. There were no schools; hospitals had been destroyed. It was near impossible to find even basic essentials, and there was little drinking water. The sewer system was not functioning.

It reminded Mangkusubroto of the images he had seen of Hiroshima after the Japanese city was flattened by an atomic bomb. The analogy was apt – physicists have calculated that the energy in the tsunami was equivalent to about eighty Hiroshima atomic bombs.[2]

On 26 December 2004, in the Indian Ocean just off the coast of Sumatra, a massive undersea earthquake on the fault line between the Burma and India tectonic plates registered 9.1–9.3 on the Richter Scale, the third-largest quake ever recorded. It lasted at least ten minutes and moved the sea floor by as much as 15 metres, creating a series of massive waves that devastated coastal communities in Sri Lanka, India, Thailand, Malaysia, the Maldives and Myanmar. The tsunami travelled the span of the Indian Ocean, killing hundreds as far away as the East African nation of Somalia. Altogether, some 230,000 people died, making it one of the deadliest disasters in history.[3]

Where Mangkusubroto sat was ground zero. The Indonesian province of Aceh, at the tip of the Sumatran Peninsula, was just 160 kilometres from the quake's epicentre. In its capital, Banda Aceh, an estimated 167,000 people died, more than the death toll of all the other countries combined. With 110,000 houses lost, a further 500,000 people in Aceh were displaced.[4]

About twenty minutes after the initial quake, three large waves hit the city. The first rose gently to the foundations of buildings before the sea receded. This was followed by two steep, black-coloured waves, which travelled inland into Banda Aceh. They were each between 6 and 9 metres – taller than a two-storey building. In some locations, they stretched taller still; at the tsunami's highest point, just south of Banda Aceh, one wave reached 51 metres, higher than the Arc de Triomphe in Paris or Nelson's Column in Trafalgar Square, London.[5]

Mangkusubroto had been sent by newly elected Indonesian president Susilo Bambang Yudhoyono to lead the reconstruction efforts in Aceh and on the nearby island of Nias. He had just arrived in Aceh for a four-year posting as director of the new Aceh-Nias Reconstruction and Rehabilitation Agency (Badan Rehabilitasi dan Rekonstruksi, BRR). Though overwhelmed, he was not alone. Billions of dollars of donations had flooded in as people around the world were touched by what they had seen on the news and sought to help. Staff from hundreds of aid organisations, ranging from the Red Cross and Oxfam to Islamic and Christian faith groups, had started to arrive in Aceh; only a handful of these had any existing presence in the province.[6] By the time Mangkusubroto arrived, the emergency response was well underway. His challenge was to ensure a coherent approach to recovery. This would encompass everything from the initial clean-up to large-scale infrastructure projects. It demanded the construction of thousands of houses, schools and government buildings, along with the rebuilding of airports, seaports and roads.

The reconstruction effort in Aceh and Nias represented the largest humanitarian operation in the world's history. While by no means perfect, Aceh's recovery has been widely hailed a success and a model for others to emulate.[7] In this chapter we'll see that not only was the reconstruction of enormous scale, but with the deep involvement of local communities, it maintained a focus on 'building back better'. Due to its transparency and accountability, donors from around the world saw a process they could trust, so donations continued to flow. And while in the decades before the tsunami Aceh was wracked by years of civil war, recovery has been accompanied by peace, and living standards are now higher than they were before the disaster.

Alongside Aceh, this chapter considers the long recovery in Christchurch, New Zealand, after the earthquakes of 2010 and 2011. This recovery, while beset by leadership and governance tensions, has given birth to impressive grassroots initiatives driving social change.

Natural disasters often strike without warning. Recovery is a long, difficult process. While reconstructing buildings and infrastructure is central, recovery also involves rebuilding communities and economies. In this chapter, we'll see that with a dedicated response from government and the involvement of citizens, crisis can give way to a brighter future.

The power of community

When I reached out to Dr Mangkusubroto for an interview, his assistant came back to me within hours. Almost before I had a chance to reflect, he was speaking with me via video link from Jakarta, where he is now based.

In his mid-seventies, Mangkusubroto projects a rare combination of humility and strength. His greatest concern during our discussion was that I gained all the information I needed. And while clearly proud of what was accomplished in Aceh and Nias, he was frequently drawn to reflect on those aspects of the recovery that had been less successful.

Mangkusubroto is finishing his career the same way he began it – as an academic. While he first trained as an engineer, he is now professor and chair of the governing council at Bandung Institute of Technology's School of Business and Management, which he helped found in 2003. In between, he's had an impressive career in government. In the early 1980s, he was hand-picked by Indonesia's state secretary to become a policy specialist, where he 'learnt a lot about politics in the capital city, politics in government, politics in the environment'. These lessons stood him in good stead during the recovery in Aceh. He went on to run several government-owned mining companies before becoming Director General of Mining, and from 1998 to 2000 he was Minister for Mines and Energy during President Suharto's regime. After returning to academia for a time, the tsunami struck, 'and the president wanted me to become the head of this new agency in charge of the construction, rebuilding of Aceh and Nias'.

Soon after he began at the BRR, Mangkusubroto had to work out how to negotiate the available assistance. 'All of a sudden you are surrounded by 800 international and local NGOs, ready to help you.' The key question was: how to make effective use of them? 'You have your own budget. You have a purpose, the donors are ready with their aid agencies, the NGOs ready with their funds and agreements,' Mangkusubroto says. 'Though even planning how to make use of these things coming from your friends is not easy.'

Much had happened before Mangkusubroto arrived in Aceh. The emergency response phase had involved the provision of drinking water, food, shelter and medical treatment to hundreds of thousands of people. Within a month of the tsunami, the Indonesian government had assessed the damage, assisted by an international team coordinated by the World Bank. Drawing on intelligence from staff on the ground, satellite imagery and aerial photography, it calculated losses at US$4.45 billion, representing about 97 per cent of Aceh's annual gross domestic product. From a total population of 4.4 million people, 2.8 million were impacted by the disaster. The damage assessment document articulated a set of principles that would underlie the recovery strategy. Key among these was a 'people-centred and participative process, in which the administration would listen to and understand the feelings and aspirations of the people'.[8]

A master plan released in April 2005 – only four months after the tsunami – elaborated on these principles, emphasising a community-oriented process with a focus on the most vulnerable, transparency and accountability, and robust evaluation.[9] The government was determined that the recovery would be community-driven. While this risked taking longer, it recognised that public support for rebuilding efforts was likely to yield effective long-term dividends.

About the same time as the master plan was released, the World Bank established the Multi-Donor Trust Fund for Aceh and North Sumatra, which was designed to pool donor funds. A steering committee of representatives from government, Aceh civil society and major donors would determine how the money would be used. As projects needed to be consistent with the principles of the master plan, in practice it meant consideration only of projects proposed by Mangkusubroto's agency, the BRR, which was established at the same time. Reporting directly to the Indonesian president, the BRR was guided by a fifteen-member advisory board consisting of ministers, provincial governors and prominent representatives from civil society. There was also a nine-member oversight board, to monitor and evaluate the organisation.[10]

When the BRR was first established, four months after the tsunami, Mangkusubroto started with a team of twelve, a borrowed office, a donated computer and no funds. Donors and agencies quickly began to contribute though, and government money began flowing from September 2005.[11] In the first year, considerable progress was made. The construction of temporary facilities meant that more than 90 per cent of children were able to return to school, and most of the affected areas had basic healthcare services restored. Although unemployment remained high, temporary work programs employed 35,000 people.[12]

Arguably more important to the reconstruction than the flow of aid money was the peace process. Aceh practises a more conservative form of Islam than the rest of Indonesia, and since 1976 the Free Aceh Movement had been running an insurgency with the goal of making Aceh independent. More than 15,000 people had died in the conflict between the Indonesian government and the rebels.[13]

'I just told the president, "How can I rebuild Aceh if people are still shooting behind my back?"' Mangkusubroto says. 'It makes people very nervous, especially coming from abroad. What will happen if, say, an Australian is killed because a bullet is shot? For sure the whole of Australia will stop sending their donations to Indonesia.' Peace was essential if international aid was to flow.

Within Aceh, the tsunami created the conditions for peace. The guerrillas had families in coastal areas but, due to fears of capture, were unable to come down from mountain areas to assist. They were fatigued with fighting, and to many the insurgency seemed less important than the devastation caused by the tsunami. According to one academic assessment, while the tsunami may not have been the cause of peace, it 'accelerated and amplified the prevalent social and political dynamics towards peace on the ground'.[14] The guerrillas and the Indonesian government negotiated a settlement: Aceh would receive limited autonomy in return for remaining part of Indonesia.[15] On 15 August 2005 in Helsinki, Finland, the two sides signed a peace agreement.

With the peace process going well, Mangkusubroto found himself with 'thousands of ex-combatants coming down the hill' looking to restart their lives. He developed programs to train former guerrillas in skills such as farming or bricklaying. 'A peace process is seldom successful if it relies only on politics,' Mangkusubroto says. 'It has to be combined with economics. And that means welfare for those people who don't have any skills, a life skill for them to survive.'

After years of conflict, 'the level of trust between people, between neighbourhoods, was at the minimum', Mangkusubroto says. The BRR's focus on community engagement meant tsunami survivors could have a say in basic decisions that affected their future. 'I was always saying to them, "The future is yours. It's in your hands. You decide how your village should look, in what shape or what structure, and these kinds of things."'

Community-led development was time-consuming. But it was a powerfully important process to rebuild trust among a fragile population. 'All of a sudden, they have to work together with their neighbours, where they are village mates, to discuss the future of their village and how the village will be built back better than before,' Mangkusubroto says. If the villagers decided they wanted an elementary school, a mosque or a health clinic, they needed to identify an appropriate parcel of land. This required negotiation and compromise, especially since the tsunami had erased many boundary markers between properties. Consultants worked with community members to prepare the plans. 'Once the map is finished, then we step in to rebuild their village,' Mangkusubroto says. 'One thing that I'm really proud of is that there has been no conflict whatsoever, between neighbours, between villages, between subdistricts.'

The phrase 'build back better' is now ubiquitous. It is the name for US president Joe Biden's economic recovery plan, it's been used by campaigners in the United Kingdom seeking a coronavirus recovery plan, and both the New Zealand prime minister, Jacinda Ardern, and the OECD have used it in reference to green recovery plans. In 2015, it was adopted by the United Nations as part of its framework for disaster recovery, which referenced the need to 'Build Back Better in recovery, rehabilitation and reconstruction'.[16] But in 2004 it did not yet exist – Mangkusubroto is credited with coining it. He says that it 'came from a discussion with President Bill Clinton', when the former US president was serving as United Nations Special Envoy for Tsunami Recovery.[17] 'We came up with the agreement "let's build it back better",' Mangkusubroto says. The catchcry of 'build back better' underpinned recovery in Aceh, and it has undoubtedly been implemented. Banda Aceh is a far superior city post-tsunami. Roads are paved and wide; modern waste management and drainage is in place. Five enormous concrete tsunami evacuation buildings tower over the city.

Yet there are aspects in which the recovery was less than perfect. In fishing communities, you'll find unused boats on the shore; local fisherman have found them of insufficient quality and not fit for purpose. A large portion of residents still live in poverty, and Aceh remains one of the poorest parts of Indonesia.[18]

To get another perspective on recovery in Aceh, I spoke with Harry Masyrafah, who hails from the region. Fortunately for him, he was away studying in Malaysia when the tsunami hit, and his immediate family was not directly impacted either. A former analyst at the World Bank, Masyrafah prepared a substantial report on the recovery process for American think tank the Brookings Institution.

'Life is much better now in Aceh,' he says. While he says many of the aid agencies failed to fulfil commitments and ensure high-quality, long-term developments, 'the creation of a single agency in the form of the BRR to coordinate the government's response, together with the pooling of funds by donors into a multi-donor fund, had direct and significantly positive effects on coordination.' It meant costs were contained and waste was reduced. Similarly, a financial tracking system worked well to manage the hundreds of projects being undertaken by aid organisations, he says.[19]

The model pursued in Aceh has served as a template for subsequent recoveries in other parts of Indonesia. For example, when a magnitude 6.3 earthquake struck Yogyakarta, damaging 260,000 houses, the government adopted the Aceh model of community-based housing reconstruction. It also established a reconstruction fund to manage and coordinate donor funds. This approach became formally embedded in Indonesia's disaster management framework and was applied after a major West Sumatran earthquake in 2009 and again following the 2010 eruption of Mount Merapi, near Yogyakarta.[20]

It's not hard to be impressed by what has been achieved in Aceh. The scale of construction was immense: over 140,000 houses; 3696 kilometres of road; 1759 schools; 1115 health facilities; 996 government buildings; 363 bridges; twenty-three ports; eleven airports or airstrips. More than 7000 fishing boats were built or provided. The scale of investment in people was also enormous: over 155,000 labourers and almost 40,000 teachers were trained, while 195,000 small businesses received assistance.[21] And accompanying all of this, there is peace.

I n a quiet corner of the South Pacific, almost exactly on the opposite side of the earth from London, you will find Christchurch. It is New Zealand's second-largest city, but is only about the size of Norwich in the United Kingdom, or Chattanooga, Tennessee, in the United States. Built around the gentle Avon River, it once prided itself on its Englishness. It was famous for its Gothic cathedral, green parks and old-money establishment.

New Zealand lies at the edge of two major tectonic plates – the Australian and the Pacific plates – which are slowly moving past each other. This movement is accompanied by regular earthquakes, and Christchurch has always been alert to the risk. In 1869, brick and stone buildings in the city were damaged in an earthquake; another strong quake hit in 1870.[22] The top of Christchurch Cathedral's stone spire collapsed in a magnitude 7.3 earthquake in 1888, and again in a magnitude 6.9 quake in 1901.[23]

In September 2010, the sleepy city was once more awoken with force when a magnitude 7.1 earthquake struck 44 kilometres west of the central business district. There were few injuries and no fatalities, but the quake caused NZ$5 billion (US$3.5 billion) in damage. In the months following, Christchurch continued to be wracked by thousands of aftershocks, including earthquakes of magnitude 5.0, 4.9 and 5.1.[24]

Things got much worse on 22 February 2011, when a magnitude 6.3 earthquake struck. Although smaller than the September earthquake – and technically part of its aftershock sequence – its epicentre was just 6 kilometres from the city centre and only 5 kilometres underground.[25]

Tara Tonkings, a former housemate of mine, is a Christchurch resident who lived through it all. 'It was the most terrifying experience of my life,' she tells me. Then a new mother with a five-week-old baby, she describes thinking her son was dead as the earthquake shook him from the bassinet onto the floor. 'The scream that came out of me – I didn't think was possible.'

This time 185 people died, mostly in the collapse of two buildings in the central city – the six-storey 1980s Canterbury Television building and the five-storey 1960s Pyne Gould building.[26] Weakened by the earlier quakes, several heritage buildings also collapsed. For safety reasons, 4 square kilometres (about 1000 acres) of the central business district had to be cordoned off for almost three years. Eventually, about half of the 2000 commercial buildings in the area were demolished.[27]

Throughout the city, parks and riverbanks were riddled with slumps and other ground failures. Some neighbourhoods experienced liquefaction, where water-saturated sediment loses its strength and acts as a fluid. The scientists at the United States Geological Survey describe this as being 'like when you wiggle your toes in the wet sand near the water at the beach.'[28] Most of Christchurch's 160,000 homes suffered damage.

The aftershocks kept coming over the following year and included one of 6.0 and another of 5.9. Each quake caused further damage and liquefaction, raising doubts about the viability of whole neighbourhoods. Altogether, there were more than 430,000 valid insurance claims for buildings, contents and land damage. The total cost of rebuilding was ultimately assessed at

NZ$40 billion (US$28 billion), about 20 per cent of New Zealand's annual gross domestic product.[29]

The management of the immediate response to the crisis was widely lauded. New Zealand's largest-ever 'public information management' team was assembled to develop and communicate critical safety messages. Christchurch mayor Bob Parker, the national controller of the emergency response, became the face of the recovery, speaking at every press conference.[30] Parker had seemed headed for defeat at the local elections of October 2010, but due to his calm and effective leadership during the earthquake response, he was soundly re-elected.

Yet Christchurch soon became wracked by bitter leadership and governance tensions that bedevilled much of the recovery period. In the immediate aftermath of the first earthquakes, the national parliament established the Canterbury Earthquake Recovery Commission (Canterbury is the region in which Christchurch is located), composed of the mayors of the three impacted local authorities and four government appointees. Its main purpose was to better facilitate coordination between local communities and the central government. It lacked executive powers and had made little progress by the time the February earthquake hit.[31] The parliament disbanded the commission and established the Canterbury Earthquake Recovery Authority (CERA) as a government department, reporting directly to the minister. Lianne Dalziel, then a Member of Parliament representing Christchurch East, was critical of the decision not to follow international example and have a layer of governance between the authority and the politicians (like the model adopted in Aceh). 'They have replaced an independent body with no power with a powerful body without independence,' she said at the time.[32]

Dalziel was elected mayor of Christchurch in 2013, and I spoke with her to better understand Christchurch's recovery. Formerly a lawyer in the union movement, a government minister and an MP (for twenty-three years), Dalziel is familiar with the tribulations of a long political career. With a deep voice and a robust New Zealand accent, she projects resilience, and it is easy to imagine that she's not the type to give up easily. Yet she clearly struggled with the government control over CERA. 'CERA was a powerful body, but it was not independent, so it was completely controlled by the minister,' Dalziel says. 'As an opposition MP I was in the wrong party, and I had no access to information other than that filtered through the minister.'

Not long after the February 2011 earthquake, the Christchurch City Council began the process of preparing a recovery plan for the central city. It kicked off with a community-consultation measure known as Share an Idea. More than 106,000 suggestions from the public were garnered. The council analysed the ideas, emerging with five themes that would shape the recovery. These painted a picture of a green, low-rise, liveable city with a compact central business district, new housing options, many recreation and cultural facilities, and public transport and cycling infrastructure.[33] However, the Minister for Canterbury Earthquake Recovery, Gerry Brownlee, expressed reservations and announced that CERA would take over the recovery planning. The final plan – developed without further public consultation – was endorsed in 2012. While it was broadly consistent with the council's plan, it significantly reduced the size of the central business district and removed reference to consideration of light rail. Key construction projects – such as a convention centre and a sports centre – were still included, but their location or size had changed. Others, including a performing arts centre and a stadium, had been added.[34]

At the heart of Christchurch's recovery was an unresolved tension between a top-down approach and one that was community-led. Dalziel, clearly an advocate of community involvement, becomes energised when the conversation turns to the subject. 'If the community aren't engaged in the recovery process, then you just leave them in a position of dependency and on the receiving end of other people's decisions,' she says. 'I always think now, with the benefit of what I've learned, that a crisis represents an opportunity to build capacity. The "build back better" theme has always been sitting in at the heart of it. That doesn't just mean the buildings. It means communities. It means the environment.'

While debate raged about leadership and governance, a grassroots movement of community and participatory projects sprung up from the rubble. Christchurch became internationally renowned for a flourishing creative movement as local organisations experimented with temporary projects, using a collaborative approach. Greening the Rubble worked with landowners, sponsors and the community to create temporary public parks on land left empty in the wake of the earthquakes; Life in Vacant Spaces also worked with landowners and project partners to activate vacant sites and spaces with temporary creative projects. The Festival of Transitional Architecture encouraged Christchurch residents to experience a reimagined city, through architectural installations, workshops, family events and live performances over the course of a weekend.[35] In 2013, Lonely Planet named Christchurch as one of the world's top ten cities to visit, citing the 'positive and innovative urban solutions' and the 'sense of energy in Christchurch that is transforming and inspiring the city's renewal'.[36]

At the forefront of this movement has been Dr Ryan Reynolds, founder of Gap Filler, a social enterprise that designs and delivers 'creative, experimental civic installations'. Reynolds studied electrical engineering in his native Chicago before a study abroad program took him to New Zealand, where he became enmeshed in the theatre and film scene. It's an unusual combination of talents, but he tells me that much of his engineering degree consisted of 'small group design work for a social purpose' – in retrospect, an ideal preparation for what was to come.

With his collaborators, Reynolds saw the vacant spaces created after the demolition of damaged buildings as opportunities for experimentation. One of their early projects was the Dance-O-Mat, where they 'just put a dance floor and some towers with speakers on it, and the little coin-operated mechanism, like a jukebox, where you play your own music'. Suddenly, people were dancing on the street corner – 'which is always possible, but it was a behaviour no one was engaging in there. You just frame the space in a certain way and kind of make an invitation.' Other projects included the Pallet Pavilion, a large-scale temporary community building built from 3000 pallets, which hosted more than 250 events, and a cycle-powered cinema, screening cycle-themed films.[37]

Reynolds found himself in conversation with people about their 'weird, wacky hopes and dreams'. The projects became catalysts. 'We managed to help people see these vacant sites as a space of opportunity where they can project some of their latent unfulfilled desires, in a way, and see that as a space to play or try something.'

With temporary projects like these, the cost of failure was low – in multiple senses. 'You don't have to sign a lease and commit to three years of your life,' Reynolds says. 'The reputational cost as well – when it's a two-week thing, some people aren't going to like it, but they'll probably not complain too much because it's only for a couple of weeks.' The temporary state of many of the city's spaces led people to experiment with creative, innovative projects they might not otherwise have been game to try.

Reynolds argues that this experimentation is central to economic recovery following a crisis like the one Christchurch experienced. He contrasts it with purely commercial activity that replicates what is happening in suburban shopping malls. 'It's the weird stuff that's not happening in the suburbs,' he says. 'That's the stuff that's going to start to pull people back into the central city and make them brave enough to come back in.' While Christchurch once had a reputation as one of the most conservative cities in New Zealand, a more experimental, creative approach has begun to permeate even the institutional fabric of the city. 'Now the identity has shifted and in Christchurch we have much more of a sense that things are possible,' Reynolds says. In 2018, Christchurch adopted a new vision: 'A city of opportunity for all. Open to new ideas, new people and new ways of doing things – a city where everything is possible.'[38] Reynolds cried when he saw that, because it encompassed 'part of what my peers and I had been trying to make happen in Christchurch for the previous eight years'.

'The city is definitely coming out the other side,' Tara Tonkings says. 'Now, it's really exciting if you go into the city. There are no recognisable landmarks; there are all these new and exciting places that you've never been to before. And I think it has become a more creative city – there's lots of really cool bars, restaurants and pop-up things that would never have happened if it wasn't for the earthquake. For a while, everything was temporary, but now it's becoming more permanent.'

It's taken time, but a new Christchurch is emerging. Striking commercial buildings, a new bus interchange, a performing arts centre and a stunning convention centre have been built.[39] At the 2018 census, 27,000 more people lived in the city than five years earlier; not exactly a population boom, but a solid 8 per cent increase. Fuelled by the rebuild, between 2011 and 2016 the Canterbury region's economy grew by 31 per cent, more than the increase in national GDP of 24 per cent over the same period. Pre-COVID, the number of passengers moving through Christchurch's airport had increased 21 per cent over five years, with international visitors from places such as China increasing faster than the rest of the country.[40]

'There is a real sense that this is becoming a city of choice in a way that it simply wasn't before,' Dalziel says. 'We are going to have facilities that are second to none for a city our size.' Christchurch has affordability on its side, along with a size that makes it extremely liveable. 'There's a strong sense of optimism and hope for what the future holds.'

The importance of resilience

Natural disasters have bedevilled humanity for as long as we have walked the earth. The eruption of Mount Vesuvius in 79 AD buried the Roman city of Pompeii in a thick layer of volcanic ash. In 1815, Indonesia's Mount Tambora erupted in the most devastating volcanic event of the past 1000 years, blocking sunlight and contributing to a 3-degree drop in global temperatures, crop failures and famine. In 1931, central China experienced a devastating flood that inundated an area the size of England, killing at least two million people, mostly through the famine and disease that resulted. More recently, the 2010 earthquake in Haiti killed an estimated

230,000 people, injured 300,000 more and displaced 1.5 million. In 2008, Cyclone Nargis struck Myanmar, killing 140,000, and in the summer of 2003, record high temperatures across Europe killed 70,000 people.

The World Bank reports that since 1980, more than two million people and US$3 trillion have been lost to natural disasters. In recent decades, damages from natural disasters have increased dramatically, from US$23 billion a year in the 1980s to US$150 billion per year over the past decade – an increase of some 600 per cent.[41] On average, more than 60,000 people are killed by natural disasters each year and more than 200 million are impacted. While earthquakes (and associated tsunamis) cause more deaths than all other types of disasters put together, extreme weather events such as hurricanes, storms and floods are the most expensive.[42] This risk is increasing, due to population growth and rapid urbanisation. The expansion of cities in developing countries has been accompanied by large informal settlements, many of which are on floodplains or in other high-risk areas.[43]

Climate change is increasing the frequency and severity of natural disasters. Since the 1950s, the number of extremely hot days has increased; in most of the world's regions, there has been at least one additional heatwave day each decade since then.[44] And as the air warms, 'its water-holding capacity increases, particularly over the oceans', writes climate scientist Dr Joëlle Gergis.[45] This means we are likely to experience more extreme rainfall events.

Since 2000, the annual number of climate-related disasters has been double that of the 1980s.[46] Scientists on the Intergovernmental Panel on Climate Change predict more frequent hot days throughout this century, along with more heavy rain events. Their modelling projects an increase in heatwaves across Europe, in hurricanes across the United States and the Caribbean, in wildfires in North America and in flooding across the world. Small island states face a very likely prospect of sea level rises and storm surges.[47] Climate scientists are anxious about what's yet to come. 'It's going to get A LOT worse,' says climate scientist Dr Kim Cobb. 'I say that with emphasis because it does challenge the imagination. And that's the scary thing to know as a climate scientist.'[48]

Natural disasters tend to be experienced very differently in rich and poor countries. Between 1994 and 2013, low- and lower-middle-income countries experienced 44 per cent of the world's disasters but suffered 68 per cent of global deaths. On average, three times more people died per disaster in lower-income countries than in high-income countries. On a per capita basis, there were forty-three deaths per million people in low-income countries and just nine per million in high-income countries.[49] In considering the risk of death from natural disasters, the developmental level of a country is a much more important factor than a country's exposure to earthquakes or weather events.

An earthquake, storm or flood can be devastating, but if it affects people who have almost nothing and earn very little, it will have a relatively small impact on a country's wealth. While rich countries experience fewer deaths from natural disasters, they do suffer enormous economic losses, as they have more expensive housing and infrastructure. Between 1994 and 2013, high- and upper-middle-income countries reported 90 per cent of all economic losses resulting from natural disaster.[50] The United States has frequent hurricanes, storms, floods and wildfires, and due to high asset values, it experiences greater economic loss from natural disasters than any other country. Between 1998 and 2017, it suffered losses amounting to US$945 billion.[51] However, while the economic losses in high-income countries might be greater in absolute terms, lower-income countries suffer more in a relative sense – losses amount to just 0.3 per cent of GDP in high-income countries, but 5.1 per cent of GDP in low-income countries.[52]

The tsunami had a far-reaching effect on livelihoods in Aceh. Fishing families lost everything – their assets and their income stream. Demand for fish plummeted for months afterwards, as locals thought fish caught in waters where so many had died were unclean. Farmers, small businesses and informal traders were also badly affected; crops were flattened, animals were lost and markets, roads and warehouses were destroyed. The price of goods increased by between 80 and 225 per cent. A month after the tsunami, 15 per cent of those surveyed were still only eating one meal per day.[53]

In general, poor people receive less support from governments, financial institutions, family and friends. As a result, natural disasters keep people in or push them into poverty. This in turn makes them more vulnerable to future disasters. Within countries, people with low incomes or low levels of education are generally less prepared for disasters. This is partly because much disaster preparation is expensive – building insurance, strengthening a home to be more earthquake-resilient. In New Orleans, for example, low socioeconomic districts had lower levels of flood insurance, leaving residents unprepared when Hurricane Katrina struck in 2005.[54] The disadvantage many suffered before the disaster may only be exacerbated during recovery as they struggle to negotiate the bureaucracy to access support.[55] For example, following the Humboldt County earthquakes in California in 1992, researchers found that higher-income residents were able to 'work the system, fill out the forms, and acquire the financial aid they needed', but lower-income residents could not, meaning they did not apply for funds they were entitled to.[56]

The effect of inequality has been seen in Christchurch too. Those living in the city's more affluent western suburbs were impacted by the earthquakes far less than those in the poorer eastern suburbs. Money and resources have flowed more freely in the west, enabling these areas to return to pre-earthquake conditions, 'whereas those living in the poorer central and eastern suburbs continue to battle toward recovery with far fewer resources to call upon'.[57]

Natural disasters have multi-generational impacts, not dissimilar to the impacts of recession. Disasters force poorer households to make choices that have long-lasting effects, such as withdrawing a child from school or cutting back on health expenditure. Children often suffer the most. For example, 2005's Hurricane Stan led to a 7 per cent increase in child labour in Guatemala. In Ethiopia, children under the age of three at the time of the 1984 famine were less likely to finish school, and hence will end up with lifetime earnings between 3 and 8 per cent lower. A long-term study into the effects of a 1970 earthquake in Peru found that males in utero at the time of the earthquake completed half a year less of schooling, and females 0.8 years less, than those born earlier. This effect flowed through to the next generation, with children of mothers who were in utero at the time of the earthquake completing an average of 0.4 years less of schooling. The reasons for this are not entirely clear. Researchers speculate it could be because of negative health shocks during pregnancy, subsequent food shortages or damage to school and healthcare facilities.[58] What's clear is that the social costs of natural disasters are at least as great as the economic ones.

This is why international organisations such as the World Bank regard disaster risk management as inseparable from poverty reduction. Natural disasters exacerbate poverty, but poorer people are more vulnerable to natural disasters. If we want to reduce the future impact of natural disasters, reducing poverty is clearly part of the answer. Improving the preparedness of poor communities also needs to be a key part of our response to poverty.

The impact of a natural disaster on a community is influenced by factors such as the quality of buildings, urban planning, infrastructure and services. Early warning systems and public response measures are also important.[59] With urban areas around the world adding 1.4 million people per week, nearly one billion new housing units will need to be constructed by 2060, mostly in the developing world.[60] Unless cities become more resilient, tens of millions of city-dwellers will be forced into poverty and the cost of natural disasters will increase by billions each year. Yet if institutional capital (such as pension funds and sovereign wealth funds) can be unlocked, the World Bank sees a significant opportunity to build resilience into cities as they develop. This requires improvements to local government capacity, so they can create the right context to enable private-sector investment.[61]

But in addition to measures that focus on reducing the risks to assets, it's also important to help *people* improve their ability to cope with shocks. Insurance and social-security safety nets increase resilience and reduce the psychological effects of natural disasters. The World Bank argues that an investment in improving the resilience of people in low-income countries would reduce 'wellbeing losses' by billions of dollars.[62]

This brings us to a key point: the impact of natural disasters is more or less a function of the conditions that exist prior to the event. These conditions also shape the subsequent recovery. Poverty and conflict in Aceh contributed to the impact of the tsunami. Earlier earthquakes in both Aceh and Christchurch meant many buildings were already weakened. Local governments in Aceh and Christchurch were relatively weak, impacting on their ability to contribute significantly to recovery efforts. With Christchurch's central business district cordoned off for three years, the existing urban form, with its suburban, car-dependent culture, was reinforced during the recovery process, making revitalisation of the city more challenging.[63]

While after a disaster it's the acute healthcare needs that usually receive the most attention, the biggest disease burden almost always comes from chronic pre-existing health conditions, such as kidney failure, diabetes and cardiovascular disease. People with pre-existing psychiatric conditions are particularly vulnerable.[64] Countries with better population health and well-developed primary healthcare systems are more resilient and better prepared when disaster hits.

In short, building resilience ahead of time to mitigate the impact of disaster is critical. This is an idea we'll return to later in the book.

How to recover well from natural disaster

Given the frequency of natural disasters, and how many communities have had to recover following their devastation, there is ample opportunity to assemble detailed insights into how we can maximise recovery efforts. The lessons that emerge from natural disasters are potentially applicable to recovery from other crises too.

While pre-existing conditions shape the impact of a disaster on a community, decisions made during the recovery process have an enormous effect on the overall outcome. In an analysis of ten earthquakes, British researcher Stephen Platt found that the critical factor explaining the difference in the speed and quality of recovery was 'the quality of decision-making'. In other words, how well a community recovers is 'within the control of government decision-makers, recovery planners and local communities'.[65]

In the aftermath of a natural disaster, it's important to act quickly. Especially in developing countries, lives are precarious even in the absence of disaster, so speed matters a great deal. A slow recovery risks the economic pain and deprivation of families and communities becoming engrained.

Eager to share its hard-earned lessons, Dr Mangkusubroto's Reconstruction and Recovery Agency published *10 Management Lessons for Host Governments Coordinating Post-Disaster Reconstruction*. One of the recommendations is to 'maintain a "crisis mindset" through the entire reconstruction effort' – it's essential to 'develop a culture of speed if affected communities are to recover quickly'.[66] To help maintain a sense of urgency, it's useful to set challenging targets, broken down into milestones. Bureaucratic processes – which are generally not designed for emergencies – need to be streamlined too. In Aceh, a one-stop shop was established to aggregate administrative services from multiple government agencies, helping aid organisations to navigate services such as immigration, taxation and customs.

BALANCE SPEED AND DELIBERATION

The challenge of speed versus deliberation is at the heart of all recoveries. It's necessary to act decisively, but we should also be prepared to change course if things aren't working.

In Aceh, acting decisively meant implementing different projects concurrently, rather than sequentially. This sped things up, but sometimes led to poorer-quality outcomes. The BRR was upfront about the trade-off – a central operating principle in Aceh was that 'it could not afford the luxury of letting the perfect become the enemy of the good'. It was 'better to have 100,000 houses built and rectify mistakes for a few thousand than to have 20,000 perfect houses' that took much longer to build.[67]

Laurie Johnson, author of the post–Hurricane Katrina recovery plan for New Orleans, wrote *After Great Disasters* with her colleague Robert Olshansky. It analyses how six countries recovered following major natural disasters and argues that 'planning and action need to happen in parallel through a constant learning process that involves continuous monitoring, evaluating, and correcting'. Recovery agencies need to quickly build their planning capacity by hiring staff. Decentralisation of information-gathering and decision-making is also important: 'to be fast and smart, decision-making must be distributed among all the recovery actors and take full advantage of local knowledge and capacity'. With implementation and planning happening together during a short period, planning decisions need to be revised over time.[68] Those involved in recovery planning are essentially building the plane while flying it!

While buildings can be reconstructed relatively quickly, community and economic recovery takes longer. In Aceh, Mangkusubroto says most of the initial focus was on hard infrastructure – roads, bridges, hospitals, schools, power plants, harbours and airports. 'Everything was achieved,' he says, 'some of them more than 100 per cent. So I can say it's a great success.' But what he calls the 'soft infrastructure' could not be achieved during the four years he was in Aceh. 'We had political conflict, armed conflict for twenty-five years before 2005. This conflict is a wound that is very difficult to heal, and it's not possible to do it in four years. We need more time. My feeling is it will take at least fifteen years. To build trust takes time.' Recovery doesn't have a clear end point; it gradually merges with those activities that are business as usual.

'You have to be very serious when you are dealing with crisis,' says Mangkusubroto. 'And that means you set an organization that works full time to attack the problem.' Learning from its experience in Aceh, the BRR advises governments to quickly establish a coordinating agency to take charge of the reconstruction effort. This shouldn't be the same organisation that leads the emergency relief effort. The coordination agency needs to 'take the lead in setting priorities and establishing an overall direction for reconstruction activities'. Given the overwhelming challenges faced in the aftermath of disasters, the BRR recommends starting with the most urgent: 'meeting basic needs, filling gaps in the supply chain, building a coordination war room based on reliable data, and getting community input'. This will lay an effective foundation for medium- and long-term recovery efforts.[69]

The establishment of a new entity made sense in Aceh, as local government was weak and conflict meant there was a deep mistrust of central government. Nevertheless, there were steep learning curves for Mangkusubroto and his team. For a smaller-scale disaster, an existing local or central government agency may be better suited to oversee the recovery efforts.

Whatever its origin, the reconstruction and recovery agency needs to have adequate powers. If it is to secure the full support of other government agencies and the donor community, it must have a strong and experienced leadership team. And it needs the capacity to implement programs; while its main function is to coordinate the activities of others, there will inevitably be gaps in the reconstruction effort that it will have to fill directly. The main challenge will be to coordinate recovery efforts to avoid double-up and bureaucratic infighting. While aid agencies may not coordinate among themselves effectively (because they are not equipped to do so or they regard other agencies as competitors), they will take direction from government or a designated coordinating agency.[70]

Aceh's recovery was built on the deep involvement of local communities. Community-led solutions are often seen as time-consuming and Mangkusubroto and his team took a risky move in adopting this approach. Many stakeholders dissented.[71] Yet it was highly successful and the model has since been applied to other recovery efforts in Indonesia.

Involving the community in recovery is often more effective than top-down approaches. The BRR reports that in Aceh 'community-managed projects were 30 per cent cheaper than contractor-managed projects, and 96 per cent of people were satisfied with the quality'.[72] Community involvement enables the recovery to draw on local resources – both human and material – and it ensures that there is widespread local ownership of the process, increasing its legitimacy.[73]

Community organisations have a valuable role to play during recovery as a conduit for information. 'There are always existing community groups who you must engage through the whole of the recovery process,' says Lianne Dalziel. 'They've got to be reached out to straight away. They're a rich source of information. But they're also a great source for dissemination of information because they're already trusted in their own communities.'

Working with communities during recovery doesn't just have instrumental value, though. Communities learn new decision-making processes and skills, and the resulting increase in community capacity is important in itself. 'A disaster or a crisis always represents an opportunity to build capacity,' Dalziel says.

Of course, communities don't have all the answers. Expert knowledge has a lot to contribute. 'The wisdom of the community, when combined with the knowledge of the experts, always exceeds what one can offer without the other,' Dalziel observes. 'You cannot just listen to experts and you can't just listen to community either; there has to be the narrative of the two.'

Local governments are often best placed to work with local communities to identify needs and oversee recovery projects. Yet local governments are sometimes devastated by natural disasters along with their communities and may lack capacity. After the tsunami hit Aceh, 'the local government was also paralysed,' Mangkusubroto says, 'because there were so many people killed.' Coordination agencies face a tension between stepping in and trying to build the capacity of local government. With coordination agencies generally dissolving after several years, it's important that local government has the capacity to continue the work through the medium and long term. 'This is something that should be given more weight,' Mangkusubroto says. 'Local government should be managed well in order to continue the development of the province.'

Successful recoveries also rely on central governments. With the deepest pockets, they will need to stump up much of the funding for reconstruction, but central governments should partner with local governments and communities. Dalziel feels that is the biggest lesson from Christchurch. 'Most of the problems that I could identify for what went wrong stem from the decision of the government to put in place a government department to run the city's recovery. That to me is fundamentally flawed. The better approach would have been to look at what the strengths of the city council were.'

Mangkusubroto agrees, saying that a 'top-down and bottom-up' approach is best, with both local organisations and national governments playing a role. 'You have to have a bottom-up approach because organisations in the district, they are the ones who are dealing with the issues and also have direct communication with the people there,' Mangkusubroto says. 'But at the top, they are the ones who design the organisation, they are the ones who decide about the budget and also procedures.' Both levels need to come together through shared governance: 'In the organization, and the budget, and the procedures, you should include the governor and the district head, to ensure they don't feel left behind.'

ENSURE ACCESS TO INFORMATION

Along with money, information is the 'fuel of the recovery process'.[74] It helps everyone involved make good decisions. Information needs to be gathered and shared regularly and openly. This transparency will drive accountability.

A free press plays an important role in facilitating transparency during disaster response. In his book *Poverty and Famines*, Indian economist Amartya Sen compares the response to famine in India in the 1950s with the response to famine under Mao's communist regime in China. He concludes that the Indian response was better, partly due to press freedom that facilitated reporting on food shortages.[75]

A public database of all recovery projects was useful in Aceh, and there is clear value in replicating this approach elsewhere. All aid agencies were asked to provide project details and targets for the database and encouraged to give updates on progress, including money spent. Through a geospatial information system, all houses and assets rebuilt were mapped. Initially compliance with the database was poor, though with the right incentives (for example, aid agencies had to be registered with the database if they wanted access to streamlined government services through the one-stop shop), this improved after the first couple of years. And because the database was public, there was external pressure on agencies – from constituents, donors and auditors – to be transparent about their progress.

The database was invaluable in helping the BRR to identify gaps in the reconstruction efforts and make informed decisions about how to allocate remaining funds. 'The ability to know who is doing what, when, and where is the core data requirement for an effective coordinating agency,' the BRR writes. 'This information is needed to understand the overall progress of the reconstruction program and to be able to quickly identify emerging project overlaps and reconstruction gaps.'[76]

Because of the number of organisations and interests involved in recovery from natural disaster, information alone won't be enough to ensure that money and resources flow to where they are most needed. The coordinating agency should use its influence to ensure this happens. The BRR suggests a mix of flexibility, collaboration and diplomacy, with formal authority as a last resort. Mangkusubroto chaired the multi-donor fund to 'steer partners to work in underfunded sectors and regions'. He also went out of his way to ensure donor organisations were acknowledged, while he 'coaxed and cajoled donors to honour their pledges and to adapt their priorities to unmet needs'.[77]

Following a natural disaster, economic output typically drops dramatically before rebounding strongly, as the reconstruction process serves as an enormous economic stimulus. Once the reconstruction process winds down though, what's left is the strength – or otherwise – of the private-sector economy. Joanna Norris, chief executive of ChristchurchNZ, the city's economic development agency, says in Christchurch, 'construction fuelled GDP growth and created what in some ways was an artificial sugar hit that disguised the fact that the economy wasn't fundamentally changing over the long term'. Once construction projects finished, growth stalled. 'Though construction still supports about 30,000 jobs in Canterbury, pre-COVID economic growth in the region was nearing zero,' she writes. 'The urgent search was on to find new forms of activity to replace the construction stimulus.'[78]

Aceh found itself in a similar position. The BRR supported existing livelihoods, such as fishing and rice farming, but largely left long-term economic development to other agencies. While the province now has excellent transport infrastructure, Mangkusubroto says it principally facilitates the movement of people; there is very little outbound freight. He points to the newly reconstructed Port of Malahayati, not far from Banda Aceh. 'Imports are 99 per cent,' he says. 'Exports are 1 per cent.' A key reason for the lack of economic progress in Aceh is the absence of significant private-sector investment. 'Nobody is willing to invest, let alone foreigners.' He puts this down partly to the Sharia law that governs the province, which deters tourists and makes foreign investment less likely. 'Rich people of Aceh origin, they live in Medan [in the adjacent province of North Sumatra], but they have their shops in Aceh. So that means that actually they are trying to do their business in Aceh, but when it comes to spending their profits, they're spending them outside the province.'

While it's understandable that during the short term, the focus is on reconstruction – funded by governments, donors and insurance – it's also critical that the role of private-sector investment is considered early on, as this is what will drive recovery over the longer term. Disaster is usually accompanied by uncertainty, which makes investment far riskier. Whatever certainty governments and recovery agencies can provide will go a long way towards instilling confidence. Strategic planning frameworks, land-use plans, reconstruction schedules and economic development strategies all help to create a more receptive business environment.

The wealth of a city or community is mostly determined by the economic output it can produce. A recovery built only on construction won't enable a city to become more competitive. 'Investment cannot be one-dimensional, and can look beyond the easy and tangible, albeit expensive, stimulus provided by construction', writes Norris.[79] Instead, cities should undertake the challenging work of considering their strengths and opportunities, and looking for ways to grow industry sectors that can yield the greatest economic gain. This will require investment to foster appropriate skills and address gaps in supply chains, and the innovation to develop unique new capabilities.

To get this work underway, Christchurch City Council under Lianne Dalziel's leadership established ChristchurchNZ, the agency headed by Norris that brought together economic development functions with tourism and events. In 2017, it also developed an Economic Development Strategy, which prioritised plans such as improving the commercialisation of innovation and positioning Christchurch as the international gateway to New

Zealand's South Island.[80] ChristchurchNZ has gone on to identify and pursue what it calls 'supernodes' – sectors such as aerospace, food and fibre, and high-tech services in which Christchurch stands a chance of being globally competitive.[81]

Mangkusubroto stared out of the car window in a reflective mood. Soon he would be at Sultan Iskandar Muda Airport, leaving Aceh after four demanding years. The window revealed a view in enormous contrast to the scene when he arrived. The city centre was bustling with activity. The streets were a kaleidoscope of colours and shapes, a mix of rusty roofs, new construction and the impressive minarets of the Baiturrahman Grand Mosque. Heading away from the city centre, neat lines of blue squares marked the roofs of new villages; it represented thousands of people with the chance to rebuild their lives after the devastation of four years earlier. Four years ago, the airport was where aid for tsunami survivors had arrived. Now, pulling up at the shiny new terminal on a smooth road, Mangkusubroto marvelled that Aceh had an international airport.

His mission had been to build back better, and the city was undoubtedly improved. Aside from the new buildings and infrastructure, there was peace. Poverty levels were lower than before the tsunami.[82] It had been a gruelling, demanding four years, but he felt proud of what had been achieved, and optimistic about the future.

FIVE STEPS FORWARD

1. **Establish or designate an agency to coordinate the recovery.**
A dedicated agency has the advantage of not being limited by a 'business as usual' approach. It has a mandate to lead recovery and the capacity to coordinate the magnitude of work required. It will need to work closely with established economic-planning agencies, which can take the lead in aligning recovery with long-term development objectives, setting the policy framework and approving funding for larger projects. To ensure accountability and transparency, recovery agencies should have access to appropriate information and data and be governed by boards that include stakeholder representatives. Aside from Aceh, examples of this approach include the Lower Manhattan Development Corporation, established to rebuild Lower Manhattan in New York City following 9/11, and the Louisiana Recovery Authority, set up to guide recovery in the aftermath of Hurricanes Katrina and Rita.

2. **Engage the community in its own recovery.** This leads to more appropriate and targeted recovery plans. At a minimum, engagement means effective communication – through media briefings, public forums and social media. But bottom-up, participatory approaches are more likely to bind stakeholders together under a common purpose, ensure project outcomes are tailored to local needs and build the capacity to better respond to future disasters. It may include working through existing mechanisms that communities already use, wide-scale consultation and involving communities directly in the organisation and delivery of projects, including reconstruction of housing and community facilities.

3. **Strengthen local government.** As the tier of government closest to the community, local government plays a critical leadership and coordination role in recovery. But after a natural disaster, local governments might not have capacity to manage recovery alone or may need additional staff, funds or resources. Local governments should consider establishing formal partnerships with other governments at national, regional and local levels.

4. **Invest in arts and culture.** While built structures and infrastructure are important, culture creates the city's identity. The reconstruction of cultural landmarks and sites of significance (such as religious buildings or historic urban areas) can serve as initial focal points for recovery. Public art is often a way of processing post-crisis trauma, and experimental art installations and temporary community spaces – such as those in Christchurch – create a sense of possibility. Arts and culture also drive tourism and fuel the creative economy. Decades before the Christchurch earthquakes, artists took advantage of abandoned buildings in East Berlin after the fall of the Berlin Wall, transforming the city with a new creative energy. Detroit is similarly bouncing back from decades of neglect as it is revitalised by young creative artists.

5. **Support local economic development.** A large proportion of businesses are owned by community members, and these businesses provide the employment that helps people recover. Once the reconstruction boom is over, recovery and community prosperity will be largely dependent on the strength of business activity. Economic recovery is a long-term process that can last a decade or more. Economic development typically involves investment in skills development (for people of all ages), support for networks, and the development of supply chains and niche industries that have a global competitive advantage.

4

WAR

Hundreds of white doves circle into the blue sky above Jamsil Olympic Stadium in Seoul, accompanied by the Olympic Anthem. The giant Olympic flag flutters. Runners carry the Olympic flame into the stadium and hand it to the three who will light the cauldron: schoolteacher Chung Sun-man, dancer Sohn Mi-chung and marathoner Kim Won-tak. They rise on a steel ring towards the cauldron, perched high up in the stadium. Unfortunately, eleven of the doves take a fancy to the cauldron and are tragically barbequed as the cauldron is lit. Yet the Olympic oath is sworn and the Korean national anthem sung. Hundreds of dancers and schoolchildren in traditional dress form synchronised displays. South Korean paratroopers land in the stadium's centre, bedecked in the colours of the Olympic rings. The event concludes with the mascots of former Olympic Games together with groups from different countries dancing to the event's official song, 'Hand in Hand', performed by pop group Koreana.

The 1988 Seoul Olympics were a big deal for South Korea. An elaborate coming-out party, they were a chance to show the world the economic miracle that had emerged from the rubble of the

Korean War thirty-five years earlier. More than 8000 athletes from 159 countries competed, watched by more than 11,000 media and countless spectators across the world. Florence Griffith Joyner, the flamboyant US sprinter known as Flo-Jo, set records in the 100- and 200-metre sprints and medalled in relay events. Canadian Ben Johnson won the men's 100 metres in record-breaking time, around twenty-four hours before being disqualified for steroid use. Great Britain stunned the hockey world, defeating West Germany to win the gold medal for the only time since World War II.

Bidding for the games was originally conceived of as a way of shoring up the legitimacy of South Korea's authoritarian regime amid pressure for democratisation, and to provide some form of protection against an increasingly aggressive North Korea. In 1981, not long after the International Olympic Committee awarded the games to Seoul, North Korea began aggressively campaigning to jointly host them.[1] The objectives of this campaign remain unclear. Was it an attempt to find a convenient pretext to ruin the games by placing the South Koreans in a difficult position? Or was it a genuine attempt to share the games and bask in Olympic glory? In any event, the crusade ended tragically in 1987, when North Korean agents blew up a Korean Air plane en route to Seoul, killing 115 passengers.[2] North Korea ultimately boycotted the games, along with its ally, Cuba. Despite the tensions with North Korea, the Games were seen as a sign that Cold War tensions were thawing, with the United States and the Soviet Union competing against each other at the first Olympics since 1976. The medal count was dominated by the Soviet Union, which won fifty-five gold and 132 medals in total in what was to be its last ever games before it ceased to exist as a country.[3]

The Olympics followed a year of exciting political change in South Korea. The constitutionally limited term of then president, Chun Doo-Hwan, had come to an end, but he had sought to foil, delay or defer efforts to amend the constitution to permit direct election of a successor. In 1987, the June Democratic Struggle saw hundreds of thousands take to the streets across the country, agitating for free and fair elections, the release of political prisoners and press freedom. On 18 June, 1.5 million people in sixteen cities turned out, and on 26 June at least a million participated in the Great National March of Peace. Facing international scrutiny in the lead-up to the Olympics, the government was unwilling to use violence to suppress the protests and believed that its candidate could win an election anyway, given divisions within the opposition. The regime's candidate, Roe Tae Woo, was elected, but South Korea's democratic transition was well and truly underway, ironically enabled by the event that was meant to shore up the earlier dictatorship.[4]

South Korea was booming, with its economy growing faster than any in the world. Over the previous two decades, its annual growth rate had averaged an incredible 8.8 per cent. Less than thirty years earlier, per capita income had been just US$120 per year, making South Korea poorer than Sudan or the Congo. By the year of the Olympics, per capita incomes had increased thirty-sevenfold to US$4,520, about the same as Portugal.[5] It would subsequently go on to earn a place high on the list of the world's most developed nations.

The country had financed its enormous expansion by running up billions in foreign debt. Yet exports were booming, growing by more than 30 per cent each year. As a consequence, by 1986 South Korea recorded its first current account surplus. This meant it was exporting more than it was importing, thereby enabling it to reduce foreign debt.[6] The country had become a leading shipbuilder. The automotive sector – with brands such as Hyundai and Kia – was becoming a major growth industry. The electronics industry (think Samsung and LG, then called LuckyGoldstar) had started to take off in a big way too.

The period of rapid economic growth following the end of the Korean War in 1953 is often referred to as the 'miracle on the Han', named after the large river that flows through Seoul. The Korean War left the country devastated, but South Korea quickly rebuilt. In just a few decades, it managed to transform from an impoverished developing country to one of the world's industrial and technological powerhouses. South Korea's history shows us that while reconstruction after a crisis is important, it's the medium-term policy settings that help create globally competitive, export-oriented industries with the potential to transform the lives of generations to follow.

South Korea's recovery took its inspiration from a similar economic transformation that began to take place a decade earlier in Germany, following World War II: the 'miracle on the Rhine'. Adopting a different approach, Germany has largely managed to put the trauma of war and fascism behind it to grow into one of the world's richest countries, with enormous manufacturing capability and a robust liberal democracy. This chapter explores how in both cases, the nations had the chance to build back better after conflict.

A time of miracles

By 1953, Korea was at rock bottom. A devastating occupation by the Japanese had only ended in 1945, with Japan's surrender in World

War II. At the war's conclusion, the Korean Peninsula was occupied by Allied forces – in the vague notion that that this was only until Korea was ready for self-government. The Americans and Soviets had agreed that Soviet troops would occupy areas of Korea north of the 38th parallel, while Americans would occupy areas south of the parallel. By 1948, as a result of Cold War tensions, the occupation zones each became sovereign states – a socialist state in the north (the Democratic People's Republic of Korea, or North Korea) and a capitalist state in the south (the Republic of Korea, or South Korea) – with neither accepting the border as permanent.

In 1950, North Korean forces had invaded the south. Twenty-one members of the United Nations combined in a UN force to repel the invasion, with the United States providing 90 per cent of the troops. The fighting was brutal, resulting in the deaths of 1.25 million people and the complete destruction of almost all of Korea's major cities.[7] Seoul was captured four times. The two sides agreed to a ceasefire in 1953, although they are technically still at war. The armistice agreement created the 4-kilometre-wide demilitarised zone separating the two countries, with thousands of pieces of artillery aimed across the border on each side. In ruins, Korea's future looked bleak.

To understand how South Korea emerged from this period into prosperity, I sought out Kwan S. Kim, an emeritus professor of economics at the Kellogg Institute for International Studies in the United States. Now in his eighties, Professor Kim connected with me via telephone, and was earnest and warm in his responses to my questions.

Professor Kim is uniquely qualified to reflect on South Korea's success. Not only is he a globally recognised expert in development economics, but he also spent his formative years in South

Korea, before moving to the United States in 1961 to further his studies. In the aftermath of the war, 'the country was ruined', Kim says. 'Ninety per cent of the country was devastated and there was absolutely no hope. If ever there was an economic basket case, Korea of the 1950s was it.'

South Korea's economic recovery didn't start right away. For eight years following the war, the economy grew painfully slowly, with per capita gross domestic product (GDP) increasing at just 2 per cent per annum.[8] 'We had an inefficient civilian government led by Syngman Rhee,' Kim says. 'He didn't have any pragmatic solutions for the country. The government remained corrupt.' Rather than develop a coherent development strategy, Rhee's government relied largely on US aid. At one point in the mid-1950s, this aid represented some 80 per cent of government revenue.[9] There wasn't much to show for it though, with most going to food and building materials for reconstruction, with little applied to long-term development. A *New York Times* reporter wrote at the time that South Korea, 'the poorer half of one of the poorest nations in the world', is 'trying to exist with too many people and too few resources'. He suspected that South Korea would be 'dependent for the foreseeable future, perhaps for decades, on the self-interest and charity ... of the United States'.[10]

This state of affairs precipitated a military revolution in 1961, with General Park Chung-hee coming to power. 'Initially people hated him because of the military coup,' Kim says. 'But then he turned out to be a very effective leader with pragmatic, sustainable development policies in mind. He was able to amass national consensus.'

The newly installed dictator found South Korea in a difficult position. 'All the mineral resources were located in North Korea,'

Kim says. 'South Korea had no resources, only about 20 per cent of the country is arable land and the country was overpopulated.' Furthermore, South Korea possessed almost no financial capital.

There were some opportunities, though. 'Korea had strength in human capital,' Kim says. 'Because of the Confucian system, education is a high priority as a national culture. Ninety per cent of people were numerate and could at least read.' After liberation from the Japanese in 1945, schools had sprung up across the country, with the number of enrolments exploding. The expansion continued through the Korean War, with classes of often up to 100 students held wherever space could be found, including in tents or abandoned warehouses. By 1960, primary schooling was nearly universal and families were prepared to make enormous sacrifices to invest in their children's education. As a result, South Korea entered the 1960s with a better-educated population than other countries at similar stages of development.[11]

Other factors also lent new energy to the nation. Massive social transformation was leading to a more fluid society, open to change and prepared to take risks. There had been a massive exodus from rural areas to the cities. Land reform had been implemented during the 1950s, redistributing land from conservative landlords to peasants who became entrepreneurial farmers. The former landlords redirected their energies towards business and education. South Korea also had a pool of talented government bureaucrats, many of whom had received US support to train in economics, engineering or finance.[12]

Despite resentment over the brutal Japanese occupation, the Japanese economy offered inspiration. Park was a keen observer of Japan and admired its emphasis on big industries, large firms, capital accumulation and government guidance for industry. Park

signed a treaty with Japan in 1965 that normalised diplomatic relationships. This resulted in the payment of hundreds of millions of
dollars in reparations to South Korea, which supported the government's economic development efforts.[13] 'Initially, he used the
money to support poor, labour-intensive sectors,' Kim says. 'Hair
wigs, toys, silk, clothing – the kind of stuff that can be done by a
rural household. And he'd use massive cheap labour and it had a
good market at that time. All of a sudden, things were growing.'

Park's resolute focus was on increasing South Korea's exports
and diversifying into manufactured goods. Initially the focus was
on light, labour-intensive industries, such as textiles, clothing and
plywood. These were chosen because they didn't need massive
capital investments, but relied instead on labour, which Korea had
in abundance.

Because the private sector was relatively weak, the government
felt that it needed to play a leading role in developing industries
and supporting trade. 'The basic strategy to develop industry
called for the targeting of a few sectors of the economy that were
expected to perform well in international markets. Those firms
entering them would be granted special incentives,' Kim writes.[14]
Given that the cost of manufacturing declines with increasing volume, a focus on exports would enable production volumes to be
much greater than if companies had been producing for a domestic market alone. This would enable businesses to become more
competitive – a virtuous cycle.

When the government identified an exportable product
for development, eligible manufacturers would be showered
with incentives. These measures included tax reductions, tariff
exemptions for materials that needed to be imported to support
export production, discounted finance and export insurance.[15]

Export manufacturers could access subsidised loans from institutions such as the Korea Development Bank, the Export–Import Bank of Korea, the Technology Development Corporation and the National Investment Fund. A range of institutions were established to promote Korean exports, including the Korea Trade-Investment Promotion Agency (KOTRA), with offices all around the world. Still in existence today, it arranges trade missions, facilitates participation in trade fairs and liaises with potential overseas purchasers of South Korean products.[16]

Park's regime was not afraid to pick winners. In a series of five-year plans, the government channelled investment funds to 'promising strategic industries'. By the third and fourth plans (1971–1981), the focus switched from light, labour-intensive industries to 'heavy and chemical industrialisation'. Industries such as shipbuilding, machinery, petrochemicals and automobile manufacturing were developed from scratch. The government saw basic materials such as metals, petrochemicals and refined oil as the backbone of a modern economy. As a result, it 'continued to undertake risks that cautious entrepreneurs would tend to avoid', Kim writes, 'by providing heavy capital investment in these industries'. As China developed into a major competitor in the 1980s, the Korean government shifted focus from industrial to technology policy, dramatically increasing expenditure on research and development.[17] This period saw an enormous rise in high-tech exports, with South Korean products becoming ubiquitous. You have almost certainly watched an LG television or sent a text on a Samsung smartphone.

Interestingly, the focus of government support was not small companies. Because the focus was on large industries, the government decided to support very large industrial conglomerates, referred to as 'chaebols' – groups of firms usually owned by a single entrepreneur and their family members. The four largest chaebols were Samsung, Hyundai, Daewoo and LG. These firms became very close to government and were involved in policy-making. While in a democratic nation this would have significant potential for corruption, in Park's autocratic regime it actually provided a check on government power, leading to better policy decisions. While the chaebols received very favourable incentives, the government demanded a high level of performance, setting ever-escalating export targets.[18]

Kim is clear that the South Korean approach was driven by pragmatism. 'This is an important point,' he says. 'The policy was non-ideological – neither communist, as in North Korea, or neoclassical economics, as in the UK–US system. Park devised policies suitable for Korea.' It has resulted in a form of 'guided capitalism'. 'We accept the open market, we need it, because as we develop the new industries, we're ready to compete. But we have our own national pragmatic goals. We still decide which industry is suitable for technology-intensive exports.'

While this strategy has been highly successful, South Korea did have some lucky breaks that contributed to its impressive outcomes. The Vietnam War in the 1960s and 1970s provided an important stimulus, driving demand for international construction and cement. With the deployment of South Korean troops to Vietnam, the government took full advantage of funding from the United States to modernise its defence forces. Over the period of South Korea's deployment (1963–1973), its GDP increased four-fold, with some academics estimating that the financial gains from war between 1966 and 1969 amounted to 7 to 8 per cent of GDP.[19] Later on, the global demand for Middle Eastern oil created a

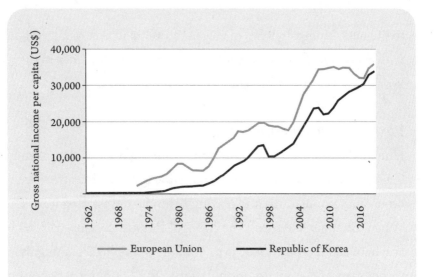

Figure 5. In 1972, per capita incomes in the European Union were more than seven times the size of incomes in Korea, but by 2019 Korea had caught up.

shipping boom. With Japanese shipbuilders at capacity, this created opportunities for new South Korean shipbuilders.[20]

South Korea's recovery following decades of occupation and war has been nothing short of stunning. Over the period 1962–1979, Korea's economy grew at an average of 9.3 per cent a year, and exports at an amazing 33.7 per cent annually. Exports are now equivalent to 40 per cent of South Korea's GDP, up from 11.4 per cent in 1970.[21] South Korea has grown into the tenth-largest economy in the world, and in 1996 it joined the OECD, the network of the world's most advanced economies.[22] As Figure 5 shows, since the early 1960s there has been a 280-fold increase in gross national income per capita, which in 2019 was US$33,790.

Some 70 per cent of 25- to 34-year-old South Koreans have a tertiary degree, the highest rate in the OECD (in the United States, the figure is 50 per cent; in the United Kingdom, 52 per cent, and in Australia, 53 per cent).[23] Since its democratic transition just prior to the 1988 Olympics, it has managed to sustain its democracy too, with Freedom House giving it 83 out of 100 in its Freedom in the World report – the same score as the United States.[24]

Post-war recovery can be vigorous

Humans have waged wars since the beginning of time, slaughtering each other brutally in battle, inflicting unthinkable atrocities on civilian populations and leaving behind a devastating legacy. When Ghengis Khan and the Mongol Empire conquered Eurasia between 1206 and 1242, 35 to 37 million people died (roughly 10 per cent of the world's population). The Qing dynasty conquest of the Ming dynasty in China resulted in the deaths of some 25 million people between 1618 and 1683. The Napoleonic Wars of 1803–1815 killed about five million people. In more recent memory, up to 20 million people died in World War I, and World War II was the deadliest in history, with about 60 million fatalities.

It's really quite tricky to assess how many people actually die in wars. Obviously, soldiers and civilians are killed in battle – that's fairly straightforward to measure. But surges in unprovoked violence also kill people during war (including executions of prisoners of war or genocidal campaigns such as the Holocaust or the Rwandan genocide). Deaths also arise from criminal behaviour in the absence of local policing and from non-violent consequences of war, including disease and famine. The figures from earlier wars I quote above include deaths from all sources, including genocide, famine and disease, and are consequently a little rubbery. It's hard to judge whether an event such as a famine or a riot would have happened in the absence of war. Because of this difficulty, and to ensure accuracy, many contemporary tallies of war deaths include only combatants or civilians who die in battle.[25] Table 1 shows the

Table 1: Conflicts with the Largest Number of Battle Deaths,
1946 to present

Conflict	Years	Best estimate of battle deaths
Vietnam War	1955–1975	2.098 million
Korean War	1950–1953	1.255 million
Chinese Civil War	1946–1949	1.2 million
Iran–Iraq War	1980–1988	644,500
Afghan Civil War	1978–2002	562,995

Source: Bethany Lacina and Nils Petter Gleditsch, 'Monitoring Trends in Global Combat', *European Journal of Population*, vol. 21, pp. 147–48.

conflicts with the largest number of battle deaths since the end of World War II. As you can see, the largest wars of the last seventy-five years have been in Asia or the Middle East. Notably, although there have been many wars since World War II, the scale of deaths from each crisis has progressively decreased.

The first half of the twentieth century was one of the most brutal periods in history, with deaths from war higher than at any point over the previous 600 years. However, when viewed in historical context, the last seventy or so years have been comparatively peaceful, with humanity today safer from war than ever before. In 2019, just 63,000 deaths were attributable to conflict or terrorism; for every 100,000 deaths, only about one was due to conflict.[26] Cardiovascular diseases such as strokes and heart attacks are a far greater killer, causing 18.3 million deaths in 2019 and making it the number-one cause of death.[27]

Author and academic Steven Pinker argues that the rise of democracy, capitalism, industrial civilisation and multilateral institutions such as the United Nations have made our world fundamentally different. He is convinced that this trend is likely to continue. But Nassim Nicholas Talem, author of *The Black Swan*, who's built his career studying unpredictable events that have massive consequences, cautions us that peace in our recent past does not guarantee peace in the future – just as a rising stock market doesn't mean there won't eventually be a crash.[28]

Deaths from war are only the tip of the iceberg. The effects of war are catastrophic for the health and wellbeing of communities. For every person killed, somewhere between 1.9 and thirteen additional people are injured, often leading to permanent disabilities.[29] The immediate health effects of conflict are severe, with mental illness, higher rates of infectious diseases, malnutrition and sexual violence. Stressors such as trauma, infection and malnutrition are exacerbated by disruptions to education and health systems and by social factors such as increases in alcohol consumption and violence among the civilian population.[30] These effects play out over the long term, impacting children and even grandchildren. In Gaza, children of mothers experiencing depression, anxiety or post-traumatic stress disorder (PTSD) are more likely to have PTSD themselves. In Rwanda and Darfur, children born of rape are at an increased risk of abandonment, neglect or abuse. In Australia, children of Vietnam veterans have a suicide rate three times higher than the general population. Israeli mothers who are children of Holocaust survivors have 'higher levels of psychological distress and less positive parenting'. The effects are felt even at the third generation, with adolescent grandchildren of Holocaust survivors having lower self-perception and 'inferior emotional, instrumental and social functioning'.[31]

Another significant consequence of war is displacement or forced migration. Throughout recent history, war has forced an enormous number of people to leave their homes. Sixty million were displaced in World War II, more than 11 million in the

ongoing Syrian conflict, five million in the Israeli–Palestine conflict, up to five million in the Korean War, four million in the Iraq
War and three million in the Vietnam War.[32] In 2018, 25.9 million people around the world fled from extreme violence (such
as that inflicted on the Rohingyas, who are forced to find safety
in Bangladesh) or from conflicts in places such as Syria, Yemen,
the Central African Republic, the Democratic Republic of Congo
and South Sudan.[33] Half of all refugees are children, and the vast
majority are hosted in developing countries. As with war, the ref-
ugee experience carries with it a long-term legacy of trauma that
is still evident in subsequent generations.[34]

War causes economic devastation, with infrastructure such
as transport and telecommunications networks destroyed, institutions such as courts unable to function and business activity
disrupted. Loss of life and forced migration can impact the size
of the labour force. Even a country that engages in war remotely
suffers economically. In the United States, for example, public
debt and taxation increased through most conflicts, while investment and consumer spending as a percentage of GDP decreased.
Additional spending due to war does have some short-term benefits, but engaging in war hurts the economy over the long term
because military spending is not as productive as other types of
spending, such as investment in education or infrastructure.[35]

Many of the long-term impacts of war can be mitigated by the
recovery of economies, societies, health systems and schools following the conflict. A long-lasting conflict is likely to lead to more
complex, long-term effects. It's incredibly important that countries do recover quickly. Not only is economic recovery important
to reverse the destruction and improve living standards; it also
plays an important role in reducing the risk of conflict reoccurring.

The United Nations reports that two major risk factors for conflict are low per capita incomes and weak economic growth.[36]

Over the long term most countries do recover, and even thrive. With the passing of years, it can even be difficult to tell which locations were impacted by war. Edward Miguel and Gérard Roland from the University of California, Berkley investigated areas of Vietnam thirty years after they had been bombed by the United States in the Vietnam War. Using a military dataset that enabled them to assess bombing intensity at district level, they identified that 10 per cent of the 584 districts received three-quarters of the bomb tonnage. Yet with the passage of time, the more intensively bombed districts were not any worse off than those less intensively bombed. Bombing did not seem to have an impact on poverty, consumption levels, infrastructure, literacy or population density. This is probably at least partly because during the recovery process, the Vietnamese government allocated more resources to regions that were most heavily bombed. Hence, the authors conclude that with the right government support, recovery from war can be relatively quick.[37]

While most countries recover strongly after war, there are plenty of countries that haven't. For example, in Africa, Eritrea has not recovered after its war with Ethiopia, ongoing political crisis has stalled reconstruction efforts in Burundi following civil war and genocide, and while Liberia has finally transitioned to democracy after twenty-five years of civil war, its economy remains in crisis.[38]

An important factor influencing recovery is the coherence of a country. Fragmented countries racked with ethnic divisions are much less likely to achieve political and economic success. In a fascinating study, Alberto Alesina, William Easterly and Janina

Matuszeski, economists from Harvard and New York universities, look at how 'artificial' a country's boundaries are by examining whether an ethnic group is partitioned between two countries. The second factor they looked at was how "squiggly" a country's borders are. A straight border is much more likely to mean that a colonial mapmaker has arbitrarily determined the borders, ignoring rivers, mountains and ethnic groups. The economists find that countries with artificial borders are invariably much poorer, even after controlling for a range of other factors.[39] 'The governments in these countries are often run to benefit one ethnic group at the expense of the others and are prone to corruption,' Professor Alesina said in an interview. 'Second, if you have a lot of people who would prefer to be part of the neighbouring country, they tend to spend their time fighting the government rather than improving schools and building roads.'[40] Viewed through that prism, the prospects for straight-edged, ethnically partitioned countries in much of Africa and the Middle East don't look great.

L ike South Korea after the Korean war, Germany's future after World War II appeared grim. German deaths totalled more than six million, including military casualties, victims of Nazi persecution and Allied bombing, and Germans who died after expulsion from central and Eastern Europe.[41] Its global standing in the world had been decimated by aggression and genocide. Bombing had destroyed five million houses, and 12 million mostly ethnically German refugees from Eastern Europe had to be accommodated somehow.[42] With infrastructure and factories destroyed, Germany's economy was barely functional. Economic output was about half of what it had been in 1938, and food production too was only half of pre-war levels. Rations set by the occupying powers varied between 1040 and 1550 calories per day, about a third of what an average American consumes today. The German currency, the Reichsmark, was effectively worthless, leading hordes of people to trek out to the countryside each weekend to barter with farmers for food.[43]

The country was occupied by the Allied powers, which brought a degree of stability, restored the rule of law and ensured the provision of basic services. The Soviet Union occupied the eastern parts of Germany, while the United Kingdom, the United States and France occupied western Germany. Still owing billions of dollars in reparations for the damage caused during World War I (which it finally paid off in 2010), Germany was also forced to pay for the ongoing costs of the occupation, amounting to US$2.4 billion per year.[44] Not wanting to risk a repeat of the conditions following World War I, which saw the rise of the Nazis, the Allies had agreed not to extract heavy reparations this time around.[45] But they did confiscate German intellectual property, including patents and trademarks, and factories were dismantled and shipped abroad to Allied nations.

Despite these challenges, Germany bounced back extraordinarily quickly. By 1949, four years after the end of the war, when the Federal Republic of Germany was established in the western occupied zones, output was almost back to pre-war levels. The 1950s saw growth in GDP average an astounding 8.3 per cent a year, while unemployment fell from 11 per cent in 1950 to 1.3 per cent in 1960. Real wages during the decade also increased at an average of 6.3 per cent annually.[46] The 1960s continued in the same vein, with strong growth, low inflation and low unemployment.[47] This period became known as the *Wirtschaftswunder*, the German 'economic miracle' or the 'miracle on the Rhine'.

In my youth, I undertook a year-long student exchange in the north of Germany. My host father, Dr Jörg Hardegen, grew up during and after the war. He has the appearance and demeanour of a good-natured professor, complete with goatee, and has always been enthusiastic about educating me on postwar German history. When I speak with him while researching this book, he tells me that his family initially had to queue in the shops with food stamps. 'We only got butter on Sundays,' he says. 'It wasn't until the mid-1950s that we could afford butter every day instead of margarine. For me this was a sign that we had made it.' Studying in London in the late 1950s, he was struck by the contrast with the recovery he had experienced in his home city of Bremen. 'In London, there was still a lot of debris in the city. That hadn't existed in Bremen for a long time; everything was cleared or newly built. As a child you notice that everything is getting better, but you don't really think about why it is.'

With her big smile and dark bob, my host mother, Sybille Hardegen, continues to cut an elegant figure. A multilingual hostess who works on cruise ships, she brings charm to every interaction. Sybille says that the *Wirtschaftswunder* enabled many Germans to become wealthy, including her family. 'My father had a tree nursery and supplied trees for landscaping as freeways were built,' she says. 'Forests were also being reforested. He made a lot of money because he did so much work for the government.'

To better understand the factors that enabled such an impressive postwar recovery, I sought out Ulrich Herbert, a history professor at the University of Freiburg and author of the 1000-page book *A History of Twentieth-Century Germany*. Between my rusty German and Professor Herbert's quite reasonable English, we managed a fascinating conversation.

Herbert says that while the initial goal of the Allies was to remove Germany's capacity to wage war by limiting its industry, Cold War tensions between the Americans and the Soviets led to a change of heart. 'By 1948 at the latest, the Americans thought that the Soviet Union would attack the West, as they did in Korea, and therefore the Germans were needed – economically, politically and militarily,' Herbert says. 'The original goal of keeping the Germans small was abandoned, and a lot of money was invested to protect West Germany as a strong and powerful power against the anticipated attack from the Soviet Union.'

The Marshall Plan was a US scheme to fund economic recovery in Western Europe. While a lot of mythology now surrounds the plan, it didn't provide an enormous amount of money to West Germany. From 1948 to 1951, it amounted to a total of about US$1.4 billion, and even at its peak in 1948 and 1949, it contributed no more than 5 per cent of West Germany's national income.[48] The scheme did come with conditions though, which drove significant structural adjustment across Western Europe, restoring price and exchange-rate stability and driving trade. This is perhaps its greatest legacy. 'Through the Marshall Plan, the Americans forced the Europeans to work together,' Herbert says. In particular, it forced them 'to work with the Germans – which many European states did not want after their experience with Nazi Germany – and to build a European trading system'. Originally, the Marshall Plan was to take place without Germany, but 'without Germany the European economy would not have recovered. In this respect the Americans are the founders of the European Economic Community.'

At around this time, the first West German government put in place a set of policies that coincided perfectly with the new, more open European economy. The 'social market economy' was aimed at establishing a market-based system, where supply and demand determined prices, wages and what was produced, while a strong social policy protected against the excesses of unrestrained capitalism. These reforms brought an end to the central planning of the Nazi era, with price and production controls abolished. A new currency, the Deutschmark, was established at the same time, largely putting an end to the black market.[49]

The more the boom progressed, the more it seemed that the war damage had been overstated. After allowing for repairs to factories, the number destroyed was actually less than the number constructed during the war, so Germany found itself with significant industrial capacity. The dismantling of industrial plants, which was supposed to weaken German armaments potential, only involved relatively few companies in the western part of the country. And although it did hurt German industry, it offered unintentional benefits too. German-American economist Henry Wallich wrote in 1955 that dismantling 'often led to the replacement of an old plant by one of the latest design and to an increase in Germany's power to compete'.[50]

Germany had been a strong exporter of finished goods even before the war. Industrial products such as machines and chemicals were a strength. But in the aftermath of the war, total imports far exceeded exports, creating a serious balance-of-payments problem, with substantial amounts of money leaving the country to pay for imports. Strengthening Germany's exports was an obvious way to address this, and the government introduced a range of export promotion schemes, including tax incentives, government guarantees that reduced the risk of international transactions, and export finance at discounted interest rates.[51] With Germany able to supply products the world needed – machinery, cars, iron and steel products, and chemicals – exports boomed during the 1950s, increasing from 8.4 billion Deutschmarks in 1950 to 31 billion in 1958 and 47.8 billion in 1960.[52]

Just as in South Korea, luck played a role in the German recovery, with the Korean War providing a major stimulus from 1950, coinciding almost exactly with the government's export push. Wallich writes that 'the world-wide Korea splurge set off some remarkable fireworks in the German export industries. These industries specialised in machinery and other capital equipment, just the things that were most in demand, and they had excess capacity.'[53] Herbert says that the Korean War led France, the United Kingdom and the United States to full capacity. They needed Germany, but 'Germany was not allowed to build armaments'. With all its industrial potential, 'Germany instead concentrated on products such as cars or even refrigerators, for which there was great demand'.

Economic recovery was not unique to Germany. 'There was an economic miracle across Europe,' Herbert says. Through the 1950s, economic growth in Italy was 6 per cent a year; in Austria, it was 5.7 per cent; Switzerland, 5.1 per cent; and France, 4.4 per cent. Only the United Kingdom stagnated, with just 2.5 per cent annual growth.[54] Other countries achieved economic growth with quite different policy settings to Germany. 'France pursued a policy that was much more strongly oriented towards the state. Large parts of the Italian economy were socialised,' says Herbert. Given the diversity of responses across Europe, he says 'national economic policy cannot be regarded as the sole or even paramount reason for the European economic upsurge'. Instead, Herbert argues that the spectacular postwar boom was due to a combination of factors: 'the spurt in population growth, the enormous backlog of demand both for consumption goods and investment goods, the liberalisation of international trade and international payments systems, the confidence felt in the superior economic strength of the US, which was decisive for the investment climate, and finally the Korean War.'[55]

Herbert is more impressed by another German miracle – 'how Germany, with a generation of Nazis, managed to build a stable liberal democracy over the years. That is really the interesting question.'

In the war's aftermath, the Allies were determined to rid Germany of Nazi ideology. But Nazism wasn't confined to a small minority; it had deep, popular support throughout the country. About 10 per cent of Germans had been members of the Nazi Party, and Nazi-related organisations such as the German Labour Front and the Hitler Youth had huge memberships too. Altogether, about 45 million Germans were members of Nazi-affiliated organisations.[56] Even in the years following Germany's defeat, Nazi ideology continued to enjoy popular support, with surveys revealing that less than 40 per cent of Germans thought Nazism an unequivocally 'bad idea'. Three years after the war, 60 per cent of Germans still insisted that Nazism was a 'good idea, gone wrong'.[57]

At the end of the war, at the Nuremberg trials, the Allies prosecuted the top twenty-four surviving Nazis for war crimes, with ten sentenced to death. In the subsequent trials against generals, SS officers, business leaders and Nazi doctors, heavy sentences were imposed. Numerous lower-level Nazis were also sentenced to shorter prison sentences, and much larger numbers of Germans were subjected to 'de-Nazification' proceedings, which involved close examination of their past activities and re-education.[58]

But given the number of Germans with a Nazi history, it was simply impossible to prosecute them all. German political leaders learnt that speaking openly about the Nazi past risked a right-wing revolt that threatened to undermine its nascent democracy.[59] Konrad Adenauer, West Germany's first chancellor, reputedly argued that 'you could have democracy in post-Nazi Germany or justice in post-Nazi Germany, but not both'.[60] As a result, there was little or no talk of Nazi crimes in West Germany for the first fifteen to twenty years after the war, so a view emerged that the Nazis' crimes were the fault of a small clique of evil leaders and that the vast majority of Germans had been innocent.[61]

An oppressive conservatism hung over West Germany for more than fifteen years following the war, with Adenauer's policy of 'amnesty and integration' a euphemism for not asking Germans what they did during the war.[62] Not that there was any particular appetite to talk about it. As my host father says, 'most Germans were working very hard on reconstruction and were trying to find financial security with their families. They generally repressed the wartime experience.' All the while, thousands of ex-Nazis continued to hold dominant roles in West German society, including in medicine, law, science and the public service.

Ultimately, the tensions between democracy and justice could not be contained. 'The crimes of the Nazis were so great that it was impossible to simply suppress them for a long time and at the same time build a democratic society,' Herbert says. The political and cultural revolution of the 1960s, driven by the first generation to grow up after the war, forced a debate. 'When you're twenty-one or twenty-two, and you are confronted with the realisation that you are living off your parents' generation, who were involved in the crimes of the Nazi regime,' Herbert says, 'that was certainly a very important motivation.' After twenty years of 'restoration and reconstruction but relatively little re-evaluation', ageing war criminals were prosecuted in West German courts, the Holocaust became a topic of discussion (it was largely unmentioned in the 1950s) and there was vigorous debate about Germany's past and its future.[63] 'Since the late 1960s, there has been uninterrupted talk in Germany about Nazi crimes every day from morning till night, tens of thousands of books and television programmes and discussions,' Herbert says. 'A long, difficult and painful process of coming to terms with the past.'

The Cold War played a part in incubating German democracy too. Democracy gained West Germany entry to NATO in 1955, bringing with it the security of a military alliance with the United States. The partition with East Germany also threw into sharp relief the difference between the democratic west and the authoritarian, Soviet-controlled east. In the midst of the Cold War, American cultural influence was important – it stood for freedom, modernity and youth. Germans had been drawn to the American way of life as early as the 1920s, and even during the Nazi era. Herbert points out that until 1940 the most popular actor in Germany was an American, Cary Grant.

German democracy is not without its problems. As David Thrum writes in *The Atlantic*, it experiences 'neo-Nazi crimes against immigrants; immigrant crimes against German Jews; far-right parties gaining seats in state legislatures; the post-communists cannibalizing the democratic left'.[64] And yet the triumph of German democracy is there for all to see. It's built a more complex national identity based on memory, East Germany has been successfully incorporated into the Federal Republic and Germany has pledged itself to even tighter European integration.

Giving Germany's democracy a score of 94 out of 100 (the same as the United Kingdom, and eight points more than the United States), Freedom House writes that 'Germany is a representative democracy with a vibrant political culture and civil society. Political rights and civil liberties are largely assured both in law and practice.'[65] Germany's postwar economic miracle has now been accompanied by a democratic one too.

How to recover well from war

It's unlikely that your country is directly impacted by war at the moment. Let us hope that it won't be anytime soon. Nevertheless, the experiences of South Korea and Germany offer many insights that are relevant to recovery from other crises.

As we've seen, recovery in both South Korea and Germany in the postwar decades was rapid, with extraordinarily strong economic growth. This should reassure us that even after the most devastating crisis, recovery can be relatively quick, and countries can bounce back to become far more prosperous than before. While this growth is sparked by the massive investment needed for reconstruction, recovery also has the potential to lead to a boom that lasts for decades, involving major growth in output, productivity and living standards. South Korea's and Germany's experiences, while impressive, are not unique. Over the past seventy or so years, there have been quite a few postwar economic booms, as Table 2 shows.

You'll see that across these examples, average annual growth in GDP per capita ranges from about 5 to 8 per cent in the decades after war. For comparison, note that between 1950 and 1973, growth in GDP per capita across the world averaged just 2.9 per cent, and between 1973 and 1997 an even lower 1.4 per cent.[66] To understand

Table 2: Postwar Growth Periods

Country	Period	War	Growth of GDP (annual %)	Growth of GDP per capita (annual %)
China	1978–2006	Post-Mao period	8.1	6.9
West Germany	1950–1973	World War II	6.0	5.0
Indonesia	1967–1997	War of Independence	6.8	4.8
Japan	1946–1973	World War II	9.3	8.0
South Korea	1952–1997	Korean War	8.2	6.3
Malaysia	1968–1997	World War II and the Malayan Emergency	7.5	5.1
Singapore	1960–1973	World War II	10.0	7.6
Taiwan	1962–1973	World War II	11.4	8.7
Vietnam	1992–2005	Vietnam War	7.6	6.1

Source: data from Adam Szirmai, 'Explaining Success and Failure in Development', MERIT Working Paper No. 2008-013, United Nations University, Maastricht Economic and Social Research Institute on Innovation and Technology (MERIT), Maastricht, 2008, p. 13.

the difference that rapid growth makes, consider some maths. If annual growth averages just 2 per cent, living standards will be about 50 per cent better in twenty years. But if growth averages 6 per cent, living standards in twenty years will be about 220 per cent better, or 3.2 times what they were at the start of the period. Over the long run, faster economic growth makes an enormous difference. Last century, most of the countries in Table 2 were impoverished. Now, following decades of rapid economic growth, they have living standards comparable with the world's richest countries. South Korea and Japan have higher living standards than New Zealand; Germany has higher living standards than Australia, Canada and the United Kingdom; and Singapore's living standards are 40 per cent higher than the United States.[67]

The experience of postwar economic growth shows us that there is at least initially a rubber-band effect, with economies catching up on growth that that they sacrificed during the war. One of the reasons for this is the reconstruction process, which requires lots of money to be spent on rebuilding housing and infra-structure. Typically, this involves a great deal of money flowing in from overseas, in the form of loans, direct foreign investment, for-eign aid, debt relief and the transfer of private money. All of this serves to stimulate the economy through spending and enables more money to be saved.[68]

In Germany, for example, recovery in the decade following the war was fuelled by massive investment in the reconstruction of damaged factories, infrastructure and houses. This was partly enabled by US funds and loans provided through the Marshall Plan, as well as tax incentives and low-interest loans that supported reinvestment in important areas such as transport, housing, iron and steel. However, the success of Germany's export performance also meant that by the early 1950s, foreign funds were pouring into the country – much of which was available to finance recon-struction.[69] As a result, in the years after the war Germany was constructing some 500,000 houses and apartments each year, three times as many as in the pre-war period.[70]

A FRESH START

One key reason that countries recover so quickly after war is that reconstruction often involves upgrading to the latest technology. This can mean 'leapfrogging' multiple generations of technology to catch up with the world's best. After the Allies dismantled old factories in Germany, new factories were built, often equipped with the most up-to-date machinery. South Korea was a latecomer to the steel industry, but it was able to exploit existing technology and benefit from economies of scale by leapfrogging the plant size of other countries.[71] The reconstruction process enabled West Germany and South Korea to benefit from the best of international technology without bearing the costs or the risks of technology development.

This notion of 'technological catch-up' is widely recognised by economists, with one going so far as to argue that 'there is not a single example of successful catch-up since 1868 which did not involve tapping into international technology'.[72] Globalisation and increases in digital technology make technological catch-up even more likely in future.

The more backward a country is when reconstruction commences, the more rapid growth will be, as it has more ground to catch up. But it all depends, of course, on a country's existing capabilities and its capacity to absorb the new technology. There's no point in having the latest technology if no one in the country knows how to use it, or if there are no skilled workers available to operate it. South Korea and Germany both adopted deliberate approaches to facilitate technological catch-up in the aftermath of war. South Korea identified industry sectors it wished to build and ensured low-cost financing was available to conglomerates – its chaebols – through the state-owned banking system to build scale, enabling companies to procure state-of-the-art production equipment.[73]

Another benefit after war is that pre-war interest groups are no longer powerful, so with less institutional inertia, necessary reforms are more likely to be achieved. In his book *The Rise and Decline of Nations*, American economist Mancur Olson argues that interest groups such as business associations, cartels (groups of businesses who collude to improve profits and dominate a market) and trade unions limit growth by resisting the change that has to accompany economic progress. 'The longer any society is stable, the more groups will have been formed,' he said.[74] This leads to gridlock, with fixed wages, fixed prices, monopolies and closed shops.

According to Olson, a key reason for Western Europe's rapid postwar economic development was the dismantling of pre-war interest groups and alliances. In Germany, for instance, industrial conglomerates were broken up, unleashing rivalry, supported by tough new competition laws, courtesy of the Americans. 'We wiped the institutional slate clean for them,' Olson said.[75] He argued that this explains the difference between Western Europe and the relatively slow economic growth of the United Kingdom, which had 'with age ... acquired so many strong organizations and collusions that it suffers from an institutional sclerosis that slows its adaption to changing circumstances and technologies'.[76]

Both West Germany and South Korea found that natural and mineral resources were located on the other side of the partition. East Germany ended up with large supplies of lignite (brown coal). North Korea retained the country's hydroelectric power potential, and almost all of the Korean Peninsula's mineral resources, such as coal and iron ore. Yet for both West Germany and South Korea, this ended up being a blessing in disguise. It eliminated any hope of building a postwar economy based on resources and forced the development of more technically advanced industries.

Throughout history, natural resources have been a curse on those countries that are endowed with them, bringing high inflation, extreme indebtedness and sometimes corruption or civil war. Economists who investigated the 'resource curse' found that between 1960 and 1990, the economies of countries poor in natural resources grew three times faster than resource-rich nations. While countries rich in oil, such as Nigeria, Mexico and Venezuela, went bankrupt, countries without natural resources boomed, including Singapore, Taiwan, Hong Kong and South Korea.[77] They invested instead in education and the development of globally competitive industries.

Strong economic growth over the longer term needs investment to ensure that businesses and industries remain competitive. This means improvements in workforce skill levels, substantial investment in technology and the development of globally competitive industries. The countries that do this succeed over the long run. It's a lesson that applies universally. Resource-rich countries such as Norway, Australia, Saudi Arabia and Canada risk falling prey to the resource curse if they lock in an unhealthy dependence on resources. They will need to take conscious steps to ensure they stay competitive and productive in the decades ahead.

Productivity is the primary influencer of a nation's standard of living. According to Harvard academic Professor Michael Porter, 'the central goal of government policy toward the economy is to deploy a nation's resources (labour and capital) with high and rising levels of productivity'. 'To achieve productivity growth, an economy must be continually upgrading,' he writes. 'This requires relentless improvement and innovation in existing industries and the capacity to compete successfully in *new* industries.'[78] Countries such as South Korea and Germany exemplify this approach to economic development.

Neither Germany nor South Korea has been content to produce products only for a domestic market. Both countries recognised that economic development required the export of goods and services to the world. Other countries will only purchase international products if they are cheaper or of superior quality, so an economy oriented towards exports is forced to become competitive with other countries, and to work hard to stay competitive. Relentless global competition is a major driver of productivity and innovation. Over the past seventy years, industrialisation with a focus on exports has been behind all developing countries that have experienced rapid growth.[79]

Postwar 'catch up' enabled South Korea and Germany to develop rapidly, leveraging technology developed by others to improve productivity. Yet a technology adoption strategy is based on following others; it has a natural ceiling. In the later stages of postwar development, both South Korea and Germany realised that to continue their vigorous growth, it was necessary to develop their own world-leading capability, particularly if they were to out-compete newly industrialising countries such as China. This would enable them to offer the rest of the world goods and services that compete on quality, not just price. For example, Samsung now sells twice as many smartphones as Apple,[80] and German car brands such as Porsche, Mercedes, BMW and Audi are among the world's most desirable. At the frontier of innovation, countries such as South Korea and Germany are now largely immune from price-based competition from emerging manufacturing nations such as China. Consequently, they have been able to sustain large manufacturing sectors, at a time when other advanced nations have seen dramatic declines in manufacturing. In South Korea, manufacturing's share of economic activity is 27.7 per cent, while in Germany it is 21.2 per cent – far more than manufacturing's 11.7 per cent share in the United States, 9.7 per cent in the United Kingdom and 6.1 per cent in Australia.[81] Both Germany and South Korea now export significantly more than they import.[82]

Being at the forefront of technology doesn't just happen. Determined government leadership has elevated keeping ahead of the competition to a national priority. The South Korean government has been prepared to pick winners: industrial sectors in which the country has the potential to lead the world. Most recently, these have included manufacture of semiconductors, mobile phones, digital televisions, cars and shipbuilding. Both countries have focused on improving the conditions that help underpin innovation, through investments in science, research and development. Clustering of like-minded companies has been encouraged through the establishment of industrial centres in fields grouped around education institutes. Investment in research and development is a feature of both countries, with Germany spending an amount equal to 3.1 per cent of GDP. South Korea now spends 4.5 per cent of GDP on research and development, second in the OECD only to Israel (4.9 per cent). Canada (1.5 per cent), the United Kingdom (1.7 per cent) and Australia (1.8 per cent) spend significantly less.[83]

Investment in education and workforce training is a key driver of economic development around the world. A skilled workforce is the most important ingredient in a strong economy. But education is a long-term investment. There is a lag – potentially many decades – between an initial investment and the ultimate payoff of stronger economic development. South Korea has focused on tertiary education, with more young people receiving a university education than any other OECD nation.[84] Germany instead emphasises vocational training, with strong industry collaboration. About half a million Germans enter the workforce through apprenticeship schemes each year.

Investment in human capital and the expansion of education has been one of the great success stories of the last seventy years. Often starting from scratch, formerly poor countries such as Singapore, Hong Kong, South Korea and Taiwan have built education systems that are now among the world's best. This will surely underpin further success for these countries in the decades ahead.

AN HONEST SELF-APPRAISAL

A crisis brings out the best and worst in a nation. Some people do horrible, evil things. Others are heroic and selfless. At times of stress and great fragility, our institutions serve us well or they are shown to be part of the problem. Crisis sometimes reveals things about ourselves that we would rather not think about. Yet once the genie is out of the bottle, it won't go back in.

The contradictions at the heart of a nation linger corrosively until dealt with. Such conflicts undermine national coherence; while they can be papered over, until they are repaired the cracks only get wider with time. Some Germans would have preferred never to speak of the war, but the next generation understood that if Germany was to develop a coherent postwar identity, its democracy needed to be accompanied by justice and an honest accounting of history.

War has left the Korean Peninsula divided. With a conflict that is not yet officially over, the question of reconciliation hangs, unresolved, over North and South. While most South Koreans support reunification,[85] they are divided over what it means, torn by the contradictions that arise between a desire for greater strategic autonomy and a fear of being abandoned by the United States. Many believe the country should continue to maintain a relationship with the United States, but a majority also feel that a unified Korea should align with China. This dilemma at the heart of South Korea's national affairs won't be resolved easily.[86]

Other nations, too, are damaged by unhealed wounds. How can a modern Australia go forward with pride when it has never righted the injustice of the Indigenous dispossession and genocide on which the nation is built? In 2017, representatives of Australia's First Nations peoples gathered in Central Australia to attend the First Nations National Constitutional Convention. There, they released the Uluru Statement from the Heart, a document developed after two years of intense deliberation. It maps out a process inviting non-Indigenous Australians to join with First Nations peoples on structural reform, including the constitutional enshrinement of a First Nations 'Voice to Parliament', empowering First Nations peoples to have their views heard in the government. It also proposes a treaty process between the government and First Nations peoples, as well as a process of 'truth telling' to reveal past injustices to Aboriginal and Torres Strait Islander people.[87] This proposal is a gift to the Australian people and presents a genuine opportunity to heal the trauma that lies at Australia's heart, yet it has not been adopted by the government.

How can the United States move on until it can reconcile the intense political polarisation that threatens its democracy? Or the persistence of racism across American history and society? Some have suggested the United States needs to chart a path towards 'reconciliation and reunification'. The country has been there before – in 1913, on the fiftieth anniversary of Gettysburg, former Union and Confederate soldiers embraced in a 'festival of national reconciliation'. This warming encounter notably excluded black, brown and Native Americans, and any future reconciliation will need to be overt and deliberate in including them.[88] It could possibly involve a 'truth and reconciliation commission', like that in South Africa.[89] American healing will be difficult and slow, but to safeguard the country's future, it needs to be done.

Other pre-existing issues will also be thrown into stark relief by crises. In crisis, the most vulnerable are the ones to suffer, our health systems aren't up to the task and the implications of a changing climate become too obvious to ignore. It's then that we really need to work things through as a nation: to have the conversations we've been putting off because they've been too hard; to genuinely listen to the perspectives that confront us. Crisis therefore presents us with a challenge, a choice. We either grow as a nation, with a more mature, nuanced, coherent sense of national identity, or we keep our fingers in our ears, pretending that if we don't talk about the painful schisms at our nation's heart, they will eventually disappear. The only problem is that time doesn't wash away the pain. Working through these issues isn't quick, it isn't neat, and it is perhaps never finished. But an honest nation, a mature nation, faces up to its past. Germany understood that, and for fifty years has done the demanding, painful work that has forged a contemporary German identity to accompany the nation's economic success. By getting uncomfortable, we set ourselves up for a stronger future.

The music pumps through the stadium, coloured lights under each seat flashing through the darkness. A young woman in an elegant white dress adorned with what look like ice crystals holds a sign that says, simply, 'Korea'. Wearing white, knee-length winter coats that resemble lab coats, athletes from North and South Korea walk out into the stadium together. In contrast to the rest of the highly choreographed opening ceremony of the 2018 PyeongChang Winter Olympics, the athletes are informal, clearly excited, some filming the experience on their phones. They march under the Korean Unification Flag, which displays the entire Korean Peninsula in blue against a white backdrop, held jointly by a North and South Korean athlete. Cheering them on, mascot Soohorang, the white tiger, is dancing wildly. The stadium roars with the cheers from the largely Korean crowd, while the South Korean president, Moon Jae-in, and his wife, Kim Jung-sook, wearing the same uniform as the athletes, wave to them. Kim Yo-jong, sister of the North Korean president, is more subdued and wears black, but turns to politely shake the hand of the South Korean leader.

Thirty years after the Seoul Olympics, North and South Korea remain divided by the heavily fortified demilitarized zone, but there has been some rapprochement. While continuing to compete as separate nations, they form a joint women's ice-hockey team, the first time they have contributed athletes to the same team at an Olympics.[90]

Yet the two countries, which share the same peninsula and people, are now quite different. While South Korea has built a modern democratic nation and a competitive economy, North Korea is a secretive, repressive country, with an isolated, tightly controlled command economy dominated by state-owned industry and collective farms. The average per capita income in South Korea is now twenty-seven times that of North Korea.[91] Whereas 60 per cent of North Koreans live in poverty, those in the South have living standards roughly the same as those in Japan or New Zealand. South Koreans have some of the fastest internet speeds in the world and the highest rates of tertiary education.[92] Children in South Korea are 7 to 8 centimetres taller on average than North Korean children, with increased height strongly associated with reduced mortality, and will live at least eleven years longer than the average North Korean.[93] Life expectancy at birth is now 82.7 years, about the same as in Australia, and four years more than in the United States.[94]

Until reconciliation with the North can be achieved, South Korea won't truly be able to put the war behind it. Yet while North Korea remains an international pariah, South Korea's recovery has been an incredible – and ongoing – postwar success story.

FIVE STEPS FORWARD

1. **Upgrade with the latest technology.** A crisis is an ideal
   opportunity for companies and nations to catch up to the
   world's technological leaders. Due to COVID-19, companies
   have had to stay abreast of the latest technology, with
   customers moving towards online channels and staff working
   remotely. Many are investing in data security and artificial
   intelligence to further enhance their operations. Government
   can support the adoption of technology by investing in related
   infrastructure, updating regulations, making finance available
   and providing diagnostic tools or advice. For example, Germany,
   as part of its recovery plan, is obliging all petrol stations to offer
   electric car–changing facilities, and Australia is investing to
   improve its relatively slow fixed broadband speeds. Canada is
   supporting small- and medium-sized businesses with advice
   and funding on how to adopt the latest technology.

2. **Support export-oriented businesses.** Nations become richer by developing products and services that the rest of the world wants to buy. National and state governments should help businesses to export by facilitating introductions to overseas markets (for example, through trade missions or exhibitions), providing export credit or assisting smaller businesses to participate in global supply chains. While countries invariably have export strengths in particular sectors, export success stories can emerge from a diverse range of areas. Consequently, all companies should be supported to export, no matter which sector they are from.

3. **Pick winning industries and back them.** Governments should form a view on the industries that stand a chance of becoming globally competitive and prioritise them for support. Government policy can assist by incentivising research and development, facilitating links between research and industry, supporting startups and using its own procurement to drive innovation.

4. **Invest in education.** While the payoff can take decades, lifting the educational level of a population is one of the best long-term investments a nation can make. A more highly trained workforce will contribute to greater innovation and improved productivity, and therefore a stronger economy and higher living standards. Key to this is investment in quality early childhood education, improvement in the prestige and quality of teaching, and ensuring the supply of higher-education graduates matches labour-market needs.

5. **Facilitate a national conversation.** If a crisis has revealed
    underlying tensions, the post-crisis period is an opportunity
    for introspection and debate. What has been revealed about
    the nation? What does that mean for its future? For example,
    COVID-19 has brought significant pre-existing economic and
    health inequalities into stark relief in many countries. While
    such a conversation is likely to be unruly and political, it should
    ideally create space for different views to be heard. In Australia,
    for example, COVID-19 coincides with the findings of a Royal
    Commission into Aged Care Quality and Safety, which sparked
    a national debate with its revelations of 'a shocking tale of
    neglect' and a need for serious reform. A change of government
    in the United States during COVID-19 opens up the potential for
    a national process of reconciliation and national healing.

5

OUR POST-PANDEMIC FUTURE

Phew. The end is in sight. The vaccine has arrived for many of us and we're looking forward to waving the virus good-bye, or at least learning to live with it. Perhaps we'll even be able to ease our way into some sort of post-pandemic normalcy.

But even after we've figured out a global vaccine rollout and the re-establishment of international travel, we have an enormous recovery ahead of us. With millions dead, COVID-19 has been traumatic and devastating. Many continue to suffer the aftereffects of the virus, with extreme fatigue, shortness of breath and brain fog. The pandemic has led to a surge in mental illness and a rise in family violence. Vulnerable young people unable to attend school have fallen further behind their more advantaged peers.

The pandemic is an economic crisis too, with government restrictions shutting down whole economies. The global economy contracted by 3.5 per cent in 2020, making it the deepest recession since World War II. Across the developed nations of the OECD, the contraction is estimated at 4.8 per cent. Europe was hit particularly hard, with the economy shrinking by 6.7 per cent.[1] Around the world, the recession has tipped some with low incomes back into poverty. Uncertainty associated with the pandemic has discouraged investment, and disruptions to education have slowed the growth in 'human capital'. With a disproportionate impact on vulnerable groups – such as the young and those with low skills – the COVID-19 recession is only likely to worsen inequality. Even with the economy seeming to bounce back quickly in many countries, a recession of this magnitude will leave scars that will last for years.

In many nations, the pandemic has also been amplified by a crisis in democracy. Countries led by right-wing populist leaders – the United States, the United Kingdom, Brazil and Russia – have fared particularly badly during the pandemic, showing up the limits of this type of government. With government letting citizens down and intense partisanship in many countries undermining its functioning, restoring trust in government institutions is a significant challenge ahead.

So, the crisis we are seeking to recover from has up to three dimensions: the health impact of the pandemic itself; the economic crisis of a deep recession; and a crisis of trust in government.

And before we get too carried away with our plans for recovery, we need to remind ourselves that COVID-19 is almost certainly not going to be our last crisis. With human-induced climate change worsening, natural disasters such as floods, fires, droughts, heatwaves and storms are becoming far more frequent and damaging. We are entering an age of crisis. Responding to, recovering from and planning for crises is a skill set in which we're going to need to become expert.

Lessons from past crises

Our current situation is unique. Following the Spanish flu, the world was recovering from war as well as a pandemic. The COVID-19 recession is deep, but it's nothing like the Great

Depression. And we're not grappling with the physical reconstruction required after a tsunami, earthquake or war. Yet that doesn't mean history has nothing to provide us with. The lessons of past crises offer us insights that can inform the decisions ahead and help us to expand our ideas about just what might be possible as part of our recovery.

It is likely that many countries will return to economic growth in the short term. For a while, we may even see slightly faster growth than normal, particularly if governments maintain an adequate level of economic stimulus after the vaccine rollout. Certainly, major economic bodies such as the OECD, the International Monetary Fund and the World Bank are all projecting global growth of up to 6 per cent in 2021 and more than 4 per cent in 2022, which is stronger growth than prior to the pandemic.[2] Experience of past recoveries demonstrates that once the acute phase of the crisis is over, people tend to start spending and investing again, releasing demand that was pent up during the crisis. We saw this 'reconstruction bounce' following World War II and in Christchurch after the earthquakes. With house prices in countries such as Australia, New Zealand and Canada skyrocketing and the share market booming, we are perhaps already seeing the signs of a post-crisis surge.[3]

What's not clear is whether we'll see a boom beyond the initial bounce – like the Roaring Twenties after the Spanish flu – or a decade of sluggish growth and stagnating living standards, like after the Great Recession of 2010. The World Bank is pessimistic about growth prospects over the longer term, worried that 'unless there are substantial and effective reforms, the global economy is heading for a decade of disappointing growth outcomes'.[4]

A focus on economic development will make a huge difference. In this book, we've seen the incredible transformation in

Germany and South Korea flowing from economic growth following war. The United States was able to emerge strongly from the Spanish flu into a decade of growth, while New York made decisions that drove its growth in the aftermath of the Great Recession. Strong economic growth underpins rising living standards and provides abundant jobs, which pay more and more as the economy flourishes. A strong economy enables a country to respond to the social, political and environmental challenges it faces. With better economic circumstances, parents are more likely to invest in the education of their children. Stronger economies are associated with longer life expectancy and greater happiness. Following a crisis, the decisions that set a country up for long-run economic growth are some of the most critical that governments will make. It will require upgrading of technology, support for export-oriented companies, backing of industries that have the potential to be globally competitive and an acceleration of decarbonisation. In the next chapter, we'll look at the detail of the policy interventions that will support this economic growth in the years ahead.

There will be political impacts of the pandemic too. Anger at the British following the Spanish flu strengthened the Indian independence movement. The New Deal led to a long-term shift in Americans' views on the role of government. The Great Recession of 2010 generated the discontent that led to Brexit and the Trump presidency. This pandemic has affected us all, whether through deaths of loved ones, health worries, lockdowns or loss of income. It has elevated fringe political views and conspiracy theories – from the notion that Washington is controlled by Satan-worshipping paedophiles to the idea that the pandemic is a subterfuge for Bill Gates to plant trackable microchips in people through vaccination. When conspiracy theorists stormed the

Capitol Building in Washington, DC, this sentiment manifested in real-world violence. It's possible that anger and blame will form part of the post-pandemic political context, yielding an unpredictable outcome.

Crises also disrupt the geopolitical order. The Great Depression contributed to the rise of Germany's Nazi regime and World War II. World War II redefined global civilisation. It established the United States as a global power and moral arbiter, resulted in the Cold War and led to the establishment of multilateral institutions such as the United Nations. COVID-19 too is likely to have geopolitical consequences. The pandemic experience is highly dependent on which country you are in. In the United States, Brazil and the United Kingdom, the virus has run rampant, killing hundreds of thousands of people. Australia and New Zealand have escaped the worst horrors, but have spent extended periods under severe restrictions and isolated from the rest of the world. Other places – such as Taiwan and South Korea – have been mostly successful at holding the virus at bay without extensive lockdowns, by using masks and sophisticated testing and tracing. Based on how they handled the acute phase of the virus, some countries will recover faster than others. The International Monetary Fund estimates that the Spanish economy contracted by 11 per cent in 2020, the UK economy by 9.9 per cent and Italy's by 8.9 per cent. By contrast, the Chinese economy *grew* by 2.3 per cent and Taiwan's by 3.1 per cent. Expect to see a highly varied recovery across the world. Forecasts for growth in 2022 range from 2.0 per cent in South Africa through to 6.9 per cent in India.[5] Of course, economic forecasting is a mug's game, particularly with so much uncertainty. The point is that the global economic leader board is likely to change. With the disastrous impacts of COVID-19 coinciding with the start of Brexit, the United Kingdom will emerge from this period significantly weakened. China and Taiwan, by contrast, will start the recovery in a relatively strong position. This recasting of the world economic order is likely to have profound long-term implications.

It's inevitable there will be lasting social consequences of the pandemic. Recovery following the Spanish flu involved an intensification of social activity and led to permanent changes in gender roles. The very identity of Christchurch changed following the earthquakes, with the city shaking off its conservative reputation to become a place where 'everything is possible'. If the Spanish flu is any guide, following an enforced period of reduced human interaction we may be drawn to intensify our social lives, making up for lost time. A decade of parties ahead, perhaps? Alternatively, after many have reconfigured their relationship with the office during the pandemic, maybe people will be more inclined to keep working from home, connecting with their local neighbourhoods.

Not all of these effects will be positive. Increased prevalence of mental illness is a consequence of almost every crisis we've explored in this book; after the Spanish flu in particular, there was a huge increase in hospitalisations due to mental illness. Experts are expecting a 'tsunami of psychiatric illness' in the years ahead. The effects of quarantine, lockdown and social distancing include 'anxiety, anger, depression, post-traumatic stress symptoms, alcohol abuse, and behavioural changes' lasting up to three years.[6] People recovering from a COVID-19 infection experience similar effects. Up to 60 per cent of frontline healthcare professionals working during the pandemic have had symptoms such as anxiety, depression and insomnia, and these will probably persist for several years too. Furthermore, the economic consequences of

COVID-19, including recession and inequality, are likely to lead to 'increases in the prevalence of psychological distress, anxiety, depression, substance abuse disorders, and suicide and suicidal behaviour'.[7] It's therefore quite possible that the peak of the mental-health challenge is still ahead of us.

To mitigate the spread of COVID-19, many countries have closed their schools for extended periods, with students transitioning to remote learning, including through online platforms. During extended school closures in Europe and the Americas in the past, evidence shows that students learnt less than they would have in school. This has long-term consequences. Studies on the impact of extended teacher strikes in Belgium, Canada and Argentina show that impacted students were more likely to repeat a level, less likely to complete a tertiary degree and suffered salary losses of 2 to 3 per cent.[8] Similarly, in the 1960s Germany had two shortened school years, in an effort to standardise the start of the school year. Impacted students are now in their fifties and sixties and still show lower maths skills. They have earned about 5 per cent less over their lifetimes than their peers.[9]

The long-term impacts of disrupted learning are likely to be enormous, since more schooling is associated with skill development and higher lifetime incomes. The OECD calculates that if students in 2020 lost the equivalent of one-third of a school year, GDP will be an average of 1.5 per cent lower for the rest of the century. Students at school in 2020 can expect to earn 3 per cent lower incomes over their lifetimes.[10] Further, the impacts on learning are likely to be greatest for disadvantaged children. On average, these students started behind in their learning, were less able to get help from their parents and were less likely to have a computer, good internet and a quiet place to study. The effects of recession will only exacerbate this if disadvantaged students have to deal with the stress of a parent who slips into long-term unemployment after losing a job in a precarious economy.[11] Returning to normal won't address these impacts; only *improving* schooling will make up for the learning losses.

Crises also provide an opportunity to sort out festering internal conflicts. Countries that can emerge from crisis with coherence and long-running tensions resolved set themselves up for success in subsequent decades. Following years of separatist conflict, Aceh was able to find peace in the aftermath of the tsunami. It took a long time, but Germany is now much stronger for having taken action to confront its responsibility for wartime horrors. Nations that have come to terms with the trauma of their pasts and are acting to heal any deep-seated schisms will be best placed to work constructively towards long-term recovery.

Recoveries from crises are rarely neat, linear progressions. They play out in the context of complex histories and pre-existing structural issues. But they invariably bump into other issues along the way too. The reality is that there will be future crises, and they won't wait until recovery is complete. The pandemic arrived to an Australia still reeling from devastating bushfires. And when New York was starting to bounce back from the Great Recession, it was hit by Hurricane Sandy, which destroyed 300 homes, left hundreds of thousands without critical services and caused US$19 billion in damage.[12]

How well a city or country responds to a crisis is partly a function of how well it recovered from the last one. And our recovery from this crisis will impact our ability to respond to the next one. Unfortunately, we can't assume that this recovery will be simple; it must involve contemplation of an uncertain future.

What we've learnt during the pandemic

The pandemic has provided us with many insights, and it's important we remember these as and when we enter our recovery. Many of the insights are not new. We have learnt – and subsequently forgotten – these lessons before, as we've recovered from past crises. The fact that these are old truths should make them more powerful, as if we've been able to tap into some long-lost wisdom. But it is extra important that we don't lose sight of the lessons this time around.

The COVID-19 pandemic has reminded us – again – that we're all connected. Health is a not just a private matter, of concern only to an individual and their family. Health is a *public* concern. What happens in the community impacts all of us. All the private health insurance in the world can't protect us if the public health system is not up to the task of containing the virus, or if significant numbers of people fail to comply with public health directions.

The importance of public health was revealed starkly during the Spanish flu. Yet it was soon forgotten, as medicine became obsessed with a focus on individualised treatments. When we move on from COVID-19, our challenge will be to remember that health is a public concern, not just a matter for individuals, and that investment in a strong healthcare system needs to be sustained.

We've also learnt that what happens around the world impacts us at home. The virus might have originated in China, but the extent to which the virus was allowed to grow exponentially and spread around the world was a function of how other countries responded. It's likely that only when most of the world's population is vaccinated will we be able to truly say that the pandemic is over. How well we cooperate at a global level is critically important – whether through the sharing of early intelligence on emerging infectious diseases, developed nations lending support for global vaccination or even sharing approaches to post-conflict reconstruction in places such as Syria. Getting it right at the global scale benefits us all.

Might we take this lesson and draw parallels with other global crises, such as climate change? We all breathe the same air; a warming earth impacts us all. No matter what action we take at home, in the absence of a global response climate change will continue to worsen. It's in everyone's interest that each country makes a bold and constructive contribution to the global response.

As we scoured the supermarket shelves searching for toilet paper that wasn't there, it no doubt occurred to many us that some parts of our existence are more fragile than we thought, more vulnerable to shocks. While globalisation has contributed to enormous economic growth and price reductions, it has been accompanied by long and complex supply chains, with components being shipped back and forth across the globe. A 'just in time' approach means that only small quantities of stock are stored in warehouses. Consequently, disruption to air and sea freight movements means that shortages in even one component can disrupt supply. In many countries, stockpiles of essential medical equipment were inadequate, and there were shortages of masks. In Australia, there was no shortage of food, but disruptions to imported packaging meant many products could not be supplied to consumers. At times, it was hard to find a bag of rice or a jar of pasta sauce.[13]

We've also experienced the consequences of the inequality that pervades our society. Precarious and underpaid work served only to exacerbate the pandemic. Lacking sick leave and needing to feed their families, some attended work while sick. Factory labourers took second jobs as Uber drivers. Multiple generations of the same family could not keep their distance in overcrowded housing. All of these factors create opportunities for the virus to spread to vulnerable groups. All crises expose the fault lines in society, and this pandemic has been no different.

We've learnt that at times like this, it's actually quite important to have a competent government. Competent government is perhaps a boring concept and is largely invisible much of the time. We understand its value most clearly when it is absent. Countries such as the United Kingdom and the United States have been characterised by flip-flops in public health advice, botched test and trace regimes, and chaotic and ever-changing lockdown arrangements. Furthermore, certain US leaders catered to populist sentiment and opposed the mask mandates recommended by experts.

Competent governments rely on the existence of institutions that have the capacity and authority to do things properly. These institutions need to have the staff, expertise, resources and powers to respond to complex situations. To be effective, they also need to be supported with a legal and political culture that is committed to public administration. Political leaders that value public administration have been critical during our most recent crisis.

Smaller units of government have proven to be particularly important during the crisis. Many smaller jurisdictions – such as New Zealand, Taiwan, Iceland and Australia – have been remarkably successful in containing the virus. In federations, state and provincial governments have played an important leadership role. Small nations and state governments have often been more agile than their larger counterparts, better equipped to develop a rapid policy response.[14] New Zealand, for example, moved quickly to close its borders in March 2020 and implemented snap lockdowns when cases were detected. Iceland has used science to contain the virus. From the first days of the pandemic, it has tracked the health of every person who tested positive for COVID-19 and sequenced the genetic material of each positive test.[15]

Governments and citizens have a symbiotic relationship. During a crisis, people need to trust experts, governments and one another. In the absence of trust, governments find it much more challenging to respond competently. But the incompetence of government is likely to further undermine trust, leading to a downward spiral of declining trust and poorly functioning government. Trust and capable public sectors are national assets that need to be nurtured over many years. The pandemic has shown us what can happen when they are left to wither.

Intersecting challenges

Unfortunately, recovery following the COVID-19 pandemic is not the only challenge we are facing. The recovery intersects with some serious – even existential – pre-existing issues that provide the context for the task ahead.

Climate change

Floods, storms, fires, heatwaves and droughts: climate change is revealing itself at increasingly frequent intervals in dramatic fashion. Each one of these natural disasters represents a crisis. While risks will differ depending on location, all of us can expect to encounter some form of extreme weather. For example, my city, Melbourne, will see bushfires of increasing frequency and intensity, decade-long droughts, severe heatwaves and devastating floods.[16] While such events will impact those in rural areas most, the effects on city-dwellers are profound too. Dense bushfire smoke will blanket streets for weeks, making breathing difficult, droughts will lead to severe water restrictions, and heatwaves will contribute to hundreds of deaths.[17]

We can't pin any natural disaster directly on climate change, but as we saw in Chapter 3, the trend is clear: the overall frequency and severity of natural disasters is increasing. The world has to face the notion that the post-COVID recovery will be accompanied by climate-related natural disasters.

Yet climate change is not merely a set of dramatic weather events. It is a slow-onset crisis that is transforming life on earth. Left unchecked, it represents an overwhelming threat to the very existence of humanity. Since the Industrial Revolution, human activities have caused temperatures to rise by 1 degree Celsius (1.8 degrees Fahrenheit). Scientists for the Intergovernmental Panel on Climate Change have concluded that if we keep emitting carbon dioxide and other greenhouse gases at the current rate, the earth is on track to be 1.5 degrees Celsius (2.7 degrees Fahrenheit) warmer somewhere between 2030 and 2052. This level of warming means 14 per cent of the global population will be exposed to a severe heatwave at least once every five years, sea levels will rise by 40 centimetres by 2100, 8 per cent of plant species will be lost forever, and 70 to 90 per cent of coral reefs will decline further. This will affect the poor and the vulnerable disproportionately, as they are the most likely to be displaced by rising sea levels and impacted by natural disaster, food insecurity and disease.[18]

Incredibly, a global temperature rise of 1.5 degrees Celsius represents an optimistic scenario. To achieve this, we need to reach net-zero emissions by or before 2050.[19] Net zero is achieved when human-caused carbon emissions (such as from burning fossil fuels) are reduced to close to zero, with remaining emissions balanced out by removing carbon from the atmosphere (for example, by planting trees). It will require a dramatic reduction in global demand for energy, materials and food. It will probably necessitate modifications to our diets and the way we travel – for example, by flying less. We need to use energy and materials more efficiently, and we will have to become much better at agriculture, reducing emissions and water use. And finally, we're going to need a massive transformation of our energy supply. Renewables such as wind, solar, hydropower and biomass will need to supply half to two-thirds of our energy by mid-century.[20]

Unfortunately, we're not yet on track to do any of these things. Even if countries meet all the (legally binding) commitments they made in the 2015 Paris Agreement, the world is currently heading for warming of at least 3 degrees Celsius (5.4 degrees Fahrenheit) sometime this century. This would put the earth in a perilous position, with mass extinctions and entire regions uninhabitable.[21]

The Paris Agreement seeks to limit the rise in global temperature 'to well below two, preferably to 1.5 degrees Celsius'.[22] Two degrees Celsius (3.6 degrees Fahrenheit) is about the limit beyond which life on earth starts to get particularly challenging. It would mean the Arctic would be free of ice one year in every ten, seas would rise by 46 centimetres, 16 per cent of plant species would be lost and crop yields would be reduced by 7 per cent. We need to act urgently and decisively if we are to limit warming to 1.5 degrees. We have to halve global emissions by 2030 to have a chance of avoiding the worst impacts. Christiana Figueres, the architect of the Paris Agreement, argues that the coming decade is critical. 'What we do regarding emissions reductions between now and 2030 will determine the quality of human life on this planet for hundreds of years to come, if not more,' she writes.[23] This imperative is the backdrop to our coming recovery.

With or without government intervention, the need to respond to climate change will continue to drive alterations in our economy. Decarbonisation is happening. It's not happening quickly enough, but it's definitely picking up speed. More and more companies are making choices to reduce their carbon emissions, through investments in new technology or changes to their business models. Strategies to decarbonise through technological innovation can also lead to reduced operating costs through improved efficiencies or low-cost energy.

Furthermore, with pressure from investors and risk-averse banks and capital markets, it's becoming harder and harder to secure finance for dirty industries. Investors increasingly view carbon-intensive industries as a major risk. For example, to limit global warming to 2 degrees, 80 per cent of coal reserves will need to be left intact,[24] meaning many coal assets have the potential to become redundant. Consequently, a wave of investors and insurers have begun reducing their exposure to coal by actively divesting. BlackRock, one of the world's largest institutional investors, which manages US$7 trillion of funds, announced that it would withdraw funds from any firm generating more than 25 per cent of its revenue from thermal coal. It has since called on large energy companies to hasten the closure of coal-fired power stations.[25] Chubb, the largest commercial insurance company in the United States, announced that it 'will not underwrite risks related to the construction and operation of new coal-fired plants' or 'risks for companies that generate more than 30 per cent of their energy production from coal'.[26]

Societal pressure is also leading firms to change behaviour. The need to attract and retain quality employees and a desire to improve customer loyalty means many firms are choosing to position themselves as carbon neutral.[27] Fewer and fewer people want to be associated with dirty, polluting businesses. Even big mining firms such as Rio Tinto and BHP have committed to reducing carbon emissions to net zero by 2050, and are investing billions of dollars in climate-related projects.[28]

Myriad other forces are leading in the direction of decarbonisation of the economy. Enormous technological advances mean that in almost all parts of the world, renewable energy is now the cheapest form of new generation capacity, even without government subsidies. In 2020, more than 80 per cent of all new generation capacity installed across the globe was in the form of renewables.[29] As generators powered by coal and gas are retired, they are mostly being replaced with wind, solar or other forms of renewable energy.

Government policy, too, is driving the trend towards decarbonisation. There are more than sixty carbon pricing schemes in place or being implemented around the world. About half of these are emissions trading regimes and half are carbon taxes.[30] Even countries without such a scheme in place, such as Australia, may be impacted through 'border carbon adjustments', which are effectively a tariff on imports from countries that don't have a carbon price in place. For example, to avoid being undercut on price, the European Union is proposing to apply a tax on imported energy-intensive products, such as steel, cement and chemicals, from countries that don't have robust carbon pricing in place.[31]

Decarbonisation's acceleration will coincide almost perfectly with the coming recovery. The only question is which countries will be able to make good use of this opportunity and eke out a comparative advantage. In the next chapter, we'll explore how we can leverage the enormous fiscal stimulus being used to support recovery from COVID-19 to ensure it contributes to a further acceleration of decarbonisation.

Threats to democracy

Democracy has been struggling for some time. Dictators have been working to stamp out the last of domestic dissent. Many freely elected leaders have been rejecting pluralism and demanding unchecked powers to act in the interest of their supporters. Ethnic, religious and other minorities have borne the brunt of abuse. Washington-based think tank Freedom House reports that 2020 was the fifteenth consecutive year of decline in global freedom, with the number of countries becoming more democratic outweighed by countries experiencing erosion of political rights and civil liberties. Since 2005, twenty-five of the world's forty-one established democracies – including the United States, the United Kingdom and India – have suffered deterioration.[32] The Economist Intelligence Unit reports that in 2020, the average score for democracy fell to its lowest level since it first produced its Democracy Index in 2006. It argues that just 8.4 per cent of the world's people now live in 'full democracies' – countries with political freedoms and civil liberties, as well as a political culture that is conducive to the flourishing of democracy. More than half of the global population live under authoritarian rule or in a 'hybrid regime'.[33] These countries are dictatorships, or they have elections with irregularities substantial enough to prevent them from being free or fair. Media is state-owned or controlled, there is repression of any criticism of government and no independent judiciary.

Democracy has further retreated during the pandemic. As country after country locked down, the Democracy Index recorded a democratic decline in almost 70 per cent of countries.[34] Repressive leaders leveraged the pandemic to suit their political interests, often with little regard for health impacts or basic freedoms. In the Philippines, for example, the government employed a ban on spreading 'false information' to punish those criticising its pandemic response. In Hungary, the government used the pandemic to amass emergency powers that allowed it to rule by decree and exercised those powers to remove funding from municipalities ruled by opposition parties.[35] Freedom House is concerned that 'even open societies face pressure to accept restrictions that may outlive the crisis and have a lasting effect on liberty'.[36] Rebuilding democracy will need to be a key element of our recovery. By engaging communities in decisions that impact on them and drawing on a diverse range of voices to plan our recovery – mediated through democratic institutions such as parliaments – we can make better decisions while strengthening our democracy.

Inequality

In recent decades, we've seen enormous reductions in the number of people living in extreme poverty. In the decade to 2018, the proportion living on less than US$1.90 per day fell from 18.1 to 8.6 per cent of the world's population. In 2015, at least a billion fewer people were living in extreme poverty than in 1990. This progress has been driven largely by strong economic growth, particularly in East and South Asia.[37]

With the economies of rising countries such as China and India growing much faster than developed countries, the gap between the richest and poorest nations is getting smaller. But *within* countries, the gap between rich and poor is increasing nearly everywhere. Since 1990, inequality has increased within most developed countries, as well as some middle-income countries. Seventy per cent of the world's population live in countries in which inequality has been increasing in recent decades.[38] In the United States, the top 1 per cent of income earners now earn 20 per cent of the nation's income while the bottom quarter of Americans earn just 3.7 per cent of the income. The average income of those in the top 1 per cent is about US$1.7 million per year, about twenty times the average income among all American taxpayers.[39]

And while the world's ten richest billionaires have increased their wealth by more than half a trillion dollars during the pandemic, the World Bank estimates that as a result of COVID-19, an additional 88 to 115 million people will be forced back into extreme poverty.[40] It seems likely that in the absence of a concerted response, a legacy of the pandemic will be still greater inequality.

Inequality leads to poorer outcomes in almost any area you care to think of. It harms economic growth because poorer people under-invest in their education, leading to lost productivity. Inequality reduces social mobility, causing families to become trapped in an intergenerational cycle of poverty. It contributes to poorer health outcomes, more crime and reduced support for democracy.[41] Building a brighter future after the pandemic will need to involve efforts to reduce inequality, by investing in education and housing, improving universal services and redistributing income through a progressive taxation system.

Geopolitical context

The COVID-19 recovery will occur against a global backdrop of geopolitical risks and opportunities. In the wake of Brexit, Europe is seeking to become more 'ambitious, strategic and assertive in the way that [it acts] in the world'.[42] In particular, it will continue to play a leadership role in shaping global norms for digital regulation and environmental policy. However, when Europe's dominant leader, German chancellor Dr Angela Merkel, steps down, it will create a European leadership vacuum. This will bring with it some uncertainty about Europe's future direction.[43]

A Biden presidency is seeing the United States return to global engagement, working through multilateral forums. Biden's administration is mobilising to tackle climate change assertively, re-establishing a leadership role within the global climate community. This is likely to re-energise global efforts to make substantial progress on carbon emissions.

China continues to rise to superpower status, restoring the ascendency it enjoyed in centuries past. Its strong economic growth through the pandemic only accelerates this progression. This creates economic, political and military challenges for rival countries such as the United States. China and the United States – the world's two biggest carbon polluters – have agreed to 'cooperate to tackle the climate crisis'.[44] Yet at the same time, tensions between them manifest in an acrimonious trade relationship and technological competition in areas such as 5G. Both countries will invest in domestic industries to become more self-reliant. And there will be ongoing friction associated with China's sovereignty in areas such as its maritime territorial boundaries and its engagement with Taiwan.[45] This conflict creates dilemmas for middle powers such as Australia, who are caught between their trading relationship with China and their security relationship with the United States.

These and a host of other geopolitical issues will both enable and constrain the choices we make in the recovery period. For example, companies in China and in the West are likely to face greater regulatory scrutiny when investing in each other's jurisdictions. If the European Union imposes 'carbon tariffs' so that imports are priced to reflect their carbon content, new opportunities and challenges will be created for exporters. A push towards greater self-reliance from too many countries has the potential to weaken multilateral institutions such as the World Trade Organization.

Economic stagnation

Emerging economies have seen strong growth in recent years. Between 2010 and 2018, GDP per capita in China grew by an average of nearly 7 per cent a year. In India and Bangladesh, per capita GDP growth averaged 5.2 per cent per year. Other emerging economies recorded similar rates of growth.[46]

Yet in the advanced economies, it's a different story. Over the same period, per capita growth rates in the Eurozone, Japan and Australia averaged just 1.1 per cent a year. The United Kingdom and the United States didn't fare much better, averaging 1.3 per cent a year.[47] This weak economic growth is a function of weak productivity growth. Essentially, over a decade, advanced countries didn't get much better at producing things. When productivity is increasing, we see more output for each hour of labour contributed, but here, each hour of work continued to produce about the same amount of output as it did a decade ago. This weak productivity growth has led to a stagnation in living standards, particularly for poorer and middle-class households. Between 2009 and 2017 in Australia, for example, the annual income of the average household *fell* by A\$542 (US\$416).[48]

Weak productivity growth is a function of companies under-investing in machinery and equipment as well as inadequate movement of workers and capital from low productivity sectors to more productive ones.[49] The World Bank is concerned that the uncertainty and disruption resulting from the pandemic is likely to lead to a further weakening of productivity growth.[50] It will be critical that countries do what they can to support economic development: for example, through technology upgrades and support for emerging technology sectors.

How we can improve in the short term

Most countries are well advanced in tackling their immediate recovery challenges. The vaccine rollout is progressing rapidly in most developed countries, although many nations have had to deal with renewed outbreaks, and we've discovered new variants with the potential to be particularly infectious. Even after much of the world is vaccinated, it seems COVID-19 will remain an endemic disease similar to seasonal flu, causing illness but not devastation. Countries such as Australia and New Zealand, whose strategy has been to isolate, are figuring out how to open borders and re-engage, while living alongside the virus.

The ongoing health consequences of COVID-19 are continuing to put pressure on health systems, particularly in those countries where infections have been widespread. 'Long-haulers' report symptoms such as 'extreme fatigue, muscle and joint pain, breathlessness, heart palpitations, loss or alteration of taste and smell, gastrointestinal distress, and problems with attention, memory and cognition'.[51] Systematic follow up of COVID-19 patients is occurring in many places around the world. Given that COVID-19 interacts with pre-existing health concerns, we may need to find new ways of providing integrated care.[52] Similarly, enhanced access to mental-health services will require proactive screening and provision of support services to specific groups, such as frontline health workers. To tackle an increase in family violence, governments will need to dramatically increase funding for the services that support women and children.

Some nations are trialling ways to overcome significant disengagement from school and the curbing of student aspirations. In France, between 5 and 8 per cent of students could not be reached by their teachers two weeks after school closures. In Los Angeles, teachers report that 13 per cent of high-school students had not had any contact with teaching staff three weeks into the lockdown.[53] To limit the number of school dropouts following the pandemic, governments are developing strategies to re-engage students, learning from other nations. In Spain, for example, vulnerable students have benefited from individualised phone follow-ups, to discuss academic, health and personal issues. In Germany, 'transition coaches' are supporting students to ensure they finish school or vocational education.[54]

Cities have been hit hard by the pandemic. With office workers at home and tourists absent, many central business districts are eerily quiet. While restrictions have mostly lifted, enabling office workers to return – along with cafes, restaurants, bars and retailers – many cities remain subdued. Some continue to move in and out of lockdown. Reactivating the central business district, giving people the confidence and purpose to return, means providing a sense of safety. Enhanced cleaning, along with transport systems that give nervous visitors some extra space, has helped. Many cities will keep their enhanced bicycle lanes and outdoor dining schemes, established to allow venues to seat more patrons under social distancing requirements. Councils are also working hard to provide reasons to visit, including events, art installations and other exciting offerings.

As we've seen throughout this book, time and again nations have recovered from crises to come back even better than before. Crisis provides an opportunity to create a future that might not have been possible otherwise. What matters more than the crisis itself are the decisions we make during the recovery, as that's what sets us up for a successful future.

So far in this chapter, we've reviewed the lessons from past recoveries, considered the insights gained during the COVID-19 pandemic and contemplated the intersecting challenges that we'll have to tackle during our recovery. Armed with this information, how do we make sense of our situation? The diagram on the next page provides an overview of how we might begin to position ourselves for success.

We'll have to overcome many weaknesses during our recovery, many of which have been exposed by the pandemic. The fault lines are stark, with inequalities leading to significant differences in health outcomes. Trust levels are low in many nations, and democracy is in retreat throughout much of the world. Our global economy has been revealed as fragile, and advanced economies have experienced an extended period of low productivity growth. These weaknesses will be amplified by the threats ahead of us. Future crises are inevitable, and the risks associated with climate change grow with every day that we fail to respond with adequate determination.

Yet we will enter recovery with the benefit of the insights we've gained through the trauma of the pandemic. We've built new consensus around the need for economic stimulus and the value of competent government informed by expert advice. We've seen how small nations have been particularly effective at responding to the virus and have appreciated the important role local and state governments play at a time of crisis.

Strengths

We've (re)learnt the importance of government. A competent government is a big asset at a time of crisis.

We know there is value in smaller units of government. In many federations, state governments have taken the lead. Small nation-states have performed well too.

Fiscal stimulus is no longer contentious. Leaders of all political persuasions have embraced fiscal stimulus as an important crisis-response tool.

Experts have been elevated. Experts – from a variety of disciplines – play an important role in responding to crisis and delivering competent government.

Weaknesses

We see the limits of science. Even with vaccines, we can't quickly vaccinate people because we need to take time to test for safety and efficacy.

Public health system capabilities are mixed. The pandemic has revealed significant weaknesses in some nations' public health systems, even those previously thought of as high-performing.

Structural inequality is evident. COVID-19 has exposed long-standing drivers of poor health, including inequality, precarious work and inadequate housing.

Trust has fallen. Trust between citizens and government is extremely low in some countries, contributing to adverse consequences.

Democracy has retreated. Democracy was in decline before the pandemic and retreated further during 2020.

We have fragile supply chains. Complex global supply chains have been exposed as highly vulnerable to disruption.

We have weak productivity growth. In advanced economies, productivity growth has essentially stalled, contributing to lower living standards.

Our current situation

Opportunities

Align fiscal stimulus with other strategic priorities. We can direct the billions government is spending on stimulus towards challenges such as climate change, inequality and productivity.

Embrace a democratic, experimental approach to recovery. An inclusive, innovative approach to recovery has the potential to strengthen democracy.

Build resilience into systems. Improving the resilience of communities, infrastructure and the economy will mean we are better prepared for the next crisis.

Adopt a global approach. Given how much economic, health and security outcomes are influenced by what happens around the world, it is in everyone's interest to supporting developing countries to become more resilient.

Threats

Future crises. Whether pandemic, war, natural disaster or recession, it's highly likely that we'll be affected by future crises.

Climate change. Fire, floods, storms, heatwaves and droughts are becoming more frequent, prevalent and intense. A warming planet risks climate catastrophe.

Economic growth. With low productivity growth, developed nations risk a long period of economic stagnation.

Democratic regression. A further retreat of democracy in many parts of the world is likely.

Consequently, we find ourselves with some powerful opportunities to recover from the crisis, tackle our biggest problems and create a brighter future. Billions of dollars of stimulus will – and should – continue to flow for some time. If these funds are directed with purpose, they can yield positive outcomes in addressing climate change, inequality and economic productivity. As we retool our cities, we have an opportunity to ensure that our communities, infrastructure and economies become more resilient to future crises. National resilience will be enhanced if we can cooperate globally. And if we draw on a range of perspectives to shape our recovery, there's the potential to try exciting new approaches.

Building back better

A recovery strategy leveraging these opportunities will allow us to 'build back better'. The OECD describes this as an approach that will 'trigger investment and behavioural changes that will reduce the likelihood of future shocks and increase society's resilience to them when they do occur'.[55] It has two dimensions: taking the required steps to avoid or mitigate future crises; and learning how to become more resilient to future shocks when they do occur.

Central to building back better is a focus on the long term, even when urgent decisions need to be made. The OECD suggests screening all response and recovery proposals for their impact on long-term outcomes. A key dimension is 'the need for a people-centred recovery that focuses on wellbeing, improves inclusiveness and reduces inequality'. While economic growth and job creation is important, job quality, increased income, housing and health are important too.

Ideally, recovery initiatives should align with other long-term priorities. The OECD suggests the following considerations.

- **Long-term objectives for reducing greenhouse gas emissions.** For example, new infrastructure should not make it more difficult to achieve net-zero emissions.

- **Strengthening resilience to the impacts of climate change.** Any infrastructure should be able to withstand climate change risks across its life term.

- **Policies that halt and reverse biodiversity loss and restore ecosystem services.** Reforestation and wetland restoration are a cost-effective way of increasing climate resilience while providing employment opportunities.

- **Innovation that builds on enduring behaviour change.** Using technology, we can embed or reverse the behaviour change we've seen during the COVID-19 crisis to create more sustainable behaviours (for example, mobile apps that show the extent of crowding can provide people with the confidence to use public transport again).

- **Improving resilience of supply chains.** Efforts to strengthen local supply chains can improve resilience, and if they use 'circular economy' principles to design our waste and pollution, these initiatives can improve environmental outcomes too.

As we saw in Aceh and Christchurch, building back better also needs to have a focus on people and institutions. This helps to ensure that communities are better equipped to handle future crises.

The United Nations describes building back better as being about improving capacity 'through the creation and strengthening of recovery-focused relationships, the establishment of planning and coordination mechanisms, and the introduction of methods and procedures to ensure recovery activities are adequately informed and supported'.[56] Building back better is about these things, but it can't be just about these things. If we are aiming to maintain a long-term focus while making short-term decisions, then we need to consider a broad range of factors relevant to the future. This includes the geopolitical context, threats to democracy, productivity, inequality and the competence of government. A lot to ask, perhaps. Our challenge is to seek to find the best alignment between short-term recovery initiatives and long-term challenges.

Ultimately, if we do all this well, we become more resilient. The OECD describes resilience as 'the ability of households, communities and nations to absorb and recover from shocks, whilst positively adapting and transforming their structures and means for living in the face of long-term stresses, change and uncertainty'. That's not bad, but a bit of a mouthful. I prefer the definition in the Cambridge Dictionary, which describes resilience as 'the ability to be happy, successful etc again after something difficult or bad has happened'.[57] With the right decisions, I'm optimistic we can be happy and successful again after this crisis.

Making decisions

Governments have had to make some tough decisions during the pandemic, ranging from shutting down international borders to lockdowns and mask mandates. These decisions have been instrumental in determining how badly their country has been affected by the virus.

Expert voices have played a large role. Epidemiologists, virologists, immunologists and science communicators have become household names. Countries that have been most successful in their response have been prepared to draw experts into their decision-making. President Roosevelt similarly drew on expert opinion as he shaped the New Deal in response to the Great Depression. Experts clearly have an important role to play in informing decisions, particularly in a crisis. Yet we must temper this enthusiasm for experts with a couple of notes of caution.

First, the scientific process is exactly that – a *process*. With a novel virus, there's a lot that scientists simply don't know. Experts can be spectacularly wrong, as they were during the Spanish flu when scientists assumed that the illness was transmitted by bacteria (it was actually a virus), or in 1929, when renowned economists predicted a 'permanently high plateau' for the stock market three days before the Wall Street crash that precipitated the Great Depression.[58] Crises are incredibly complex events, and experts can only draw on the information that is available to them. As information is assembled and scientific understanding improves, advice will change. Experts from the same discipline will disagree with one another. Experts from different disciplines will bring a range of perspectives, and not all of these disciplines will be in the sciences – lawyers, economists, planners, engineers and social workers are all experts with valuable perspectives on aspects of a crisis. In a time marked by uncertainty, there are often no clear answers. Expert advice is important, but it is not always clear-cut.

Second, there are different forms of knowledge that can and should help to inform decision-making. Community perspectives provide useful intelligence. How is policy playing out in practice? How are businesses being affected by lockdowns? How could we tweak existing policy to improve it? Questions like these are best addressed by listening to members of the community.

As we saw in Aceh and Christchurch, involving communities in their own recoveries leads to better targeted and more-effective interventions.

Embedding community consultation into our decision-making strengthens our democracy. The balancing of expert opinion and community voices is fundamentally a role for elected political representatives. Once we are no longer in an emergency situation, parliament should ideally provide appropriate checks and balances on decision-making as we move forward in our recovery efforts. With democracy waning during the pandemic, strengthening and enhancing our democracy needs to be a core part of the recovery process.

While the emergency-response phase of a crisis lends itself to a command-and-control structure, during recovery it will be important to create space for different perspectives. This was the iterative, experimental approach adopted through Roosevelt's New Deal, with myriad ideas drawn from multiple sources. A bottom-up, experimental approach also worked for Christchurch, with temporary initiatives giving the arts and creative sector the remit to try things they might not have otherwise. Government stimulus will play a central role in recovery, but so will grassroots community initiatives. Our recovery will be shaped not just by the nature of the decisions that we make, but also by the *way* that we make them.

This chapter considered the issues that will shape our post-pandemic future. In the next chapter, we'll explore how we might respond practically to harness the opportunity ahead.

FIVE QUESTIONS
FOR RECOVERY

1. How do we set ourselves up for economic growth?

2. How can we address the structural issues revealed by
    the crisis?

3. What other problems will we have to tackle at the same time
    as recovery?

4. What future crises do we need to prepare for?

5. How can we strengthen our democracy through the
    recovery process?

6

A ROADMAP TO RECOVERY

The stories in this book show us that in the long run, crises are less important than the recovery periods that follow. Decades later, hard-hit places aren't necessarily worse off than those that avoided disaster. Humans can recover remarkably quickly.

Recoveries from past crises should inspire us with optimism. Other places have been able to recover from crisis to become better than before, so we should be confident that it's possible for us to do the same. The United States, Germany and South Korea show us that recovery need not be a mere return to pre-crisis conditions; rather, it can involve accelerated development, enabling nations to become world leaders. This knowledge should inspire us to lift our ambitions. A long-term perspective on past recoveries should spark a national – if not global – conversation about what transformations might be possible in this recovery.

Yet success is not a given. Now is the time for informed and inspired decisions. With the wrong policy choices, recovery could be set back by many years. If we ease restrictions too early, we risk prolonging the health crisis. If we withdraw economic stimulus before the economy is truly humming, growth will stall.

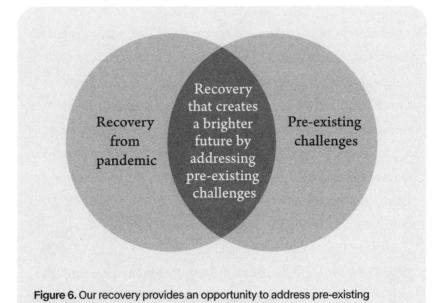

Figure 6. Our recovery provides an opportunity to address pre-existing challenges.

If we impose a top-down, bureaucratic response, the community will fail to engage. If we don't address the underlying fragilities revealed by the pandemic, we will remain weakened. And unless we learn the lessons of this pandemic, we will be vulnerable to future crises.

The decisions we make will determine the type of recovery we have. With the right choices, we won't just recover, we'll do so in a way that addresses many of the serious intersecting challenges we're facing. The task for us is to find the overlapping point in the Venn diagram where recovery initiatives also help us to decarbonise our economy, strengthen our democracy and reduce inequality.

The good news is that identifying initiatives that do this is not particularly difficult. As we'll explore later in this chapter, the most effective economic stimulus is directed precisely at these areas. Building collaboration and engaging communities in recovery can help us to become stronger and more democratic. And by addressing the fragility that has been revealed, we'll become more resilient to future shocks.

Drawing on these insights, we can form a relatively clear view of the types of things we can do to shape our recovery. We will need to employ a mix of simple and more complex measures over the short and long term. These are summarised in the diagram below. By now, the urgent response measures described in the previous chapter are mostly well underway; we are looking at the interventions still ahead of us that will set us up for long-term success.

Quick and relatively straightforward

Establish an agency to coordinate recovery

Enter into a formal partnership between local, state/province and national governments

Commission a post-pandemic inquiry

Reactivate cities to give people the confidence and purpose to return

Boost support for mental health

Relatively straightforward but take longer

Keep stimulus going for as long as it takes

Focus economic stimulus on initiatives that help drive long-term economic growth *and* help tackle intersecting challenges

Experiment – try lots of things and keep the things that work and discard those that don't

Double down on economic development, investing in technology and supporting emerging, export-oriented sectors

Support the arts and culture

Invest in education

Prepare for future pandemics and crises

Elements of our recovery

Quick but difficult

Wind down support for existing businesses and allow the economy to adjust to the new post-pandemic reality

Re-engage vulnerable students in learning

Long term and difficult

Really tackle the social determinants of health, including social inclusion, housing and working conditions

Confront the big cleavages that divide the nation and set a path towards reconciliation

Step 1: Set up the recovery

Recoveries are complex. They involve many different parts of government, ranging from the treasury to social services to health departments. Various levels of government, including local, regional and national governments, have roles to play, as do communities, along with not-for-profit organisations and other service providers. All of these organisations – and the staff working for them – also have core responsibilities that they must continue to deliver in addition to supporting recovery.

To manage this complexity, governments should consider establishing a dedicated agency to coordinate the recovery process. A clear lesson from most of the recoveries in this book is that a dedicated agency is critical, with a staff focused exclusively on the recovery process. Depending on the context, this could be done at the national, state, city or local level. While this agency must have the strong support of central government, key decisions should be determined by all major stakeholders in consultation. An agency can be time-limited and respond to a single crisis, as in Aceh, or it can be a standing agency to respond to multiple crises, as with Bushfire Recovery Victoria, established to respond to the bushfires that frequently devastate rural communities in the Australian state of Victoria.

In the current recovery, this agency will need a broad remit, encompassing both the residual health effects of the pandemic and economic recovery. It may even encompass mental health or re-engagement of students.

Local governments, as the level of government closest to communities, have a particularly important role working with towns and cities to help them recover. Yet local governments don't have the depth of resources that national governments enjoy, and they will need support. In the aftermath of COVID-19, city economies are reeling, and local governments will need extensive help to re-energise struggling economies. A formal partnership between local, state and national governments may be one way to set struggling cities up for the long recovery ahead. In Melbourne, for example, local and state governments have jointly committed hundreds of millions of dollars to economic recovery and agreed to work in partnership over a two-year period to revitalise the central city in the wake of the pandemic.[1]

Step 2: Establish a post-pandemic inquiry

Following crises, nations often undergo a bit of soul-searching. Crises reveal a lot about a country, in a fairly raw way. In this crisis, some countries have experienced a failure of government. In others, a lack of trust has undermined efforts to contain the virus spread. Elsewhere, health systems have struggled, or inequalities have revealed just how vulnerable some parts of the population really are. If there are underlying structural concerns, a crisis will invariably lay them bare. The recovery period is an opportunity to ruminate on these issues and consider whether they truly reflect the nation we'd like to be.

After the pandemic – or any crisis, for that matter – a good way to process the experience is to conduct a thorough investigation into all its aspects. Careful documentation of what was learnt is crucial, ensuring we are better prepared and better able to respond in the event of a similar crisis.

Each jurisdiction will have different mechanisms for conducting inquiries. In monarchies, such as the United Kingdom, Australia, Canada and New Zealand, royal commissions are ad-hoc public inquiries into defined issues, usually chaired by a judge.

Within their terms of reference they have considerable powers, being able to take evidence under oath, request documents and even subpoena witnesses. There is lots of precedent for royal commissions into crises. For example, a royal commission was conducted into the Christchurch earthquakes in New Zealand, while in Victoria, Australia, a royal commission examined the 2009 bushfires that killed 173 people.[2] Both resulted in robust sets of recommendations for reform, most of which have been adopted by government. In the United States, presidential commissions are quasi-judicial taskforces established by the president to inquire into particular issues. These have been used after crises such as 9/11.[3]

Given the scale of the COVID-19 pandemic, it makes sense for countries to commission inquiries on this crisis. At a minimum, these are the questions that should be addressed.

- What were the causes and circumstances of the pandemic and associated recession?

- How well prepared were we?

- How did we respond?

- How can we better prepare and plan for future pandemics?

A number of jurisdictions have completed inquiries into aspects of the pandemic. In Australia, Victoria conducted a judicial inquiry into its hotel quarantine scheme and New South Wales conducted a Special Commission of Inquiry into an outbreak arising from the *Ruby Princess* cruise ship.[4] Yet once the response phase of the pandemic is truly behind us, more comprehensive inquiries will provide a broader perspective. The UK government has announced that it will launch an independent public inquiry into its handling of the pandemic, commencing in 2022.

As inquiries are completed, nations should share their lessons with other countries. An inquiry process posing similar questions should also be conducted at the global scale. Documenting the lessons learnt during the pandemic will enable global frameworks for pandemic preparedness and response to be updated and improved.

Step 3: Keep stimulating the economy

During the acute phase of the pandemic, government spending initiatives offered relief to those directly impacted as the economy was put into hibernation. This included subsidised wages for furloughed workers, direct payments to households and increased payments for jobseekers. As the economy opened back up, these measures were supplemented by initiatives designed to get more money circulating in the economy quickly. For example, voucher schemes, such as the United Kingdom's 'Eat Out to Help Out' and Singapore's 'SingapoRediscovers', furnished citizens with cash that could only be spent in designated parts of the economy, such as on hospitality or accommodation.[5] It makes sense to target stimulus funds to parts of the economy that have been most affected: they need the greatest support and stimulus will be most effective there.

The economic effects of COVID-19 will persist in the years after the pandemic, and governments will need to provide economic stimulus until unemployment returns to low levels. A key lesson from the Great Recession of 2008 is that economic stimulus cannot be withdrawn too early. Managing director of the International Monetary Fund Dr Kristalina Georgieva argues that 'we cannot afford to withdraw support prematurely until we see the health crisis in the rear-view mirror; it is important that governments ... are there to make sure that we can build the bridge over the health crisis into recovery'.[6] Stimulus will gradually need to shift from support for the retention of existing jobs to initiatives that help create new employment and increase productivity. With interest rates at record low levels, many governments will be able to scale up public investment in projects that leave a long-term legacy, such as those related to infrastructure, energy efficiency or research and development.

With interest rates at or near zero in most countries, there is very limited capacity for monetary policy to contribute to stimulus – interest rates can't be lowered much further and unconventional monetary policy (including 'printing money') can only play a limited role.[7] Consequently, almost all of the economic stimulus will need to come from fiscal policy – that is, from government spending. With recessions causing enormous damage that lasts for years, governments will need to spend as much as it takes for as long as it takes to get the economy firing again.

As we move past the acute phase of the crisis, there is an opportunity to draw breath and consider how best to structure such a massive spending program. If we're going to be spending hundreds of billions of dollars, we should make sure we put it to good use. Stimulus can be broadly assessed on three criteria:

1. Speed of response (getting stimulus out quickly)

2. The long-run multiplier effect (how well the stimulus will contribute to long-run economic growth)

3. The impact on other strategic priorities (such as climate change)

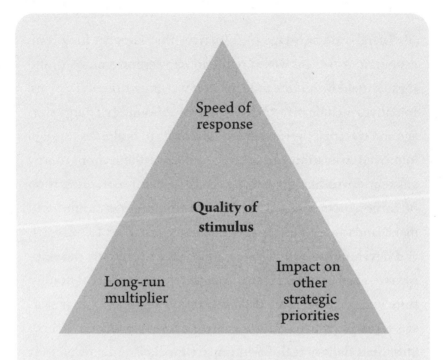

Figure 7. The iron triangle of economic stimulus. It's challenging for a single stimulus measure to achieve speed of response, a good long-run multiplier and a positive impact on other strategic priorities.

We can think of these three dimensions as the 'iron triangle' of fiscal stimulus. It's difficult to achieve more than two at any one time. Getting money out the door quickly is not generally compatible with a focus on highly considered strategic priorities. As former Australian treasurer Wayne Swan pointed out in the chapter on recession, 'shovel-ready' projects aren't always of high-quality, and 'shovel-worthy' projects mostly have longer lead times. However, with a focus on stimulus over the medium term, getting money out the door as quickly as possible is no longer the main focus. We can consider initiatives that contribute to long-run economic growth *and* help us tackle critical intersecting challenges, such as climate change or inequality.

There is no shortage of initiatives that support long-term economic growth, as well as reductions in carbon emissions, and these should be an integral part of government recovery plans. Initiatives include investments in renewable energy, energy storage and electricity grid upgrades. Retrofits of buildings through improved insulation and heating will make them more energy efficient. Investment in natural ecosystems through restoration of carbon-rich habitat and climate-friendly agriculture will make landscapes more resilient. Financial support for research and development in green technologies will support developments in areas such as electrolysis (a chemical process used to store renewable energy as hydrogen),[8] heat pumps, energy storage, plant genetics and greenhouse gas removal.[9] None of these initiatives deliver real-world impact quickly, and so were not appropriate during the acute phase of the pandemic. But with recovery now focused on the medium term, these are exactly the sorts of initiatives that should feature in government stimulus packages.

You'll recall from the last chapter that another strategic imperative is addressing inequality. Inequality has been increasing within countries, contributing to poorer outcomes in everything from economic growth and social mobility to health and crime. In Australia, forty-nine top economists were surveyed for their views on the stimulus measures that would be most effective in boosting the economy over the next couple of years. The most widely supported initiative was a big investment in social housing. This has the double benefit of supporting the building industry and reducing homelessness. The second most-supported initiative was an increase in unemployment payments. This will have the tangible effect of reducing poverty and inequality, and every cent is likely to be spent rather than saved, making it an effective stimulus measure.[10]

While some governments may be tempted to permanently lower taxes to stimulate the economy, this is not particularly effective. Wealthy households receiving tax cuts are likely to save much of the benefit, thereby reducing the stimulatory effect. And budgets will be left weakened, with reduced capacity to generate revenue once the economy recovers.

Step 4: Adopt an experimental and creative approach

Recovery doesn't require us to lock in a grand masterplan. In fact, given governments really don't know what will work and what won't, it's probably better that we try lots of different things. Governments should listen to suggestions from experts and community members and give their ideas a go. And rather than deliver everything itself, governments should be prepared to empower and fund others – such as community organisations or companies – to run a range of recovery initiatives. Creative groups might activate vacant spaces in high streets, as in Christchurch. For-profit event management companies might deliver major festivals. Not-for-profit organisations might organise volunteers to support reading remediation in schools.

Adopting an experimental approach requires accepting that not all initiatives will work. One way to manage this risk is to fund things at a modest level and scale them up rapidly if they are effective. This requires a structured approach to program evaluation, with an evaluation methodology built into new initiatives at the outset. It will enable decision-makers to be clear about what it means for a program to 'work' and what measurements will be used to determine its success. With a disciplined and structured approach, governments will be in a strong position to keep progressing measures that work and discard those that don't.

COVID-19 has impacted the arts and creative sectors more than almost any other. Yet public art and cultural expression are an important way for communities to process the trauma associated with major crises. With central cities emptier than usual, arts and creative activity should be supported to fill the gap. Governments should encourage temporary and experimental installations, leveraging vacant spaces such as shopfronts. Not only will this provide opportunities for the creative sector; it will contribute to the revitalisation of central cities by providing visitors with a reason to return.

Given the significant hit that artists have taken during the crisis, governments should provide additional financial support throughout the recovery period. Governments will also need to ensure that venues for arts and culture survive, supporting them to become safer and more accessible. It's not just government that has a role in supporting the arts and cultural sector, though. Some pockets of the sector – such as video gaming and streaming – have done extremely well during the pandemic. Successful companies should be encouraged to work in collaboration with other parts of the creative sector on joint initiatives – potentially assisting to develop capacity to engage online. Universities, too, will be well-placed to offer support for creative programming and incubation of creative activity.[11]

Many cities and countries are responding. The UK city of Manchester has released a Culture Recovery Plan, which positions culture as a key aspect of city life. It aims to reactivate high streets through music, festivals and pop-up events. Through Creative Connections – a kind of online marketplace for creatives – it will support individuals to find paid creative employment by matching

them with commissioners, producers and casting directors looking for talent.[12] Ravaged by the pandemic, German nightclubs
and live-music venues have been officially recognised as cultural
sites alongside theatre, opera, museums and concert halls, rather
than as 'entertainment venues'. This now allows them to operate in
more parts of the city and provides access to tax breaks.[13] In rec-
ognition of the impact on the cultural sector, the European Union
has doubled the funding it provides through the Creative Europe
program, significantly increasing funding for promoting female
talent, the live-music sector and small-scale projects.[14]

Step 5: Invest in economic development

When looking back from future decades, economic development
will be the factor that shaped our recovery the most. The extent to
which our economy is able to grow will have an enormous impact
on material living standards, including on education outcomes,
life expectancy and happiness. It is the foundation that will enable
us to respond to important social, political and environmental
challenges.

As we emerge from the deepest recession in a generation,
economic growth is crucial. Incrementally improving the rate of
growth won't make a huge difference in the immediate future, but
over the next decade or two, the things we do now to improve
the productivity and competitiveness of our economy will reap
enormous rewards. Throughout this book, we've seen that the
countries most successful in recovering from crises were able to
grow their economies strongly. Those places that haven't yet seen
strong growth in the aftermath of crisis – such as Aceh and Christchurch – have identified economic development as the missing
ingredient in their recoveries.

In shaping recovery packages, governments should consider the following.

- **Let the economy adjust.** Recessions are periods in which established order is upended. Businesses that were barely profitable beforehand will be found out during a recession. Inefficiency or complacency lurking within a company will be shaken out. Recessions are brutal, but they are also an opportunity for economies to become more efficient and more competitive. When failing businesses close, staff and capital can be reallocated to other, more competitive businesses. This process will drive the growth that will underpin our recovery. During our recovery, governments will need to provide enormous economic stimulus for an extended period and social supports to protect the vulnerable. The challenge for governments is to find a way of doing this while letting the economy adjust. Rents, wages and other prices will need to change to reflect the new economic reality. In time, governments will need to redirect stimulus towards emerging businesses rather than existing ones.

- **Upgrade technology.** Past recoveries have been fuelled by investments in the latest technologies. Similarly, we have seen COVID-19 condense into months changes that would otherwise have taken years. Now is the time to support companies to upgrade their technology. While companies need to make their own decisions, governments can assist by investing in enabling infrastructure, providing finance or facilitating access to technical advice. South Korea's Korean New Deal, for example, is aimed at 'setting the foundation for the next 100 years' and involves large-scale investment in digital infrastructure, grants and subsidies to expand adoption of artificial intelligence, and strengthening of cybersecurity.[15]

- **Support export-oriented businesses.** Increasing exports is one of the main ways for a country to become wealthier. Exports both generate revenue from offshore and drive increased productivity, thereby triggering a positive upward shift. The recovery period is the perfect time to support companies to build their export capability. Governments can introduce companies to overseas markets, provide export credit or assist small businesses to participate in global supply chains (with the right support, a small business can become the global supplier of a small widget that goes into a more-complex product produced by a large multinational). For example, the World Bank suggests that for Nepal, a small developing country in the Himalayas, exports will be a 'powerful platform to boost post-pandemic recovery' and recommends 'modernizing export promotion and upgrading exporters' capabilities' and 'developing an e-commerce framework'.[16] As part of its COVID-19 economic stimulus package, the Singaporean government has expanded its trade loan scheme, enabling Singaporean export businesses to borrow up to S$10 million (US$7.5 million) to finance short-term costs associated with importing and exporting.[17]

- **Back winning industries.** With high costs and high wages, it's unlikely that most companies in the world's advanced economies will be able to compete by being the cheapest. Instead, they will need to leverage better technology, a better-educated workforce and more capital investment to develop innovative and desirable products. It's likely that countries will only be able to compete globally in a relatively small number of product and industry niches. To develop industry sectors that can compete globally, government must work with industry to determine a nuanced and sophisticated range of interventions unique to that sector. Measures might include tax subsidies for investment in research and development, facilitation of collaboration between companies and academics, support for startups or use of government procurement to support innovative new products produced locally. Christchurch, for example, continues to leverage its agricultural strengths to become increasingly competitive in agritech – the use of technology and technological innovation to improve the output and efficiency of agriculture.[18] In Canada, Ontario is investing heavily to create a leading specialty in regenerative medicine, developing techniques to regrow, repair or replace diseased or damaged cells, tissues or organs.[19] The Netherlands is specialising in high-tech systems and materials, including nanoelectronics (electronics at a very, very small scale) and mechatronics (combining electronics and mechanical engineering).[20]

- **Accelerate decarbonisation.** Just as climate change is the terrifying phenomenon that is altering life on earth, decarbonisation is the exciting trend accompanying it – far too slowly, but inexorably. There is no escaping decarbonisation. Economies that decarbonise first will enjoy an enormous competitive advantage, with decarbonised industries spurring rapid economic growth. Large amounts of private-sector capital are poised and ready to be spent on decarbonisation projects. To unlock the potential of this investment, it's critical that governments provide policy certainty. This needs to involve a fast-tracked transformation of energy supply towards renewable sources and investment in infrastructure such as energy storage and transmission.[21] Germany, for example, is endeavouring to ensure that it will emerge from the crisis in a more climate-friendly manner. It has supported this goal with grants of more than €50 billion euros (US$61 billion) as part of its stimulus package. A big portion of this funding will go towards public transport, railways and charging infrastructure for electric vehicles. It is also investing large amounts of money towards research into 'green hydrogen' – a clean, energy-intensive gas made with water and renewable electricity. This is aimed at developing a next-generation export industry that will enable it to store and sell surplus renewable energy in the form of hydrogen and become a global market leader in associated production machinery and equipment.[22]

Step 6: Invest in education

As we saw in the last chapter, there are several initiatives governments and others will need to pursue urgently to re-engage students in education in the aftermath of the pandemic. Yet long-term investment in education is also one of the most important moves a country can make.

Returning to normal won't address the impacts of learning losses during the pandemic. Only *improving* schooling will make up for these losses. Angel Gurría, until recently the OECD's secretary-general, argues that 'strengthening education systems needs to be at the heart of government planning to recover from this crisis'. It's particularly important that every effort is taken 'to ensure that the crisis does not exacerbate the inequalities in education that have been revealed in many countries'.[23] Governments will urgently need to consider big investments in education, through initiatives such as small-group tutoring for struggling students or expansion of literacy and numeracy programs that can help students learn rapidly.[24] In the United States, for example, a central element of the Biden administration's economic stimulus is the largest-ever federal government investment in school education. This will support school districts to address short-term needs associated with the pandemic, as well as invest in the structural changes required to strengthen public education over the long term.[25]

Investment in education and training will better equip people to deal with the major structural shifts in the economy associated with decarbonisation and rapid technological change. While it takes years, raising overall education standards will improve the productive capacity of the economy in the long run, contributing to higher living standards. The best way to support improved education outcomes is to invest in quality early childhood education, and to enhance the prestige and quality of teaching by investing in teacher learning and development and rewarding the best teachers.

The tertiary education sector, too, will need strengthening. The closure of international borders has undermined the business model, built on international students, upon which many universities depend. The pandemic has disrupted academic programs and research and has affected the wellbeing of staff and students. The recovery period is an opportunity to grow and reframe the role of tertiary education. In particular, universities have a critical role in reskilling workers for the post-COVID-19 world and in sparking growth in new industries.[26]

Step 7: Address the social determinants of health

COVID-19 has shown us again that the conditions in which people live and work play an enormous role in influencing health outcomes. Disadvantaged people are disproportionately burdened by disease, and this includes COVID-19. 'Social determinants' impacting health outcomes include higher rates of smoking and alcohol consumption, obesity, overcrowded housing, dangerous jobs and exposure to air pollution. Reducing the impact of these social determinants will improve our preparedness for the next pandemic, but it will also improve overall health outcomes. It brings the added benefits that come with a reduction in inequality, including improved educational outcomes, greater economic growth, improved social mobility, reduced crime and greater support for democracy.

Addressing the social determinants of health is critically important, but it will not be achieved easily or quickly. Universal service provision is key, and there are certainly opportunities to strengthen universal healthcare in many countries. However, at the most fundamental level, it requires a reduction in inequality. The most effective way to achieve this is for governments to strengthen progressive taxation, with the proceeds redistributed through the welfare system. Over the medium term, the provision of adequate public housing and the strengthening of labour laws that protect workers will also be critical.[27]

Step 8: Have national conversations about difficult issues

As we put ourselves back together after the disruption of a once-in-a-generation event, we will have a unique opportunity to give meaningful consideration to the future we would like to create. We've seen that in some instances, crisis has led to the resolution of long-standing and painful national schisms. In Aceh or Germany, recovery was not truly possible until major divisions were reconciled.

Every country has cleavages, and the COVID-19 recovery won't be a panacea. Yet there is value in confronting the divisions that are likely to hinder recovery. Australia, for example, will forgo major economic opportunities associated with decarbonisation until it is able to resolve the highly polarised, decades-long bitterness associated with energy and climate policy. Deep rifts in the United Kingdom over the desirability of social change risk causing decision paralysis or 'continual reversals in public policy' that deter business investment and hinder recovery.[28] To truly enable a strong recovery, national leaders have a responsibility to facilitate open, participative discussions about the future, constructively engaging those on both sides of the divide.

Step 9: Prepare for future pandemics

This will not be the last pandemic. As we recover, it's important we don't forget the lessons we have only just learnt. By taking prevention, preparedness and response seriously, we can be in a stronger position the next time we're faced with a global health emergency.

Given how interconnected the world is, we undoubtedly need better cooperation among nations. The World Health Organization (WHO) is the best multilateral body to coordinate this, and it needs to be defended, strengthened and revitalised. One of the major factors in the severity of the COVID-19 pandemic was that much of the world ignored the WHO's warnings when it declared a 'public health emergency of international concern' on 30 January 2020. Few countries commenced testing, tracing and social distancing, and as a result, six to eight weeks later the virus had spread around the world. The World Health Assembly – the governing body of the WHO – meets annually to determine the organisation's policies. As it makes recommendations for reform following COVID-19, it will be important for countries to act on this advice.[29]

One issue the WHO – and individual nations – will need to grapple with is travel bans. While the WHO has long maintained that travel bans are ineffective, there is a growing evidence base showing that stopping travel can prevent the spread of viruses. Bans are more likely to be effective if decisions are made quickly and apply broadly, rather than targeting specific countries ('because the virus spreads so quickly, you have to assume the virus has already spread to other countries', wrote the authors of a recent academic paper).[30] As Professor Peter Doherty notes in the chapter on pandemic, a global agreement that requires countries to notify the WHO of new pathogens and rapidly shut down air travel would be wise.

After countries conduct post-pandemic reviews, a slew of areas for improvement at the national level will be identified. Countries need to be better equipped with stockpiles of personal protective equipment and medical supplies; hospitals will need to have more isolation wards and ventilators; and affordable healthcare will need to be made available to all, so that people don't deny themselves much-needed medical treatment due to fears about cost. Countries must take seriously the lessons of COVID-19 and prioritise preparedness.

Step 10: Prepare for other crises

COVID-19 has shown us just how vulnerable we are to crises. With floods, storms, droughts and fires all likely to become more severe and frequent (and earthquakes, tsunamis and volcanic eruptions always possible), we need to plan for shocks of all sorts, not just pandemics. COVID-19 is a reminder to step up preparedness now, rather than waiting for the next crisis to hit. The cost of preparing for crisis is far outweighed by the potential cost of disaster.

Government economic stimulus is an opportunity to invest in improving resilience. For example, better data and analysis will underpin improvements in early warning systems that give greater notice of storms or heatwaves, enabling communities to prepare. Ensuring that building codes provide for housing that can withstand flooding, storms or fires will be important in a world shaped by climate change, along with reconsideration of the insurance arrangements that need be in place to support vulnerable populations.

ROADMAP IN ACTION: MELBOURNE, AUSTRALIA

The suggestions outlined in this chapter provide the framework for our recovery. But what would this look like in practice?

The City of Melbourne, where I work, has framed its recovery efforts broadly along these lines. With the state and national governments providing most of the money for economic stimulus, the city's initial focus was on public health and wellbeing. It deployed teams of cleaners to sanitise frequently touched surfaces and reassure people that the central business district was safe. It worked with the state government to provide safe accommodation for people experiencing homelessness. And it rolled out a rapid program of public works, including separated bicycle lanes, to provide additional safe transport options.

Lord mayor Sally Capp explains that it also sought to respond to the crisis by 'putting in place a reactivation and recovery program to save jobs and protect vulnerable residents, foreign students, and our hospitality, retail and creative sectors'.[31] Businesses were offered funding and advice, enabling many to develop new business models or change their operations to be COVID-safe. International students were issued food vouchers. Artists and arts organisations were supported with grants.

When the easing of health restrictions allowed, the focus shifted to reactivating the central business district, giving people a reason to return. The city experimented with a range of interventions. Outdoor dining was dramatically expanded, including into on-street parking spaces. The Melbourne Money scheme encouraged diners back to the city by offering them discounts on their meals. A fulsome program of events was delivered, including 'Urban Blooms', a series of large-scale floral installations, and 'Music in the City', which deployed hundreds of buskers throughout the streets, including internationally renowned performers. Artists were commissioned to design artworks for vacant shops and to develop creative installations for laneways. Once people did start to return to the central city, they discovered it to be refreshed and exciting.

Many of these activities were delivered through a formal partnership with the state government and overseen by an advisory board of representatives from across government, industry and the universities. The *COVID-19 Reactivation and Recovery Plan*, developed through extensive public engagement, provided the framework.

Capp argues that there needs to be a focus on 'regeneration of our city in the medium and long term if Melbourne is to regain its position among the world's most liveable cities, and build confidence about our prospects to encourage ongoing participation and investment'.[32] As a result, the plan also sketched out proposals for the city's longer-term 'regeneration and ongoing resilience'. It included interventions such as 'building a thriving innovation ecosystem', improving 'health, wellbeing and prosperity' through greater inclusiveness, stimulating 'collective action on climate change' and 'strengthening community participation'.[33]

Plans for economic recovery were subsequently developed through an economic development strategy, which seeks to 'build the economy of the future, and attract and retain diverse and high-value jobs for current and future generations'.[34]

Like all of the world's cities, Melbourne has a long way to go in its recovery. However, after lockdowns totalling more than six months, a palpable sense of optimism now pervades central Melbourne, with great anticipation about the potential of the recovery ahead.

A role for all of us

The success of our recovery will depend on the choices we make. Many of these decisions will need to be made by governments. If you're a decision-maker with a state or national government, I hope you find the suggestions in this book useful, and that you're able to shape the direction of recovery using the principles underlying them. If you're in a country where trust in government has increased during the pandemic, I wish you all the best maintaining it through the recovery period. If trust in government has taken a hit in your country, competent and inclusive government leadership during the recovery is just the response needed.

If you work for a local government, you have an important leadership role in your community. By listening to the voices of stakeholders and citizens, you are well placed to assemble the services and resources the recovery needs. The challenge is to partner well with others, including with other levels of government.

But recovery is too important to be left to government alone. We all have a role to play and something to contribute. The best recoveries will be those that we collectively shape, own and drive. Remember what we have learnt during the pandemic – we're all connected, with what each of us does impacting on the lives of others. We've been through a traumatic experience together and are still a bit shaky. Many of us have lost loved ones or jobs, or are still recovering from the virus. Keep an eye on each other's mental health, and be kind – a significant number of us are struggling. If you're an artist, we need you more than ever, to give joy, to help us process what we've just experienced and to bring us together.

We all have a role in influencing government decision-making too. It might not seem like it, but governments do respond to shifting public sentiment. So if government invites participation through community consultation, participate – complete the survey, write a submission, join the workshop. Write to your member of parliament and tell them that withdrawing stimulus too early would be a mistake. Join an environment group and work together to make the case that stimulus should support decarbonisation. Hop on your child's school council or parent–teacher association and advocate for additional investment in education. Working with others who share similar views is a remarkably effective way to have your voice heard. Above all, vote. Every vote has the potential to change the government, and the direction of the country.

Many businesses are still struggling, while others are adapting to new business models. Some small-businessowners have lost everything, some are hanging in there. Still other businesses are booming and new ones forming, possibly in areas not even contemplated before the pandemic. If you're running a business, I wish you all the best. A strong economy and our prosperity depends on your success in growing and employing more people. If your business is doing well, explore how you can contribute, shaping the recovery. Share what you've learnt. Play a role in industry-wide initiatives. Participate in discussions about the future of your city.

All of us have something to contribute to recovery. The best recoveries draw on a large range of voices. If you work for a non-government organisation, you play an important role delivering services or connecting with the community. If you're an academic, your research can help inform the debate about future directions. If you work, you can help your organisation to figure out how it will adjust to the new, post-COVID world. If you're a human being, you matter. What you do influences those around you; the perspectives you bring sway others you interact with. So – very soon – it will be time to try something new, throw off the shackles of the pandemic, celebrate. As it was after the Spanish flu, recovery will be as much a social movement as a government policy. We will make it through and it will be time to dance.

The stories in this book demonstrate that crises do not have to leave a long-term legacy. We can recover. Countries and cities rebuilding from devastation have gone on to create prosperous, exciting futures. The people living in New York or Aceh or South Korea now enjoy a quality of life that far exceeds that pre-crisis. In many cases, countries which experienced a shattering crisis have not merely recovered, but have gone on to lead the world. This should provide us with the confidence that we too can recover and thrive.

History is also strewn with examples of places that failed to recover. They withdrew economic stimulus too early, or held too tightly to their pre-crisis worldview. Embarking on what – for most of us – will be the biggest recovery process of our lifetimes, it's important that we approach it in a considered fashion, learning the lessons of the past.

While the COVID-19 pandemic has been the biggest crisis in a generation, our recovery also represents an enormous opportunity. It has the potential to spark us to renewed prosperity, advance us on a path to net-zero carbon emissions, reduce inequality and strengthen our democracies. Examples from history show that with the right choices, we will go on to create a better, brighter future.

ACKNOWLEDGEMENTS

This book was made possible by contributions from a great many people. I am grateful to the experts, leaders and community members who gave so generously of their time, speaking with me and reviewing drafts. Thank you to Tsung-Mei Cheng, Hon Lianne Dalziel, Laureate Professor Peter Doherty, Dr Caitjan Gainty, Dr Jörg Hardegen, Sybille Hardegen, Professor Tim Hatton, Professor Ulrich Herbert, Professor Kwan S. Kim, Robert Lieber, Dr Kuntoro Mangkusubroto, Harry Masyrafah, Dr Ryan Reynolds, the Hon. Wayne Swan and Tara Tonkings.

Similarly, the manuscript was improved markedly by the perspectives of friends who reviewed draft chapters and provided frank feedback: Dr Alison Bryant-Smith, Mohammad Chaudhury, Andrew Giles MP, David Imber, Julian Littler, Dr Josh Mackie, Katrina McKenzie, Eamon O'Hearn-Large, Shane Potter and Fran Stephen. Any errors or omissions in the book are, of course, my responsibility alone.

The team at Black Inc. were fantastic to work with, enthusiastically supporting this project from the start. Thank you to Sophy Williams, Erin Sandiford, Kate Nash and the rest of the team.

Editor Julia Carlomagno pushed gently but firmly, and was instrumental in drawing this project together in a highly changeable environment. Agent Jeanne Ryckmans has been unwavering.

Although this project was a labour of love completed outside work hours, my pandemic experience has been shared intimately with the team at the City of Melbourne. It has been a real privilege to work alongside such a passionate and professional team, including the lord mayor and a rather impressive group of councillors. They have all influenced the thinking that has found its way into this book.

My family share much of the credit for this book. Completing a project like this while working a busy day job placed enormous demands on them. My wife, Claire, has been my rock. In what can only be described as an act of love, she encouraged and supported me to write this book, despite this already being an absurdly busy chapter of our lives. My kids, Sophie, Genevieve, Charlotte and Alice, have been incredibly patient and have supported each other – and me – through long months of winter lockdowns. My mother-in-law, Colleen Hockley, generously hosted the family over many weekends, leaving me with a quiet house in which to write. Likewise, my mum and dad, Jan and David Wear, hosted me often, allowing me to turn my younger brother's former bedroom into a work space. Their unwavering support throughout my life is the foundation upon which everything else is built.

LIST OF FIGURES

Figure 1: 'Emergency Management in the United States', Federal Emergency Management Agency, Washington, DC, p. 4-2.

Figure 2: U- and W-shaped combined influenza and pneumonia mortality, by age at death, per 100,000 persons in each age group, United States, 1911–1918, in Forrest Linder and Robert Grove, *Vital Statistics Rates in the United States: 1900–1940*, US Government Printing Office, Washington, DC, 1943.

Figure 3: Data drawn from Nicholas le Pan, 'A Visual History of Pandemics', World Economic Forum, 15 March 2020; 'Global HIV and AIDS Statistics – 2020 Fact Sheet', UNAIDS website, accessed 18 June 2021; 'Coronavirus cases', Worldometer website, accessed 18 June 2021.

Figure 4: Unemployment rates between 1890 and 1940 in Timothy Hatton and Mark Thomas, 'Labour Markets in the Interwar Period and Economic Recovery in the UK and the USA', *Oxford Review of Economic Policy*, vol. 26, no. 3, 1 October 2010, Figure 1.

NOTES

Preface

1   'Statement on the Second Meeting on the International Health
     Regulations (2005) Emergency Committee Regarding the Outbreak
     of Novel Coronavirus (2019-nCoV)', World Health Organization,
     Geneva, 30 January 2020.

2   'Pedestrian Counts the Lowest in Decades', Press Release, City of
     Melbourne, 7 August 2020.

3   As at 1 July 2021, Victoria had lost a total of 820 lives to COVID-19;
     see 'Victorian Coronavirus (COVID-19) Data', Department of Health
     and Human Services, 2021.

4   'City of Melbourne Medium-Term Economic Outlook', City of Melb-
     ourne, July 2021, p. 2, www.melbourne.vic.gov.au/SiteCollection
     Documents/medium-term-economic-outlook-report-2021.pdf

Introduction: A Bright Dawn

1   Hal Borland, *Sundial of the Seasons*, Lippincott, Philadelphia, 1964,
     p. 49.

2   Entry for 'crisis', *Merriam-Webster*, accessed 13 February 2021.

3   Entry for 'recovery', *Cambridge Dictionary*, accessed 13 February
     2021.

4   Michael Ungar, *Change Your World: The Science of Resilience and the
     True Path to Success*, Sutherland House, Toronto, 2018, pp. 32–33
     and Friedrich Nietzsche, *Twilight of the Idols* (trans. Duncan Large),
     Oxford University Press, Oxford, 1998, p. 5.

5   Jared Diamond, *Upheaval: How Nations Cope with Crisis and Change*,
     Allen Lane, London, 2019, p. 10.

6   Diamond is alert to these questions and considers some of them on
     pages 53–54 of *Upheaval*.

7   Brian Doolan and George Rutherford, 'How History of Medicine Helps Us Understand COVID-19 Challenges', *Public Health Reports*, vol. 135, no. 6, 5 October 2020, pp. 717–20.

Chapter 1: Pandemic

1   Victor Vaughan's experiences and Spanish influenza figures: Mark Honigsbaum, *The Pandemic Century: A History of Global Contagion from the Spanish Flu to Covid-19*, Penguin Random House, London, 2019, pp. 1–2, 11.

2   Victor Vaughan, *A Doctor's Memories*, Bobbs-Merrill, Indianapolis, 1926, pp. 383–84.

3   Mark Honigsbaum, *The Pandemic Century*, p. 14.

4   ibid., p. 8 and Laura Spinney, *Pale Rider: The Spanish Flu of 1918 and How it Changed the World*, Vintage, London, 2017, p. 4.

5   Mark Honigsbaum, *The Pandemic Century*, p. 3.

6   John Barry, 'The Site of Origin of the 1918 Influenza Pandemic and its Public Health Implications', *Journal of Translational Medicine*, vol. 2, article 3, 20 January 2004.

7   Mark Honigsbaum, *The Pandemic Century*, p. 10.

8   Kenneth C. Davis, 'Philadelphia Threw a WW1 Parade That Gave Thousands of Onlookers the Flu', *Smithsonian Magazine*, 21 September 2018.

9   Mark Honigsbaum, *The Pandemic Century*, p. 26.

10   Cristopher Klein, 'How America Struggled to Bury the Dead During the 1918 Flu Pandemic', *History.com*, 12 February 2020.

11   Mark Honigsbaum, *The Pandemic Century*, p. 35.

12   Kimberley Amadeo, '1920s Economy: What Made the Twenties Roar', *The Balance*, 13 April 2020.

13   Thomas A. Garrett, 'Economic Effects of the 1918 Influenza Pandemic: Implications for a Modern Day Pandemic', Federal Reserve Bank of St Louis, St Louis, 2007, p. 7 and Jerome Rosenberg and Dennis Peck, 'Megadeaths: Individual Reactions and Social Responses to Massive Loss of Life' in Clifton Bryant (ed.), *Handbook of Death and Dying*, Sage, Thousand Oaks, 2003, p. 230.

14   Andrew Noymer and Michel Garenne, 'The 1918 Influenza Epidemic's Effects on Sex Differentials in Mortality in the United States', *Population and Development Review*, vol. 26, no. 3, 27 January 2000, pp. 565–81.

15   Mark Honigsbaum, *The Pandemic Century*, p. 35 and Jeffrey Luck, Peter Gross and William Thompson, 'Observations on Mortality During the 1918 Influenza Pandemic', *Clinical Infectious Diseases*, vol. 33, no. 8, 15 October 2001, pp. 1375–78.

16   Nancy Bristow, '"It's as Bad As Anything Can Be": Patients, Identity
      and the Influenza Pandemic', *Public Health Reports*, vol. 125,
      supplement 3, 1 April 2010, pp. 134–44 and Andrew Noymer and
      Michel Garenne, 'The 1918 Influenza Epidemic's Effects', pp. 565–81.
17   Patt Morrison, 'What the Deadly 1918 Flu Epidemic Can Teach Us
      about Our Coronavirus Reaction', *Gulf News*, 15 March 2020.
18   Judith Landes, 'Poorhouses in America', *Torch Magazine*, Fall 2019,
      pp. 17–21.
19   Mark Honigsbaum, *The Pandemic Century*, pp. 27–28.
20   Soutik Biswas, 'Coronavirus: What India Can Learn from the Deadly
      1918 Flu', *BBC News*, 18 March 2020.
21   Memo to Dr Warren from Dr Armstrong, 2 May 1919, cited in John
      Barry, *The Great Influenza: The Story of the Deadliest Pandemic in
      History*, Viking Penguin, New York, 2004, p. 364.
22   John Barry, *The Great Influenza*, pp. 364–65.
23   Quoted in Richard Collier, *The Plague of the Spanish Lady: The
      Influenza Pandemic of 1918–19*, Athenaeum, New York, 1974,
      p. 266.
24   Laura Spinney, *Pale Rider*, p. 256 and Soutik Biswas, 'Coronavirus'.
25   Laura Spinney quoted in Patt Morrison, 'What the Deadly 1918 Flu
      Epidemic Can Teach Us'.
26   Mark Honigsbaum, *The Pandemic Century*, p. 7.
27   ibid., p. 35.
28   Edwin Jordan, *Epidemic Influenza: A Survey*, American Medical
      Association, Chicago, 1927 and John Barry, *The Great Influenza*,
      p. 396.
29   Nina Strochlic and Riley Champine, 'How Some Cities "Flattened the
      Curve" During the 1918 Flu Pandemic', *National Geographic*, 27 March
      2020.
30   Robert Barro, José F. Ursúa and Joanna Weng, 'The Coronavirus and
      the Great Influenza Pandemic: Lessons from the "Spanish flu" for the
      Coronavirus's Potential Effects on Mortality and Economic Activity',
      Working Paper 26866, National Bureau of Economic Research,
      Cambridge, March 2020.
31   Cited in James Grant, *The Forgotten Depression: 1921: The Crash That
      Cured Itself*, Simon & Schuster, New York, 2014, p. 70.
32   Andrew Noymer and Michel Garenne, 'The 1918 Influenza Epidemic's
      Effects', pp. 565–81.
33   US Department of Commerce, 'United States Summary: 2010:
      Population and Housing Unit Counts', 2010 Census of Population
      and Housing, US Government Printing Office, Washington, DC,
      September 2012, p. 14.

34   In 1920, 25.6 per cent of employed women worked in white-collar office jobs: 'Women in the Workplace (Issue)', Encyclopedia.com, 30 September 2020.

35   Linda Gordon, 'The Politics of Birth Control, 1920–1940: The Impact of Professionals', *International Journal of Health Services*, vol. 5, no. 2, 1975, pp. 253–77.

36   Ben Johnson, 'Bright Young Things', Historic UK website, accessed 17 June 2021.

37   'Severe Acute Respiratory Syndrome', World Health Organization website, accessed 17 June 2021.

38   Ying-Hen Hsieh et al., 'Sars Outbreak, Taiwan, 2003', *Emerging Infectious Diseases*, vol. 10, no. 2, February 2004, pp. 201–06 and Ying-Hen Hsieh et al., 'Quarantine for SARS, Taiwan', *Emerging Infectious Diseases*, vol. 11, no. 2, February 2005, pp. 278–82.

39   'In Taiwan, Officials Say SARS' Spread is Diminishing', *The New York Times*, 25 May 2003.

40   Ying-Hen Hsieh et al., 'Sars Outbreak, Taiwan, 2003', p. 201.

41   Louise Watt, 'Taiwan Says It Tried to Warn the World About Coronavirus. Here's What It Really Knew and When', *Time*, 19 May 2020.

42   C. Jason Wang et al., 'Response to COVID-19 in Taiwan: Big Data Analytics, New Technology, and Proactive Testing', *Journal of the American Medical Association*, vol. 323, no. 14, 3 March 2020, pp. 1341–42.

43   'National Health Command Center', Taiwan Centers for Disease Control website, accessed 17 June 2021.

44   C. Jason Wang et al., 'Response to COVID-19 in Taiwan'.

45   Wen-Cheng Chang, 'Taiwan's Fight against COVID-19: Constitutionalism, Laws, and the Global Pandemic', *Verfassungsblog*, 21 March 2020.

46   Numbeo, an online database, ranks Taiwan's healthcare system number one in the world, ahead of South Korea and France: 'Health Care Index by Country 2020 Mid-Year', Numbeo website, accessed 17 June 2021. *CEOWorld Magazine*'s healthcare index also ranks Taiwan's healthcare system first, ahead of South Korea and Japan: Sophie Ireland, 'Revealed: Countries with the Best Healthcare Systems 2019', *CEOWorld Magazine*, 5 August 2019.

47   Hui-Yun Kao et al., 'Taiwan's Experience in Hospital Preparedness and Response for Emerging Infectious Diseases', *Health Security*, vol. 15, no. 2, 1 April 2017, pp. 175–84.

48   Vincent Yi-Fong Su, 'Masks and Medical Care: Two Keys to Taiwan's Success in Preventing COVID-19 Spread', *Travel Medicine*

and Infectious Diseases, vol. 38, November–December (2020) and Colin Warby and Hsiao-Han Chang, 'Face Mask Use in the General Population and Optimal Resource Allocation During the COVID-19 Pandemic', *Nature Communications*, vol. 11, article 4049, 13 August 2020.

49   Helen Davidson, 'A Victim of Its Own Success: How Taiwan Failed to Plan for a Major COVID Outbreak', *The Guardian*, 7 June 2021.

50   'Coronavirus Cases', Worldometer website.

51   'Taiwan: Coronavirus Cases', ibid.; and Helen Davidson, 'A Victim of Its Own Success'.

52   Jeremiah 9:21, English Standard version.

53   Nicholas le Pan, 'Visualising the History of Pandemics', *Visual Capitalist*, 14 March 2020.

54   World Health Organization, 'What Is a Pandemic?', World Health Organization website, 24 February 2010 and 'Pandemic vs. Endemic vs. Outbreak: Terms to Know', *Medical Xpress*, 15 July 2020.

55   'Challenge Eight: Health Issues', The Millennium Project website, accessed 18 June 2021.

56   R.M. Vourou et al., 'Emerging Zoonoses and Vector-Borne Infections Affecting Humans in Europe', *Epidemiology and Infection*, vol. 135, no. 8, November 2007, p. 17, pp. 1231–47.

57   'Zoonotic Diseases', Centers for Disease Control and Prevention website, accessed 18 June 2021.

58   Angela Betsaida Laguipo, 'How Do Viruses Mutate and Jump to Humans?', *News Medical*, 7 April 2020 and Raina Plowright et al., 'Pathways to Zoonotic Spillover', *Nature Reviews Microbiology* vol. 15, no. 8, August 2007, pp. 502–10.

59   Peter Doherty, 'Lessons from the First Six Months of COVID-19 – Part One', Doherty Institute website, 6 July 2020.

60   Lucy Foster, '5 of the World's Deadliest Infectious Diseases', *World Economic Forum*, 9 April 2020.

61   R.K. Pachauri and L.A. Meyer (eds), 'Climate Change 2014: Synthesis Report', Intergovernmental Panel on Climate Change, Geneva, 2015, p. 69.

62   Mark Honigsbaum, *The Pandemic Century*, pp. xvii–xviii.

63   Laura Spinney, *Pale Rider*, pp. 240–43.

64   Marilyn Field and Harold Shapiro (eds), *Employment and Health Benefits: A Connection at Risk*, National Academies Press, Washington, DC, 1993.

65   Stephen Thacker et al., 'Public Health Surveillance in the United States: Evolution and Challenges', *Morbity and Mortality Weekly Report Supplement*, vol. 61, no. 3, 27 July 2012, pp. 3–9.

66   See for example Holly McLean and Ben Huf, 'Emergency Powers,
      Public Health and COVID-19', Research Paper No. 2, Parliament of
      Victoria, Melbourne, August 2020.

67   See for example 'Advice on the Use of Masks in the Context of
      COVID-19: Interim Guidance', World Health Organization, Geneva,
      6 April 2020 and Holger Schünemann, 'Use of Facemasks During the
      COVID-19 Pandemic', *The Lancet Respiratory Medicine*, vol. 8, no. 10, 3
      August 2020, pp. 954–55.

68   David Shukman, 'Coronavirus: WHO Advises to Wear Masks in Public
      Areas', *BBC News*, 6 June 2020; World Health Organization, 'Advice
      on the Use of Masks in the Context of COVID-19', World Health
      Organization, Geneva, 1 December 2020; and 'Which Countries Have
      Made Wearing Face Masks Compulsory?', *Al Jazeera*, 17 August 2020.

69   Parham Azini et al., 'Mechanistic Transmission Modelling of
      COVID-19 on the Diamond Princess Cruise Ship Demonstrates
      the Importance of Aerosol Transmission', *Proceedings of the National
      Academy of Sciences*, February 2021, vol. 118, no. 8; Benedict Carey
      and James Glanz, 'Aboard the Diamond Princess: A Case Study in
      Aerosol Transmission', *The New York Times*, 30 July 2020; and 'Health
      Authorities Explain How Choir Practice Causes the "Superspread" of
      52 Coronavirus Cases in US Town', *ABC News*, 13 May 2020.

70   Nancy Anoruo, '"Aerosol" vs. "Airborne" vs. "Droplets" amid
      COVID-19: What You Need to Know', *ABC News*, 3 October 2020.

71   Mark Honigsbaum, *The Pandemic Century*, p. xvii.

72   ibid., p. xiv.

73   Ethnic Communities Council of Victoria, 'ECCV Submission,
      Inquiry into the Victorian Government's Response to the COVID-19
      Pandemic', Public Accounts and Estimates Committee, Parliament of
      Victoria, Melbourne, 2020, p. 7.

74   Peter Doherty, 'Lessons From the First Six Months of COVID-19 –
      Part Three', Doherty Institute website, 20 July 2020.

75   Christine Crudo Blackburn et al., 'How the Devastating 1918 Flu
      Pandemic Helped Advance US Women's Rights', *The Conversation*, 1
      March 2018.

76   Norwegian Institute of Public Health, '1918 Influenza Pandemic
      (Spanish flu): Large Differences in Mortality between Urban and
      Isolated Rural Areas,' *ScienceDaily*, 27 April and Svenn-Erik Mamelund,
      'Geography May Explain Adult Mortality from the 1918–20 Influenza
      Pandemic', *Epidemics*, vol. 3, no. 1, March 2011, pp. 46–60.

77   Qiang Huang et al., 'Urban-Rural Differences in COVID-19 Exposures
      and Outcomes in the South: A Preliminary Analysis of South Carolina',
      PLOS ONE, vol. 16, no. 2, 3 February 2021.

78 Catherine Brinkley, 'How Pandemics Have Changed American Cities – Often for the Better', *The Conversation*, 18 May 2020.

79 Margaret Campbell, 'What Tuberculosis Did for Modernism: The Influence of a Curative Environment on Modernist Design and Architecture', *Medical History*, vol. 49, no. 4, 1 October 2005, pp. 464–88 and Norman Foster, 'The Pandemic Will Accelerate the Evolution of Our Cities', *The Guardian*, 25 September 2020.

80 Richard Florida, 'How Life in Our Cities Will Look After the Coronavirus Pandemic', *Foreign Policy*, 1 May 2020.

81 Jiajia Chen et al., 'Long Term Outcomes in Survivors of Epidemic Influenza A (H7N9) Virus Infection', *Scientific Reports*, vol. 7, article 1725, 8 December 2017 and Charles-Edouard Luyt et al., 'Long-Term Outcomes of Pandemic 2009 Influenza A (H1N1)-Associated Severe ARDS', *Chest*, vol. 142, no. 3, 2012, pp. 583–92.

82 Edwin Jordan, *Epidemic Influenza*, pp. 278–80.

83 Leah Beauchamp et al., 'Parkinsonism as a Third Wave of the COVID-19 Pandemic?', *Journal of Parkinsons Disease*, vol. 10, no. 4, pp. 1343–53, 27 October 2020 and Masashi Mizuguchi, 'Influenza Encephalopathy and Related Neuropsychiatric Syndromes' *Influenza* vol. 7, supplement 3, 12 November 2013, p. 67.

84 Haeman Jang et al., 'Viral Parkinsonism', *Biochimica et Biophysica Acta*, vol. 1792, no. 7, July 2009, pp. 714–21 and Leah Beauchamp et al., 'Parkinsonism as a Third Wave of the COVID-19 Pandemic?'.

85 Ed Yong, 'Long-Haulers are Redefining COVID-19', *The Atlantic*, 19 August 2020.

86 Svenn-Erik Mamelund, 'The Impact of Influenza on Mental Health in Norway, 1872–1929' Workshop, Carlsberg Academy, Copenhagen, May 2010.

87 Nader Salari, 'Prevalence of Stress, Anxiety, Depression Among the General Population During the COVID-19 Pandemic: A Systematic Review and Meta-Analysis' *Globalization and Health*, vol. 16, article 57, 6 July 2020.

88 'Additional COVID-19 Mental Health Support', Press Release, Minister for Health, 2 August 2020.

89 COVID-19 Disrupting Mental Health Services in Most Countries, WHO Survey', Press Release, World Health Organization, 5 October 2020.

90 Kim Usher et al., 'Family Violence and COVID-19: Increased Vulnerability and Reduced Options for Support', *International Journal of Mental Health Nursing*, vol. 29, no. 4, pp. 549–52 and Amanda Taub, 'A New COVID-19 Crisis: Domestic Abuse Rises Worldwide' *The New York Times*, 6 April 2020.

91 'COVID-19: A Global Perspective', 2020 Goalkeepers Report, Bill and Melinda Gates Foundation, Seattle, September 2020, p. 14.

92 'Pandemic Influenza Preparedness and Response', World Health Organization, Geneva, 2009, pp. 47–48.

93 Peter Doherty, 'Lessons Learned from the First Six Months of COVID-19 – Part Three'.

94 Peter Doherty, 'Lessons Learned from the First Six Months of COVID-19 – Part Two', Doherty Institute website, 13 July 2020.

95 Kelly Pyrek, '100 Years After the Spanish flu: Lessons Learned and Challenges for the Future', *Infection Control Today*, 10 October 2018.

96 'The Neglected Dimension of Global Security: A Framework to Counter Infectious Disease Crises', Commission on a Global Health Risk Framework for the Future, Washington, DC, 2016.

97 'Social Determinants of Health', World Health Organization website, accessed 20 June 2021.

98 'COVID-19 Casts Light on Respiratory Health Inequalities', *The Lancet Respiratory Medicine*, vol. 8, no. 8, August 2020, p. 743.

99 Peter Doherty, 'Lessons Learned from the First Six Months of COVID-19 – Part Three'.

100 Johan Mackenbach, 'Socioeconomic Inequalities in Health in High-Income Countries: The Facts and the Options', Roger Detels et al. (eds), *Oxford Textbook of Global Public Health*, vol. 1, 6th edition, Oxford University Press, Oxford, 2015.

101 As at 27 July 2021, the United States, Brazil, Mexico and Peru had experienced 1.612 million deaths, which represented 39 per cent of deaths from COVID-19: 'Coronavirus Cases', Worldometer website, accessed 27 July 2021. These countries all have a Gini income coefficient of more than forty, making them among the most unequal of the developed countries: 'Gini Index (World Bank Estimate)', World Bank website, accessed 27 July 2021.

102 Cheng Ting-Fang et al., 'Taiwan GDP Growth Outpaces China for First Time in Three Decades', *Nikkei Asia*, 29 January 2021.

Chapter 2: Recession

1 Chicago restaurant in Louise Armstrong, *We Too Are the People*, Little Brown & Company, Boston, 1938, p. 10; rotten vegetables and weeds in Harald Ware and Lement Harris, 1932, cited in William E. Leuchtenburg, *Franklin D. Roosevelt and the New Deal 1932–1940*, Harper & Row, New York, 1963, p. 3; and tent families in correspondence from James Myers to Olive Van Horn, 16 December 1931, cited in ibid., p. 1.

2   Lack of gas and electricity in ibid., pp. 1, 19; cave couple in Joseph
    Mitchell, *Up in the Old Hotel*, Vintage, London, 2012, pp. 136–43;
    Cameroon efforts in Samuel Freedman, *The Inheritance: How Three
    Families and the American Political Majority Moved from Left to
    Right*, Touchstone, New York, 1996, p. 50; emigration in William E.
    Leuchtenburg, *Franklin D. Roosevelt and the New Deal*, p. 28.

3   James Gregory, 'Hoovervilles and Homelessness', *The Great Depression
    in Washington State* website, accessed 20 June 2021.

4   Nicholas Crafts and Peter Fearon, 'Lessons from the 1930s Great
    Depression', *Oxford Review of Economic Policy*, vol. 26, no. 3, 2010, pp.
    285–337 and *Literary Digest*, vol. 113, 7 May 1932, p. 10.

5   John Steinbeck, *The Grapes of Wrath*, Penguin, New York, 1992,
    p. 349.

6   William E. Leuchtenburg, *Franklin D. Roosevelt and the New Deal*,
    p. 26.

7   Federal Reserve Board, *Federal Reserve Bulletin*, United States
    Government Printing Office, Washington, DC, September 1932 and
    William E. Leuchtenburg, *Franklin D. Roosevelt and the New Deal*,
    p. 19.

8   Savings and job losses in Melissa de Witte, 'The Great Depression
    Demonstrated the Indispensable Role of Government, Says Stanford
    Scholar', *Stanford News*, 29 April 2020 and ibid.; employment and
    output figures in ibid., p. 291, and Nicholas Crafts and Peter Fearon,
    'Lessons from the 1930s Great Depression', *Oxford Review of Economic
    Policy*, vol. 26, no. 3, p. 286.

9   ibid., p. 297.

10 'The Depression', *Newsweek*, 19 December 1999 and 'Miscellany', *Time*,
    23 December 1929.

11 Adrian Mastracci, 'The Great Crash of 1929, Some Key Dates' *Financial
    Post*, 24 October 2011.

12 Chistina Romer, 'The Great Crash and the Onset of the Great
    Depression', Working Paper No. 2630, National Bureau of Economic
    Research, Cambridge, MA, June 1988.

13 Roger Lowenstein, 'Economic History Repeating', *The Wall Street
    Journal*, 13 January 2015 and World Bank Group, 'Global Economic
    Prospects', International Bank for Reconstruction and Development
    and the World Bank, Washington, DC, January 2021, p. 3.

14 Christina Romer, 'Great Depression', *Britannica*, last modified 10
    September 2020.

15 Marin Carcasson, 'Herbert Hoover and the Presidential Campaign of
    1932: The Failure of Apologia', *Presidential Studies Quarterly*, vol. 28,
    no. 2, Spring 1998, pp. 350–53.

16   '1932 Presidential General Election Results', Dave Leip's Atlas of
      US Elections website, accessed 22 June 2021 and James Macgregor
      Burns, *Roosevelt: The Lion and the Fox,* Easton Press, New York, 1956,
      p. 139.

17   William E. Leuchtenburg, *Franklin D. Roosevelt and the New Deal,*
      pp. 41–62.

18   Jonathan Grossman, 'Fair Labor Standards Act of 1938: Maximum
      Struggle for a Minimum Wage', US Department of Labor website,
      accessed 21 June 2021.

19   Lary DeWitt, 'Luther Gulick Memorandum Re: Famous FRR Quote',
      Research Note #23, US Social Security website, 21 July 2005.

20   David Kennedy, *Freedom from Fear: The American People in Depression
      and War 1929–1945,* Oxford University Press, New York, 1999,
      p. 252.

21   William E. Leuchtenburg, *Franklin D. Roosevelt and the New Deal,*
      pp. 32–33.

22   Gauti Eggertsson, 'Great Expectations and the End of the Depression',
      Staff Report No 234, Federal Reserve Bank of New York, New York,
      2005.

23   Chang-Tai Hsieh, 'When the North Last Headed South: Revisiting
      the 1930s: Comment and Discussion', *Brookings Papers on Economic
      Activity,* Fall 2009, p. 273.

24   Roosevelt cited in Leonard Sloane, 'Personal Finance: Gold Danger',
      The New York Times, 23 December 1974; criticism detailed in Gary
      Richardson et al., 'Roosevelt's Gold Program', Federal Reserve History
      website, accessed 21 June 2021.

25   Cited in US Senate Committee on Agriculture and Forestry, 'Causes of
      the Loss of Export Trade and the Means of Recovery: Hearings Before
      the Committee on Agriculture and Forestry, Seventy-Fourth Congress,
      First Session, on Jan. 30, 31 Feb. 1, 2, 4–7, 1935', US Government
      Printing Office, Washington, DC, 1935, p. 247.

26   Gary Richardson et al., 'Roosevelt's Gold Program', Federal Reserve
      History website, accessed 21 June 2021 and Andrew Jalil and Gisela
      Rua, 'Inflation Expectations and Recovery from the Depression in
      1933: Evidence from the Narrative Record', Finance and Economics
      Discussion Series 2015-029, Board of Governors of the Federal
      Reserve System, Washington, DC, 2015.

27   Nicholas Crafts and Peter Fearon, 'Lessons from the 1930s Great
      Depression', *Oxford Review of Economic Policy,* vol. 26, no. 3, p. 297;
      Patricia Waiwood, 'Recession of 1937–38', Federal Reserve History
      website, accessed 21 June 2021; and Christina Romer, 'The Lessons of
      1937', *The Economist,* 18 June 2009.

28 Eugene Smolensky and Robert Plotnick, 'Inequality and Poverty in the United States: 1900 to 1990', Institute for Research on Poverty Discussion Paper No. 998–93, University of Wisconsin-Madison, Madison, 1993, p. 22.

29 David Weiman, 'Imagining a World without the New Deal', *The Washington Post*, 12 August 2011.

30 Gavin Wright, 'The New Deal and the Modernization of the South', *Federal History*, no. 2, January 2010, p. 58.

31 David Kennedy, 'What the New Deal Did', *Political Science Quarterly*, vol. 124, no. 2, Summer 2009, p. 267.

32 Richard Davenport-Hines, 'Seven Things You May Not Know about John Maynard Keynes', *The Guardian*, 5 March 2015.

33 Robert Skidelsky, 'Examining Keynes' Legacy, 80 Years On', *The Guardian*, 26 February 2016.

34 US GDP and output in Robert Rich, 'The Great Recession', Federal Reserve History website, 22 November 2013; US unemployment in Federal Reserve Bank of St Louis, 'All Employees, Total Nonfarm', FRED website, accessed 21 June 2021; Baltic states' decline in Karsten Staehr, 'Austerity in the Baltic States During the Global Financial Crisis', *Intereconomics*, vol. 48, no. 5, 2013, pp. 293–302; Russian economy in Zeljko Bogetic, 'Russia: Reform after the Great Recession', Carnegie Endowment for International Peace website, 30 March 2010; and Spain and Greece in 'Unemployment, Total (% of Total Labor Force) (modeled ILO estimate)', World Bank website, 29 January 2021.

35 Ayhan Kose and Marco Terrones, *Collapse and Revival: Understanding Global Recessions and Recoveries*, International Monetary Fund, Washington, DC, 2015, p. 4.

36 'GDP Growth (Annual %)' World Bank website, accessed 21 June 2021 and Heng Swee Keat, 'The Global Financial Crisis: Impact on Asia and Policy Challenges Ahead' in Reuven Glick and Mark Spiegel (eds), 'Asia and the Global Financial Crisis', Proceedings of the Asia Economic Policy Conference, Santa Barbara, 19–20 October 2009, p. 269.

37 Eliza Mills, '5 Things You Need to Know About Lehman Brothers', *Marketplace*, 10 September 2018 and 'GDP (Current US$)', World Bank website, accessed 3 April 2021.

38 John Kehoe, 'The GFC Remembered: Ten Years Ago It Was All About Saving the Banks', *The Australian Financial Review*, 5 October 2018.

39 ibid.

40 'Cash Rate Target', Reserve Bank of Australia website, accessed 21 June 2021.

41   Clare Newton and Lena Gan, 'Revolution or Missed Opportunity?', ArchitectureAU website, 23 April 2012.

42   The Auditor-General, 'Home Insulation Program: Department of the Environment, Water, Heritage and the Arts; Department of Climate Change and Energy Efficiency; Medicare Australia', Audit Report No. 12, Australian National Audit Office, Canberra, 2010, p. 37 and David Uren, 'Twice the Size in a Fraction of the Time: Government Responses to the Global Financial Crisis and COVID-19', United States Studies Centre website, 9 April 2020.

43   Wayne Swan, *The Good Fight: Six Years, Two Prime Ministers and Staring Down the Great Recession*, Allen & Unwin, Sydney, 2014, p. 140.

44   Ian Hanger, 'Report of the Royal Commission into the Home Insulation Program', Commonwealth of Australia, Canberra, 2014.

45   Eric Ellis, 'Finance Minister of the Year 2011: Swan Confounds His Domestic Sceptics,' *Euromoney*, 20 September 2011.

46   'Unemployment, Total', and Steve Morling and Tony McDonald, 'The Australian Economy and the Global Downturn Part 2: The Key Quarters', *Economic Roundup*, no. 2, 15 August 2011.

47   Mario González-Corzo and Vassilios Gargalas, 'Recent Trends in Employment and Wages in New York City's Finance and Insurance Sector', *Monthly Labor Review*, April 2019.

48   Madina Toure, 'NYC Sees Record Job Growth since End of Great Recession', *Observer*, 26 February 2018.

49   'Report of the Finance Division on the Fiscal 2021 Preliminary Plan, Capital Plan Overview and the Fiscal 2020 Preliminary Mayor's Management Report for the New York City Economic Development Corporation', The Council of the City of New York, New York, 11 March 2020, p. 2.

50   Bruce Berg, *New York City Politics: Governing Gotham*, Rutgers University Press, New York, 2007, pp. 32–41.

51   Chris Mitchell, 'The Killing of Murder', *New York*, 4 January 2008.

52   Patrick McGeehan, 'City Seeks Partner to Open Graduate School of Engineering', *The New York Times*, 16 December 2010 and Winnie Hu, 'This Graduate School Helped Make New York Appealing to Amazon', *The New York Times*, 17 December 2018.

53   'Cornell Tech Announces Winners of 2020 Startup Awards', Press Release, Cornell Tech, 15 May 2020.

54   David Lipke, 'The Bloomberg Effect: Fashion and the Mayor', *WWD*, 25 November 2013; Alison Gregor, 'Bringing Laboratory Space Back to New York', *The New York Times*, 21 February 2007; and 'Mayor Bloomberg Launches New Initiatives to Help New York City Continue as the Global Media Capital in the Digital Age', European American

Chamber of Commerce website, 1 October 2013; 'Mayor Bloomberg and NYC & Company Announce "Neighborhood X Neighborhood" Campaign Inviting Travelers to Explore NYC's Five Boroughs', City of New York website, 13 March 2013.

55 Scott Stringer, 'New York City's Economy Has Become More Diversified: So What?', New York City Comptroller, New York, December 2017, p. 15.

56 ibid.

57 John Irons, 'Economic Scarring: The Long-Term Impacts of the Recession', EPI Briefing Paper No. 243, Economic Policy Institute, Washington, DC, 30 September 2009.

58 Katherine Sell et al., *The Effect of Recession on Child Well-Being: A Synthesis of the Evidence by PolicyLab, The Children's Hospital of Philadelphia*, The Children's Hospital of Philadelphia Research Institute, Philadelphia, November 2010, p. 17.

59 Hannes Schwandt, 'Recession Graduates: The Long-Lasting Effects of an Unlucky Draw', Policy Brief, Stanford Institute for Economic Policy Research website, April 2019.

60 Philip Oreopolous et a., 'The Intergenerational Effects of Worker Displacement', Working Paper No. 11587, National Bureau of Economic Research, Cambridge, MA, August 2005.

61 John Irons, 'Economic Scarring'.

62 Jeffrey Haydu, *Between Craft and Class: Skilled Workers and Factory Politics in the United States and Britain 1890–1922*, University of California Press, Berkeley, 1991, pp. 27–30.

63 Stefan Gerlach and Peter Kugler, 'The Sterling-Dollar Rate and Expectations of the Return to Gold in the Early 1920s', *VoxEU*, 12 August 2015.

64 Timothy Hatton and Mark Thomas, 'Labour Markets in the Interwar Period', pp. 463–85.

65 Stephen Broadberry, 'The Emergence of Mass Unemployment: Explaining Macroeconomic Trends in Britain During the Trans-World War I Period', *Economic History Review*, vol. 43, no. 2, May 1990, pp. 272–82.

66 Ross Gittins, 'Now We're Planning Plan C to End Wage Stagnation', *The Sydney Morning Herald*, 3 May 2021.

67 'Hitler into Power 1929–1934', BBC Bitesize website, accessed 22 June 2021; 'Research Starters: Worldwide Deaths in World War II', The National World War II Museum New Orleans website, accessed 22 June 2021; and 'Documenting Numbers of Victims of the Holocaust and Nazi Persecution', United States Holocaust Memorial Museum website, accessed 22 June 2021.

68   Alan de Bromhead et al., 'Right-Wing Political Extremism in the Great Depression', *VoxEU*, 27 February 2012.

69   Emma Newburger and Tucker Higgins, 'Secretive Cabals, Fear of Immigrants and the Tea Party: How the Financial Crisis Led to the Rise of Donald Trump', *CNBC*, 11 September 2018.

70   Nicholas Sargen, 'How the Biden Administration Plans to Tackle Income Inequality', *Forbes*, 23 December 2020.

71   'The Pandemic Has Caused the World's Economies to Diverge', *The Economist*, 8 October 2020.

72   'Fiscal Monitor: A Fair Shot', International Monetary Fund, Washington, DC, April 2021.

73   OECD, 'Strengthening the Recovery: The Need for Speed', OECD Economic Outlook, Interim Report, OECD Publishing, Paris, March 2021, p. 4.

74   'World Economic Outlook: Managing Divergent Recoveries', International Monetary Fund, Washington, DC, April 2021, p. 129.

75   OECD, 'Strengthening the Recovery', p. 4.

76   Christina D. Romer, 'The Aftermath of Financial Crises: Each Time Really is Different', Sir John Hicks Lecture in Economic History, Oxford University, 28 April 2015, p. 3.

77   ibid., p. 25.

78   Ziyad Cassim et al., 'The $10 Trillion Rescue: How Governments Can Deliver Impact' McKinsey website, 5 June 2020.

79   Wayne Swan, *The Good Fight*, pp. 105–06.

80   Olivier Coibion et al., 'How did U.S. Consumers Use Their Stimulus Payments?', Working Paper 27693, National Bureau of Economic Research, August 2020 and 'How Did Americans Use Their Coronavirus Stimulus Cheques?', *The Economist*, 2 September 2020.

81   'Victoria to Employ Thousands of Tutors to Help Students Catch Up after Coronavirus Lockdown', *ABC News*, 13 October 2020.

82   Christina D. Romer, 'Lessons from the Great Depression for Economic Recovery in 2009'. Speech to the Brookings Institution, Washington, DC, 9 March 2009, p. 5.

83   Ellie McLachlan and Shay Waraker, 'Quantitative Easing: What Is It?', Canstar website, 5 November 2020.

84   Christina Romer, 'Lessons from the Great Depression', p. 8.

85   Andrew Gamble, 'The Economy', *Parliamentary Affairs*, vol. 68, no. 1, September 2015, p. 159 and John Van Reenen, 'Austerity in the UK: Past, Present and Future', Politics and Policy blog, London School of Economics website, 11 March 2015.

86   Christina Romer, 'Lessons from the Great Depression', pp. 10–11.

87   'World Economic Outlook: Managing Divergent Recoveries', p. 3, Figure 1.4.

88   Guillaume Chabert et al., 'Funding the Recovery of Low-Income Countries After COVID', *IMF Blog*, 5 April 2021.

89   Patrice Ollivaud and David Turner, 'The Effect of the Global Financial Crisis on OECD Potential Output', OECD Economics Department Working Paper No 1166, OECD Publishing, Paris, 2014.

90   OECD, 'Continued Slowdown in Productivity Growth Weighs Down on Living Standards', Press Release, OECD website, 18 May 2017 and Stephen Kennedy, 'Policy and the Evolution of Uncertainty', Speech to Australian Business Economists, 5 November 2020.

91   'Report on the Strategic Response: Strategies for Aligning Stimulus Measures with Long-Term Growth', Meeting of the Council at Ministerial Level, 24–25 June 2009, OECD, Paris, June 2009.

92   Jiawen Tang and Tania Begazo, 'Digital Stimulus Packages: Lessons Learned and What's Next', *World Bank Blogs*, 17 December 2020 and Romain Dilley, 'France to Spend $8.4 Billion on Digital as Part of Stimulus Plan', *TechCrunch*, 4 September 2020.

93   'Report on the Strategic Response', pp. 3–4.

94   Christoph Steitz and Edward Taylor, 'Germany Will Require All Petrol Stations to Provide Electric Car Charging', *Reuters*, 4 June 2020.

95   Cameron Hepburn et al., 'Will COVID-19 Fiscal Recovery Packages Accelerate or Retard Progress on Climate Change?', *Oxford Review of Economic Policy*, vol. 36, no. 1, 8 May 2020, pp. 359–81.

96   Lizbeth Cohen, 'The Lessons of the Great Depression', *The Atlantic*, 17 May 2020.

97   ibid.

Chapter 3: Natural Disaster

1   Opening description based on information in Jose Borrero et al., 'Northern Sumatra Field Survey after the 2004 Great Sumatra Earthquake and Indian Ocean Tsunami', *Earthquake Spectra*, vol. 22, no. 3S, 1 June 2006, pp. 96–97; 'Tsunami Survivor: Allah Protected the Mosques', *Ynetnews*, 23 December 2014; David Lawrence, 'The Tsunami Ship: Offbeat Tourism in Aceh, Indonesia', *World Bank Blogs*, 27 June 2012; Candida Beveridge, 'The Boat That Landed on a Roof and Saved 59 People', *BBC News*, 24 December 2014; and Jose Borrero et al., 'Northern Sumatra Field Survey', p. 96.

2   M.N.A. Halif and S.N. Sabki, 'The Physics of Tsunami: Basic Understanding of the Indian Ocean Tsunami', *American Journal of Applied Sciences*, vol. 2, no. 8, 2005, p. 1191.

3   '2004 Indian Ocean Earthquake and Tsunami: Facts, FAQs, and How to Help', World Vision website, accessed 22 June 2021 and Stephanie Pappas, 'Top 11 Deadliest Natural Disasters in History', *LiveScience*, 2 April 2018.

4   Suahasil Nazara and Budy Resosudarmo, 'Aceh-Nias Reconstruction and Rehabilitation: Progress and Challenges at End of 2006', ADB Discussion Paper No. 70, Asian Development Bank Institute, Tokyo, 2007.

5   Jose Borrero et al., 'Northern Sumatra Field Survey', p. 97 and 'Tsunami Wave Run-Ups: Indian Ocean – 2004', National Oceanic and Atmospheric Administration website, accessed 22 June 2021.

6   Jason Burke, 'Religious Aid Groups Try to Convert Victims', *The Guardian*, 16 January 2005.

7   See for example Laurie Johnson and Robert Olshansky, *After Great Disasters: An In-Depth Analysis of How Six Countries Managed Community Recovery*, Lincoln Institute of Land Policy, Cambridge, MA, 2017, p. 230.

8   Bappenas and World Bank, 'Indonesia: Damage and Loss Assessment, the December 26, 2004 Natural Disaster', World Bank Group, Washington, DC, 2005, pp. iii, 14, 94.

9   'Master Plan for the Rehabilitation and Reconstruction of the Regions and Communities of the Province of Nanggroe Aceh Darussalam and the Islands of Nias, Province of North Sumatra', Republic of Indonesia, Jakarta, 2005, pp. iii–2.

10   Laurie Johnson and Robert Olshansky, *After Great Disasters*, pp. 221, 222.

11   ibid., p. 222.

12   'Rebuilding a Better Aceh and Nias: Stocktaking of the Reconstruction Effort', Brief for the Coordination Forum Aceh and Nias (CFAN), October 2005, World Bank, Washington, DC, 2005, pp. xiv, 99.

13   'Indonesia Agrees Aceh Peace Deal', *BBC News*, 17 July 2005.

14   Arno Waizenegger and Jennifer Hyndman, 'Two Solitudes: Post-Tsunami and Post-Conflict Aceh', *Disasters*, vol. 34, no. 3, July 2010, pp. 787–808.

15   'Indonesia Agrees Aceh Peace Deal'.

16   See 'Build Back Better: Joe Biden's Jobs and Economic Recovery Plan for Working Families', Biden Harris campaign website, accessed 6 December 2020; 'The Campaign for a Coronavirus Recovery Plan That Builds Back Better', Build Back UK website, accessed 6 December 2020; Anna North, 'New Zealand Prime Minister Jacinda Ardern Wins Historic Reelection', *Vox*, 17 October 2020; 'Building Back

Better: A Sustainable, Resilient Recovery After COVID-19', OECD, 5 June 2020; and 'Sendai Framework for Disaster Risk Reduction 2015–2030', United Nations, Geneva, 2015.

17   'Kuntoro Mangkusubroto', Asia Game Changers Awards website, accessed 22 June 2021 and 'U.N. Asks Bill Clinton to Be Envoy to Tsunami Region', *The New York Times*, 1 February 2005.

18   Sonali Prasad, '15 Years After Tsunami, Aceh Reckons with an Inconsistent Fisheries Recovery', *Mongabay*, 15 September 2019 and 'Aceh Ranks One Province with Most Poor People on the Island of Sumatra, Affected by COVID-19', *VOI*, 17 February 2021.

19   Harry Masyrafah and Jock McKeon, 'Post-Tsunami Aid Effectiveness in Aceh: Proliferation and Coordination in Reconstruction', Working Paper No 6, Wolfensohn Center for Development, Washington, DC, November 2008, p. 40.

20   Laurie Johnson and Robert Olshansky, *After Great Disasters*, pp. 235–46.

21   'Story: Feat of the Daunting Launch', Badan Rehabilitasi dan Rekonstruksi, Banda Aceh, 2009, p. xiii.

22   Gaye Downes and Mark Yetton, 'Pre-2010 Historical Seismicity Near Christchurch, New Zealand: The 1869 MW 4.7–4.9 Christchurch and 1870 MW 5.6–5.8 Lake Ellesmere Earthquakes', *New Zealand Journal of Geology and Geophysics*, vol. 55, no. 3, 2012, pp. 1–7.

23   'The 1888 North Canterbury Earthquake', *Te Ara: The Encyclopedia of New Zealand*, Ministry for Culture and Heritage Works, Wellington, last modified 1 November 2017 and Daniel Hurst, 'Cathedral No Stranger to Quake Damage', *The Sydney Morning Herald*, 22 February 2011.

24   Laurie Johnson and Robert Olshansky, *After Great Disasters*, p. 59.

25   'February 2011 Christchurch Earthquake', New Zealand History website, accessed 11 April 2021.

26   Helen Goldsworthy, 'Lessons from the February 22nd Christchurch Earthquake', Proceedings of the Australian Earthquake Engineering Society Conference, Barossa Valley, 18–20 November 2011.

27   Laurie Johnson and Robert Olshansky, *After Great Disasters*, p. 61.

28   'Earthquake Glossary', United States Geological Survey website, accessed 22 June 2021.

29   Laurie Johnson and Robert Olshansky, *After Great Disasters*, p. 62.

30   Michele Poole, 'Public Information Management in Christchurch Following the February 2011 Earthquake: Lessons Learned', *Australian Journal of Emergency Manangement*, vol. 27, no. 4, October 2012, pp. 12–13.

31   Laurie Johnson and Robert Olshansky, *After Great Disasters*, p. 65.

32   'From Emergency to Urgency: the Canterbury Earthquake Recovery
      Authority', ANZSOG Case Program, 2016-189.1, Australia New
      Zealand School of Government, Melbourne, p. 4.
33   'Central City Plan: Draft Central City Recovery Plan for Ministerial
      Approval', Christchurch City Council, Christchurch, December 2011.
34   'Christchurch Central Recovery Plan: Te Mahere "Maraka Ōtautahi"',
      Canterbury Earthquake Recovery Authority, Christchurch, July 2012.
35   'Greening the Rubble', Project for Public Spaces website, accessed
      11 April 2021; 'About Life in Vacant Spaces', Life in Vacant Spaces
      website, accessed 11 April 2021; and 'Festa, 19–22 October,
      Christchurch, New Zealand', FESTA website, accessed 11 April 2021.
36   Brett Atkinson, 'Christchurch Revival: Why New Zealand's Comeback
      City Is a Must-See for 2013', Lonely Planet website, 25 October 2012.
37   'Pallet Pavilion', Gap Filler website, accessed 22 June 2021 and 'Cycle-
      Powered Cinema', Gap Filler website, accessed 22 June 2021.
38   'Our Vision', Christchurch City Council website, accessed 22 June
      2021.
39   Steve Meacham, 'Six Years On, a Startlingly Different Christchurch Is
      Rising from the Rubble', *The Australian Financial Review*, 26 July 2017
      and 'Te Pae: Christchurch Convention Centre' website, accessed 4 July
      2021.
40   2018 census in Paul Gorman, 'Christchurch Rising Despite Boom
      Times in Selwyn', *Stuff*, 23 September 2019; Canterbury economy in
      'Canterbury: The Rebuild by the Numbers', Stats NZ, Wellington,
      2018, p. 16; and Christchurch visitors in 'Our Place in the World',
      Annual Review, Christchurch Airport, Christchurch, 2019, pp. 7, 12.
41   'Disaster Risk Management', World Bank website, accessed 22 June
      2021.
42   'The Human Cost of Natural Disasters 2015: A Global Perspective',
      Center for Research on the Epidemiology of Disasters, Brussels, 2015,
      p. 7.
43   Intergovernmental Panel on Climate Change, 'Climate Change 2014:
      Impacts, Adaptation and Vulnerability, Part A Global and Sectoral
      Aspects', Working Group II Contribution to the Fifth Assessment
      Report of the Intergovernmental Panel on Climate Change,
      Cambridge University Press, Cambridge, 2014, p. 47 and 'The Human
      Cost of Natural Disasters 2015', p. 7.
44   Sarah Perkins-Kilpatrick and Sophie Lewis, 'Increasing Trends in
      Regional Heatwaves', *Nature Communications*, vol. 11, article 3357, July
      2020.
45   Joëlle Gergis, 'Yes, Australia is a Land of Flooding Rains. But Climate
      Change Could be Making it Worse' *The Conversation*, 24 March 2021.

46 'The Human Cost of Natural Disasters 2015', p. 7.
47 Intergovernmental Panel on Climate Change, *Managing the Risks of Extreme Events and Disasters to Advance Climate Change Adaptation*, Cambridge University Press, Cambridge, 2012 and *Climate Change 2014*, pp. 21–25.
48 Cited in 'Think 2020's Disasters Are Wild? Experts Say the Worst is Yet to Come', *NBN News*, 10 September 2020.
49 'The Human Cost of Natural Disasters 2015', pp. 28–29, 30.
50 ibid., p. 39.
51 'Economic Losses, Poverty and Disasters 1998–2017', Center for Research on the Epidemiology of Disasters, Brussels, 2018, p. 4.
52 'The Human Cost of Natural Disasters 2015', p. 40.
53 Patrick Webb, 'Food and Nutrition Concerns in Aceh After the Tsunami', *Food and Nutrition Bulletin*, vol. 26, no. 4, 1 December 2005, pp. 394–95.
54 Alice Fothergill and Lori Peek, 'Poverty and Disasters in the United States: A Review of Recent Sociological Findings', *Natural Hazards*, vol. 32, May 2004, pp. 89–110.
55 ibid.
56 Eugenie Rovai, 'The Social Geography of Disaster Recovery: Differential Community Response to the North Coast Earthquakes', *Yearbook of the Association of Pacific Coast Geographers*, vol. 56, 1994, pp. 49–74.
57 Morten Gjerde, 'Building Back Better: Learning from the Christchurch Rebuild', *Procedia Engineering*, vol. 198, 2017, p. 538.
58 Guatemala in Monserrat Bustelo, 'Three Essays on Investments in Children's Human Capital', PHD Dissertation, University of Illinois, Urbana-Champaign, 2011, pp. 1–37; Ethiopia in Stephan Dercon and Catherine Porter, 'Live Aid Revisited: Long-Term Impacts of the 1984 Ethiopian Famine on Children', *Journal of the European Economic Association*, vol. 12, no. 4, 1 August 2014, pp. 927–48; Peru in German Caruso and Sebastian Miller, 'Long Run Effects and Intergenerational Transmission of Natural Disasters: A Case Study on the 1970 Ancash Earthquake', *Journal of Development Economics*, vol. 117, November 2015, pp. 134–50 and Caroline Kousky, 'The Impact of Natural Disasters on Children' *The Future of Children*, vol. 26, no. 1, Spring 2016, pp. 73–92.
59 Intergovernmental Panel on Climate Change, *Climate Change 2014*, p. 548.
60 'Investing in Urban Resilience: Protecting and Promoting Development in a Changing World', World Bank, Washington, DC, 2016, p. 13.

61 ibid.
62 Stephane Hallegatte et al., *Unbreakable: Building the Resilience of the Poor in the Face of Natural Disasters*, World Bank, Washington, DC, 2017.
63 Morten Gjerde, 'Building Back Better', p. 538.
64 'Disaster Risk Management for Health: Overview', Disaster Risk Management for Health Fact Sheets, World Health Organization website, May 2011 and 'Addressing the Mental Health Impacts of Natural Disasters and Climate Change-Related Weather Events' Position Statement 35, Royal Australian and New Zealand College of Psychiatrists website, accessed 22 June 2021.
65 Stephen Platt, 'Factors Affecting the Speed and Quality of Post-Disaster Recovery and Resilience' in Rajesh Rupakhety and Simon Ólafsson (eds), *Earthquake Engineering and Structural Dynamics in Memory of Ragnar Sigbjörnsson*, Springer, Cham, 2018.
66 '10 Management Lessons for Host Governments Coordinating Post-Disaster Reconstruction', Executing Agency for Rehabilitation and Reconstruction (BRR) of Aceh–Nias, Jakarta, 2009, p. 21.
67 ibid., p. 27.
68 Laurie Johnson and Robert Olshansky, *After Great Disasters*, p. 230.
69 '10 Management Lessons for Host Governments', pp. ix, 11–15.
70 ibid., pp. 12–13.
71 'Rekompak: Rebuilding Indonesia's Communities After Disasters', Secretariat of the Multi Donor Fund for Aceh and Nias and Java Reconstruction Fund World Bank, Jakarta, 2012, p. 57.
72 '10 Management Lessons for Host Governments', p. 45.
73 'Guidelines for Community Participation in Disaster Recovery', United Nations Development Program, New York, 2020, p. 5.
74 Laurie Johnson and Robert Olshansky, *After Great Disasters*, p. 325.
75 Amartya Sen, *Poverty and Famines: An Essay on Entitlement and Deprivation*, Oxford University Press, London, 1981.
76 '10 Management Lessons for Host Governments', p. 38.
77 ibid., p. 77.
78 Joanna Norris, cited in 'COVID-19: Lessons from the Christchurch Quakes', *Newsroom*, 17 April 2020 and Joanna Norris, 'NZ Can Learn from Christchurch's Post-Quake Mistakes', *Stuff*, 31 July 2020.
79 ibid.
80 'Christchurch Economic Development Strategy: Realising Our Potential', Christchurch Economic Development Strategy, Christchurch City Council, Christchurch, 2017.
81 'ChristchurchNZ: Annual Review 2019', ChristchurchNZ, Christchurch, 2019, pp. 16–17.

82   Poverty fell to 26.5 per cent in 2006, below the pre-tsunami level:
      'Aceh Poverty Assessment 2008: The Impact of the Conflict, the
      Tsunami and Reconstruction on Poverty in Aceh', World Bank, Jakarta,
      2008, p. 8.

Chapter 4: War

1   Sergey Radchenko, 'Sport and Politics on the Korean Peninsula: North
      Korea and the 1988 Seoul Olympics', Wilson Center website, accessed
      22 June 2021.
2   Olivia Waxman, 'How Drama Between North and South Korea
      Threatened the Olympics 30 Years Ago' *Time*, 8 February 2018.
3   '1988 Summer Olympics'.
4   See Brian Bridges, 'The Seoul Olympics: Economic Miracle Meets the
      World', *The International Journal of the History of Sport*, vol. 25, no. 14,
      2008 and Jarol Manheim, 'Rites of Passage: The 1988 Seoul Olympics
      as Public Diplomacy', *The Western Political Quarterly*, vol. 43, no. 2,
      June 1990, pp. 279–95.
5   Annual growth in Barry Hillenbrand, 'Breaking Into the Big Leagues',
      Time, 12 September 1988, p. 42 and per capita incomes in 'GNI Per
      Capita, Atlas Method (Current US$)', World Bank website, accessed 6
      January 2021.
6   Barry Hillenbrand, 'Breaking Into the Big Leagues', p. 42.
7   While other sources put the death toll at up to 3 million (which
      includes deaths from one-sided massacres, starvation and disease),
      this figure includes only combatants or civilians who died as a result of
      battle: Bethany Lacina and Nils Petter Gleditsch, 'Monitoring Trends
      in Global Combat: A New Dataset of Battle Deaths', *European Journal
      of Population*, vol. 21, June 2005, pp. 145, 154.
8   Michael Seth, 'An Unpromising Recovery – South Koreas Post-Korean
      War Economic Development: 1953-1961', *Education About Asia*, vol.
      18, no. 3, Winter 2013, p. 42.
9   ibid., p. 43.
10   A.M. Rosenthal, 'Outlook Dreary for South Korea: Crowded Nation
      Has Few Resources – Long Reliance on US Held Inevitable', *The New
      York Times*, 21 March 1961.
11   Michael Seth, 'An Unpromising Recovery', p. 45.
12   ibid., p. 44.
13   Robert Hassink, 'South Korea's Economic Miracle and Crisis:
      Explanations and Regional Consequences', *European Planning
      Studies*, vol. 7, no. 2, 2007, pp. 129–30 and Jinyul Ju, 'The Japan–
      Korea Dispute over the 1965 Agreement' *The Diplomat*, 23 October
      2020.

14   Kwan S. Kim, 'The Korean Miracle (1962–1980) Revisited: Myths and Realities in Strategy and Development', Working Paper No. 166, Kellogg Institute, South Bend, November 1991, p. 12.

15   ibid., p. 21.

16   ibid., pp. 21–22.

17   Robert Hassink, 'South Korea's Economic Miracle and Crisis', p. 130.

18   Kwan S. Kim, 'The Korean Miracle', pp. 21–22 and Carter Vance, 'Assessing the Miracle on the Han River', *Medium*, 31 July 2018.

19   Glenn Baek, 'A Perspective on Korea's Participation in the Korean War' Issue Brief No. 53, *The Asan Institute for Policy Studies*, 10 April 2013, p. 4.

20   Michael Porter, *The Competitive Advantage of Nations*, The Free Press, New York, 1990, p. 476.

21   Kwan S. Kim, 'The Korean Miracle', p. 6 and 'Trade in Goods and Services, Exports, % of GDP, 2019 or latest available', OECD website, accessed 7 January 2021.

22   'World Economic Outlook, October 2020: A Long and Difficult Ascent', International Monetary Fund website, October 2020, and Peter Carroll and William Hynes, 'Korea's Accession to the OECD: A History', *OECD Observer*, vol. 1, 4 Apr 2017.

23   OECD, 'Population with Tertiary Education, 25–34-Year-Olds, % in Same Age Group, 2019 or Latest Available' OECD website, accessed 7 January 2021.

24   'Freedom in the World 2021: South Korea', Freedom House website, accessed 22 June 2021.

25   Bethany Lacina and Nils Petter Gleditsch, 'Monitoring Trends in Global Combat', pp. 147–48.

26   'Conflict and Terrorism – Level 3 Cause', *The Lancet*, vol. 396, 17 October 2020, pp. 198–99.

27   'Cardiovascular Diseases – Level 2 Cause', *The Lancet*, vol. 396, 17 October 2020, pp. 86–87.

28   Steven Pinker, *The Better Angels of Our Nature*, Penguin, London, 2011; Zack Beauchamp, 'This Fascinating Academic Debate Has Huge Implications For the Future of World Peace', *Vox*, 21 May 2015; and Pasquale Cirillo, 'What Are the Chances of War?', *Significance*, vol. 13, no. 2, 8 April 2016, pp. 44–45.

29   Robin Coupland and David Meddings, 'Mortality Associated with Use of Weapons in Armed Conflicts, Wartime Atrocities and Civilian Mass Shootings: Literature Review', *BMJ*, vol. 319, article 3207, 14 August 1999, pp. 407–10.

30   Delan Devakumar et al., 'The Intergenerational Effects of War on the Health of Children', *BMC Medicine*, vol. 12, article 57, 2 April 2014.

31   Gaza in Ruth Feldman and Adv Vengrober, 'Posttraumatic Stress
      Disorder in Infants and Young Children Exposed to War-Related
      Trauma', *Journal of the American Academy of Child & Adolescent
      Psychiatry*, vol. 50, no. 7, 7 July 2011, pp. 645–58; Rwanda in
      'Shattered Lives: Sexual Violence During the Rwandan Genocide
      and its Aftermath', Human Rights Watch, New York, 1996; Australia
      in 'Morbidity of Vietnam Veterans: Suicide in Vietnam Veterans'
      Children', Supplementary Report No. 1, Australian Institute of Health
      and Welfare, Canberra, 2000, p. 1; and Holocaust survivors in Miri
      Scharf, 'Long-Term Effects of Trauma: Psycho-Social Functioning of
      the Second and Third Generation of Holocaust Survivors', *Development
      and Psychopathology*, vol. 19, No. 2, April 2007, pp. 603, 617–18.

32   Giada Zampano et al., 'Migrant Crisis: A History of Displacement',
      The Wall Street Journal, 22 September 2015.

33   'World Migration Report 2020', International Organisation for
      Migration, Geneva, 2019, pp. 2–3.

34   Veysi Ceri et al., 'Mental Health Problems of Second-Generation
      Children and Adolescents with Migrant Background', *International
      Journal of Psychiatry in Clinical Practice*, vol. 21, no, 2, February 2017,
      pp. 142–47.

35   'Economic Consequences of War on the US Economy', Institute for
      Economics and Peace, Sydney, 2012.

36   'Post-Conflict Economic Recovery: Enabling Local Ingenuity', United
      Nations Development Program, New York, 2008, p. 8.

37   Edward Miguel and Gérard Roland, 'The Long-Run Impact of
      Bombing Vietnam', *Journal of Development Economics*, vol. 96, no. 1,
      September 2011, pp. 1–15.

38   'The World Bank in Eritrea', World Bank website, accessed 9 January
      2021; 'Burundi: The Army in Crisis', International Crisis Group
      website, 5 April 2017; 'Liberia's Economic Crisis and Corruption
      Could Lead to Violence', *The Economist*, 10 August 2019; and 'The
      World Bank in Liberia', World Bank website, accessed 9 January 2021.

39   Alberto Alesina et al., 'Artificial States', *Journal of the European
      Economic Association*, vol. 9, no. 2, 1 April 2011, pp. 246–77.

40   Cited in Austan Goolsbee, 'Count Ethnic Divisions, Not Bombs, to
      Tell if a Nation Will Recover from War', *The New York Times*, 20 July
      2006.

41   John Keegan, *The Second World War*, Penguin, New York, 1990,
      pp. 495–96.

42   Diether Raff, *A History of Germany from the Medieval Empire to the
      Present*, translated by Bruce Little, Berg Publishing, Oxford, 1988,
      p. 335.

43   Economic production in J. Bradford De Long and Barry Eichengreeen, 'The Marshall Plan: History's Most Successful Structural Adjustment Program', Working Paper No. 3899, National Bureau of Economic Research, Cambridge, MA, November 1991, p. 16; calories in David Henderson, 'German Economic Miracle', The Library of Economics and Liberty website, accessed 10 January 2021 and 'Non-Medical Determinants of Health: Food Supply and Consumption', OECD website, accessed 10 January 2021; bartering in Henry Christopher Wallich, *Mainsprings of German Revival*, Yale University Press, London, 1955, p. 65.

44   David Henderson, 'German Economic Miracle'.

45   'The Potsdam Conference 1945', Office of the Historian, United States Department of State website, accessed 10 January 2021.

46   Johannes Rittershausen, 'The Postwar West German Economic Transition: From Ordoliberalism to Keynesianism', IWB Discussion Paper No. 2007/1, Institute for Economic Policy, University of Cologne, Cologne, 2007, p. 30.

47   ibid., pp. 38–39.

48   J. Bradford De Long and Barry Eichengreeen, 'The Marshall Plan', p. 11 and David Henderson, 'German Economic Miracle'.

49   Timothy Rooks, 'Can Germany's Social Market Economy System Cope with Another 70 Years?', *DW*, 2 October 2019 and Michael Schmitz, 'The Deutsche Mark and Its Legacy', ThoughtCo website, 3 June 2019.

50   Henry Christopher Wallich, *Mainsprings of German Revival*, p. 7.

51   Wolfgang Stolper and Karl Roskamp, 'Planning a Free Economy: Germany 1945–1960', *Journal of Institutional and Theoretical Economics*, vol. 135, no. 3, September 1979, p. 392.

52   ibid., p. 397.

53   Henry Christopher Wallich, *Mainsprings of German Revival*, p. 4.

54   Werner Abelshauser, Wirtschaft in Westdeutschland 1945-48: Rekonstruction und Wachstumsbedigungen in der amerikanischen und britischen Zone, Deutsche Verlags-Anstalt, Stuttgart, 1975, p. 12.

55   Ulrich Herbert, *A History of 20th-Century Germany*, p. 502.

56   Frederick Taylor, *Exorcising Hitler: The Occupation and Denazification of Germany*, Bloomsbury Press, New York, 2013, pp. xxxiv.

57   Survey carried out on behalf of the American Military Government cited in ibid., p. 221.

58   Jared Diamond, *Upheaval*, pp. 224–25.

59   Jeffrey Herf, *Divided Memory: The Nazi Past in the Two Germanys*, Harvard University Press, Cambridge, MA, 1997, p. 7.

60   ibid.

61   Jared Diamond, *Upheaval*, pp. 225–26.

62   Norbert Frei, *Adenauer's Germany and the Nazi Past: The Politics of Amnesty and Integration*, translated by Joel Golb, Columbia University Press, New York, 2002.

63   Frederick Taylor, *Exorcising Hitler*, pp. xxxiv.

64   David Thrum, 'The Triumph of German Democracy', *The Atlantic*, 8 May 2019.

65   'Freedom in the World 2020: Germany', Freedom House website, accessed 12 January 2020.

66   ibid., p. 13.

67   New Zealand has gross national income per capita (in purchasing power parity international dollars) of $42,710; South Korea, $43,520; Japan, $44,810; UK, $47,880; Canada, $50,810, Australia, $51,670; Germany, $57,810; United States, $66,080; and Singapore, $92,270: 'GNI Per Capita, PPP (Current International $)', World Bank website, accessed 14 January 2021.

68   Adam Szirmai, 'Explaining Success and Failure in Development', p. 21.

69   Wolfgang Stolper and Karl Roskamp, 'Planning a Free Economy', pp. 374–404.

70   Robert Wertheimer, 'The Miracle of German Housing in the Postwar Period', *Land Economics*, vol. 34, no. 4, November 1958, p. 338.

71   Jang-Sup Shin, *The Economics of Latecomers: Catching Up, Technology Transfer and Institutions in Germany, Japan and South Korea*, Routledge, London, 1996.

72   Adam Szirmai, 'Explaining Success and Failure in Development', p. 39.

73   Jenn Hwang-Wang, 'From Technological Catch-Up to Innovation-Based Economic Growth: South Korea and Taiwan Compared', *Journal of Development Studies*, vol. 43, no. 6, 2007, pp. 1084–104.

74   Mancur Olson cited in Bart Barnes, 'Mancur Olson Dies at 66', *The Washington Post*, 25 February 1998.

75   Mancur Olson cited in James Lardner, 'Why America Is Outhustled Mancur', *The Washington Post*, 12 October 1982.

76   Mancur Olson cited in Bart Barnes, 'Mancur Olson Dies at 66'.

77   Natural resources as a curse, see Peter Hartcher, 'Heed the Curse of a Lucky Country', *The Sydney Morning Herald*, 9 May 2008; economic growth in Jeffrey Sachs and Andrew Warner, 'Natural Resource Abundance and Economic Growth', National Bureau of Economic Research, Working Paper 5398, December 1995; and researchers' observations in Richard Auty, *Sustaining Development in Mineral Economies: The Resource Curse Thesis*, Routledge, London, 1993.

78   Michael Porter, *The Competitive Advantage of Nations*, The Free Press, New York, 1990, pp. 617–18.

79   Adam Szirmai, 'Explaining Success and Failure in Development', p. 22.

80   Corinne Reichert, 'Samsung Sold Almost Twice as Many Phones as Apple in Q3, Gartner Says', *CNET*, 30 November 2020.

81   'Value Added by Activity, Manufacturing, % of Value Added, 2019 or latest available', OECD website, accessed 14 January 2021.

82   In 2019, Germany had a current account balance of US$273 billion; South Korea's balance was US$60 billion: 'Current Account Balance (BoP, Current US$)', World Bank website, accessed 14 January 2021.

83   'Gross Domestic Spending on R&D, Total, % of GDP, 2019 or Latest Available', OECD website, accessed 15 January 2021.

84   'Population with a Tertiary Education, 25–34 Year Olds, % in Same Age Group, 2019 or Latest Available', OECD website, accessed 15 January 2021.

85   Kitlyn Bison, 'South Korean Perceptions of Reunification', *International Policy Digest*, 15 June 2020.

86   Chung Min Lee, 'A Peninsula of Paradoxes: South Korean Public Opinion on Unification and Outside Powers', Carnegie Endowment for International Peace, Washington, DC, 2020.

87   'Voice. Treaty. Truth: Uluru Statement from the Heart', The Uluru Statement website, accessed 22 June 2021.

88   John Allen, 'Reconciling and Healing America', Brookings Institution website, 8 February 2021.

89   Sarah Souli, 'Does America Need a Truth and Reconciliation Commission?', *Politico*, 16 August 2020.

90   Zeeshan Aleem, 'North and South Korea Marched Together under One Flag at the Olympics', *Vox*, 9 February 2018.

91   Lee Jee-Young, 'North-South GNI Per Person Gap Widens in 2019', *Korea JoongAng Daily*, 28 December 2020.

92   In November 2020, South Korea ranks number two in the world for mobile internet speeds (behind the United Arab Emirates): 'November Speeds 2020', Speedtest Global Index website, accessed 15 January 2021 and 'Population with a Tertiary Education, 25–34 Year Olds'.

93   Daniel Schwekendieek and Sunyoung Pak, 'Recent Growth of Children in the Two Koreas: A Meta-Analysis', *Economics and Human Biology*, vol. 7, no. 1, March 2009, pp. 109–12 and 'Life Expectancy at Birth, Total (Years)', World Bank website, accessed 8 January 2021.

94   'Life Expectancy at Birth, Total, 2019 or latest available', OECD website, accessed 7 January 2021.

Chapter 5: Our Post-Pandemic Future

1   OECD, *OECD Economic Outlook*, volume 2021, Issue 1, preliminary version, May 2021 and Ayhan Kose and Naotaka Sugawara,

'Understanding the Depth of the 2020 Global Recession in Five Charts', *World Bank Blog*, 15 June 2020.

2 OECD, *OECD Economic Outlook*, volume 2021; World Bank, *Global Economic Prospects*, June 2021, p. 4; and International Monetary Fund, *World Economic Outlook*, April 2021, p. 8.

3 Soofia Tariq, 'House Prices in Australia and New Zealand Among World's Fastest Growing in 2021', *The Guardian*, 10 June 2021 and Emily Stewart, 'Why Stocks Soared While America Struggled', *Voxi*, 10 May 2021.

4 World Bank, *Global Economic Prospects*, January 2021, p. xviii.

5 International Monetary Fund, *World Economic Outlook: Managing Divergent Recoveries*, April 2021, pp. 8, 36.

6 Rajiv Tandon, 'COVID-19 and Mental Health: Preserving Humanity, Maintaining Sanity and Promoting Health', *Asian Journal of Psychiatry*, vol. 51, 2020, https://www.ncbi.nlm.nih.gov/pmc/articles/PMC7305748/ and Natarajan Kathirvel, 'Post COVID-19 Pandemic Mental Health Challenges', *Asian Journal of Psychiatry*, vol. 53, 2020, https://www.ncbi.nlm.nih.gov/pmc/articles/PMC7507979/.

7 Natarajan Kathirvel, 'Post COVID-19 Pandemic Mental Health Challenges'.

8 Michèle Belot, Dinand Webbink, 'Do Teacher Strikes Harm Educational Attainment of Students?', *Labour*, vol. 24, no. 4, 2010, pp. 391–406; Michael Baker, 'Industrial Actions in Schools: Strikes and Student Achievement', *Canadian Journal of Economics*, vol. 46, no. 3, 2013, pp. 1014–36; and David Jaume and Alexander Willén, 'The Long-Run Effects of Teacher Strikes: Evidence from Argentina', *Journal of Labor Economics*, vol. 73, no. 4, 2019, pp. 1097–139.

9 Kamila Cygan-Rehm, 'Is Additional Schooling Worthless? Revising the Zero Returns to Compulsory Schooling in Germany', CESifo Working Paper 7191, CESifo, Munich, 2018, and Franziska Hampf, 'The Effect of Compulsory Schooling on Skills: Evidence from a Reform in Germany', ifo Working Paper 313, ifo Institute for Economic Research, Munich, 2019.

10 Erik Hanushek and Ludgar Woessmann, *The Economic Impacts of Learning Losses*, OECD, Paris, September 2020, p. 9.

11 ibid., p. 10, and Julie Sonneman and Peter Goss, 'Disadvantaged Students May Have Lost a Months' Learning During the COVID Crisis', *The Conversation*, 15 June 2020.

12 'Impact of Hurricane Sandy', NYC Community Development Block Grant Disaster Recovery, City of New York website, accessed 25 January 2021.

13   Olga Khazan, 'Why We're Running Out of Masks', *The Atlantic*,
      10 April 2020 and Margaret Simons, 'The Real Reason Our Shelves
      Were Empty', *The Saturday Paper*, 2–8 May 2020.

14   Stephen Dziedzic, 'New Zealand Tops Lowy Institute List as Country
      with Best Response to Coronavirus, Australia Sits Eighth', *ABC News*,
      28 January 2021.

15   Megan Scudellari, 'How Iceland Hammered COVID with Science',
      Nature, 25 November 2020.

16   Department of Environment, Land, Water and Planning, *Guidelines
      for Assessing the Impact of Climate Change on Water Supplies in Victoria*,
      State Government of Victoria, 2016 and Emergency Management
      Victoria, *EMV's Strategic Plan 2020*, State Government of Victoria,
      2020, p. 17.

17   Between 2001 and 2015, Melbourne experienced 1283 heatwave
      deaths; see 'Heatwaves are More Deadly for Residents in Adelaide and
      Melbourne – Here's Why', *ABC News*, 15 August 2018.

18   'Summary for Policymakers' in Intergovernmental Panel on Climate
      Change, *Global Warming of 1.5°C: An IPCC Special Report*, Geneva,
      2018, p. 4 and Kelly Levin, '8 Things You Need to Know About the
      IPCC 1.5˚C Report', *World Resources Institute*, 7 October 2018.

19   Intergovernmental Panel on Climate Change, 'Summary for
      Policymakers', p. 12.

20   Office for Climate Education, *IPCC Special Report Global Warming of
      1.5°C: Summary for Teachers*, 2018, p. 19.

21   United Nations Environment Program, 'Emissions Gap Report 2020',
      2020, p. xxi and 'UN Emissions Report: World on Course for More
      than 3-Degree Spike, Even if Climate Commitments Are Met', *UN
      News*, 26 November 2019.

22   'The Paris Agreement', United Nations Climate Change website,
      accessed 1 February 2021.

23   Christiana Figueres and Tom Rivett-Carnac, *The Future We Choose:
      Surviving the Climate Crisis*, Manilla Press, London, 2020, p. 8.

24   Christophe McGlade and Paul Ekins, 'The Geographical Distribution
      of Fossil Fuels Unused When Limiting Global Warming to 2°C',
      Nature, vol. 517, 2015, pp. 187–190.

25   Ellie Potter, 'Wave of Institutional Divestment from Coal Mining,
      Generation Develops in 2019', *S&P Global Market Intelligence*, 20
      December 2019. BlackRock's divestment policy applies only to its
      actively managed funds; see Tim Buckley, Tom Sanzillo and Melissa
      Brown, '$7tn Investor Blackrock Announces Coal Divestment, But
      Not Across All Funds', *energypost.eu*, 20 January 2020 and Attracta
      Mooney, 'BlackRock Calls on AGL to Hasten Closure of Coal-Fired

Plants', *Financial Times*, 7 October 2020.

26 Chubb, 'Chubb Coal Policy', accessed 30 January 2021.

27 Deloitte, *Extracting Value from Decarbonisation*, 2020.

28 Gareth Hutchens, 'Rio Tinto Joins BHP in Pledging to Reduce Greenhouse Gas Emissions to Net Zero by 2050', *ABC News*, 26 February 2020.

29 International Renewable Energy Agency, *Renewable Capacity Statistics 2021*, Abu Dhabi, 2021.

30 World Bank, *State and Trends of Carbon Pricing 2020*, Washington, DC, 2020, p. 7.

31 Andrew Prag, *The Climate Challenge and Trade: Would Border Carbon Adjustments Accelerate or Hinder Climate Action?*, Background Paper for the 39th Round Table on Sustainable Development, OECD Headquarters, Paris, 25 February 2020, p. 4.

32 Freedom House, *Freedom in the World 2021: Democracy Under Siege*, London, 2021, p. 1 and Freedom House, *Freedom in the World 2020: A Leaderless Struggle for Democracy*, London, 2020, p. 10.

33 The Economist Intelligence Unit, *Democracy Index 2020: In Sickness and In Health*, 2021, pp. 3–4.

34 ibid., p. 5.

35 Freedom House, *Freedom in the World 2021: Democracy Under Siege*, p. 12.

36 'Democracy During Pandemic', Freedom House website, accessed 2 February 2021.

37 World Bank, *Poverty and Shared Prosperity 2018: Piecing Together the Poverty Puzzle*, Washington, DC, 2018.

38 United Nations, 'World Social Report 2020: Inequality in a Rapidly Changing World', 2020, p. 5.

39 Samuel Stebbins and Evan Comen, 'How Much Do You Need to Make to be in the Top 1% in Every State?', *USA Today*, 1 July 2020.

40 Oxfam International, *The Inequality Virus*, 2021, p. 12 and World Bank, *Poverty and Shared Prosperity 2020: Reversal of Fortune*, Washington, DC, World Bank, 2020, pp. 1–5.

41 OECD, 'Does Economic Inequality Hurt Economic Growth?', December 2014; David Vandivier, 'What is the Great Gatsby Curve?', *The White House*, 11 June 2013; Kate Pickett and Richard Wilkinson, 'Income Inequality and Health: A Causal Review', *Social Science and Medicine*, vol. 128, 2015, pp. 316–26; and Jonathan Krieckhaus et al., 'Economic Inequality and Democratic Support', *The Journal of Politics*, vol. 76, no. 1, 2013 pp. 139–51.

42 European Commission president Ursula von der Leyen cited in Anna Nadibaidze, 'Will the EU's Foreign Policy and Defence Ambitions be

Reflected in the Next Long-Term Budget?', *UCL Europe Blog*, 17 July 2020.

43 Mujtaba Rahman, 'We're Not Ready for Europe After Merkel', *Politico*, 14 January 2021.

44 Hyung-Jin Kim, 'US, China Agree to Cooperate on Climate Crisis with Urgency', *AP*, 18 April 2021.

45 EY, *2021 Geostrategic Outlook*, December 2020, p. 5.

46 World Bank, 'GDP Per Capita (Constant 2010 US$)', World Bank Data website, accessed 7 February 2021.

47 ibid.

48 OECD, 'Main Findings', *Under Pressure: The Squeezed Middle Class*, Paris, 2019 and Ted Tabet, 'Stagnant Wage Growth Weighs on Living Standards', *The Urban Developer*, 31 July 2019.

49 OECD, 'Continued Slowdown in Productivity Growth Weighs Down on Living Standards', 18 May 2017 and Alistair Dieppe, 'The Broad-Based Productivity Slowdown, in Seven Charts', *World Bank Blogs*, 14 July 2020.

50 Alistair Dieppe, 'The Broad-Based Productivity Slowdown, in Seven Charts', *World Bank Blogs*, 14 July 2020.

51 'Meeting the Challenge of Long COVID', *Nature Medicine*, vol. 26, 2020, p. 1803.

52 ibid.

53 OECD, 'Education and COVID-19: Focussing on the Long-Term Impact of School Closures', 29 June 2020; 'Coronavirus: «Entre 5 et 8 % des élèves» sans continuité pédagogique depuis la fermeture des écoles', *Les Echos*, 31 March 2020; Dana Goldstein, Adam Popescu and Nikole Hannah-Jones, 'As School Moves Online, Many Students Stay Logged Out', *The New York Times*, 6 April 2020.

54 European Center for the Development of Vocational Training, *Digital Gap During COVID-19 for VET Learners at Risk in Europe*, 4 June 2020, pp. 11, 12.

55 OECD, 'Building Back Better: A Sustainable, Resilient Recovery After COVID-19', Paris, 2021, p. 2. The quotation in the next paragraph and the bulleted list is also paraphrased from this report.

56 United Nations Office for Disaster Risk Reduction, *Build Back Better in Recovery, Rehabilitation and Reconstruction*, United Nations, 2017, p. 4.

57 OECD, 'Building Back Better', p. 2 and entry for 'resilience', *Cambridge Dictionary*, accessed 13 February 2021.

58 Mark Honigsbaum, *The Pandemic Century*, p. 8 and OECD, 'October 24th 1929: Stock Market Crash Hits Banks, Firms, Economists', *OECD Insights*, 24 October 2011.

Chapter 6: A Roadmap to Recovery

1   Premier of Victoria, 'Up and About: Revitalisation Push Backs City, State Recovery', Media Release, 9 May 2021.

2   Canterbury Earthquakes Royal Commission, *The Canterbury Earthquakes Royal Commission*, website accessed 20 February 2021 and Parliament of Victoria, *2009 Victorian Bushfires Royal Commission*, 2010.

3   National Commission on Terrorist Attacks, 'The 9/11 Commission Report: Final Report of the National Commission on Terrorist Attacks Upon the United States', 17 July 2004.

4   State of Victoria, 'COVID-19 Hotel Quarantine Inquiry Final Report', 2020 and State of New South Wales, *Special Commission of Inquiry into the* Ruby Princess, 2020.

5   Eat Out to Help Out offered half-price food and non-alcoholic drinks up to a limit of 10 per person, Monday to Wednesday; Chris Giles and Alice Hancock, 'Sunak's "Eat Out to Help Out" Scheme Beats Expectations', *Financial Times*, 4 September 2020. SingapoRediscovers vouchers worth S$100 were provided to each Singaporean citizen aged over eighteen and were redeemable on tours, attractions or hotels; 'SingapoRediscovers Vouchers', LifeSG website, accessed 20 February 2021.

6   International Monetary Fund, 'Joint Press Conference by IMF Managing Director, Kristalina Georgieva and IMFC Chair, Magdalena Andersson', 19 January 2021.

7   Brendan Coates and Matt Cowgill, 'RBA Should Come Off Sidelines and Play Unconventional Game', *Australian Financial Review*, 10 August 2020.

8   Zhifei Yan et al, 'Renewable Electricity Storage Using Electrolysis', *Proceedings of the National Academy of Sciences*, vol. 117, no. 23, 2020, pp. 12558–63.

9   Cameron Hepburn et al., 'Will COVID-19 Fiscal Recovery Packages Accelerate or Retard Progress on Climate Change?', *Oxford Review of Economic Policy*, vol. 36, no. 1, 2020, S359–S381.

10   Peter Martin, 'Top Economists Back Boosts to JobSeeker and Social Housing Over Tax-Cuts in Pre-Budget Poll', *The Conversation*, 27 September 2020.

11   Louis Etienne-Dubois, David Gauntlett and Ramona Pringle, 'How to Help Artists and Cultural Industries Recover from the COVID-19 Disaster', *The Conversation*, 26 January 2021.

12   Greater Manchester Combined Authority, *Protect. Restore. Heal. Grow. GM Culture Recovery Plan 2021/22*, 2021.

13   Sarah Osei, 'Those Wild Berlin Club Nights are now Officially High Culture', *Highsnobiety*, 8 May 2021.

14   European Parliament, 'MEPs Approve the EU's New Culture Programme', Media Release, 19 May 2021.

15   Sung-Young Kim et al., 'South Korea's Green New Deal Shows the World What a Smart Economic Recovery Looks Like', *The Conversation*, 9 September 2020.

16   World Bank, *Nepal Development Update: Harnessing Export Potential for a Green, Inclusive and Resilient Recovery*, April 2021, p. xi.

17   KPMG, 'Singapore: Government and Institution Measures in Response to COVID-19', accessed 23 May 2021 and Enterprise Singapore, 'Access Financing Budget 2020', accessed 23 May 2021.

18   ChristchurchNZ, *Annual Review 2019*, 2019, pp. 16–17.

19   'Ontario Continues to Establish its Role as a World-Leader in Regenerative Medicine', *Clinical Trials Ontario*, 12 September 2019.

20   'High-Tech Industry in the Netherlands', *Dutch Glory*, accessed 23 May 2021.

21   Mathew Nelson et al., 'Can We Really Make Net Zero 2050 a Reality?', *EY*, 17 February 2021.

22   'Germany', *Platform for Redesign 2020*, accessed 25 May 2021; Sonja van Renssen, 'How Germany Plans to Build on COVID-induced Emissions Dip', *Energy Monitor*, 25 March 2021; Michael Fuhrmann, 'Germany's National Hydrogen Strategy: Serious Efforts to Realise a Decarbonised Society; Development of a Green Hydrogen Supply Infrastructure is the Challenge', *Mitsui & Co Global Strategic Studies Institute Monthly Report*, December 2020.

23   OECD, 'Education Critical to Build a More Resilient Society', Media Release, 8 September 2020.

24   Julie Sonneman and Peter Goss, 'Disadvantaged Students May Have Lost a Months' Learning During the COVID Crisis', *The Conversation*, 15 June 2020.

25   Michael Griffith, 'An Unparalleled Investment in US Public Education: An Analysis of the American Rescue Plan Act of 2021', *Learning Policy Institute*, 11 March 2021.

26   For example, see PWC, *Where to Next for Tertiary Education: How the COVID-19 Crisis Can Be a Catalyst to Reboot Towards a Stronger Sector*, August 2020.

27   For example, see Céline Thévenot, *Labour Market Structure and Wages: Policies to Reduce Inequality in OECD Countries*, United Nations Expert Meeting on Policies to Tackle Inequality, 25–27 June 2017.

28   Harry Carr et al., *The Future of Towns*, Demos, London, 2020, p. 40.

29   Amy Maxmen, 'Why Did the World's Pandemic Warning System Fail When COVID Hit?', *Nature*, vol. 589, 2021, pp. 499–500.

30   Jeffrey Prince and Daniel Simon, 'The Effect of International Travel on
     the Spread of COVID-19 in the U.S.', *Social Science Research Network*,
     21 December 2020, and Jeff Prince and Daniel Simon, 'Travellers
     Coming from Italy May Have Driven First U.S. COVID-19 Wave More
     Than Those From China, Study Suggests', *The Conversation*, 29 January
     2021.
31   Sally Capp, 'Melbourne is Worth 7% of Australia's Economy. How Can it
     Build Back Post COVID?', *World Economic Forum*, 21 December 2020.
32   ibid.
33   City of Melbourne, *COVID-19 Reactivation and Recovery Plan*, 2020.
34   City of Melbourne, *Melbourne's Thriving Economic Future: Draft
     Economic Development Strategy*, 2021, p. 3.

GET IN TOUCH

If you've enjoyed this book, I would love to hear from you. Follow me on Twitter (@andrewwear), Instagram (@wearandrew) or Facebook (@andrewwearauthor) and visit my website at www.andrewwear.com.